# GENDERED RESISTANCE

NEW BLACK STUDIES

*Series Editors*
Darlene Clark Hine
Dwight A. McBride

*A list of books in the series appears
at the end of this book.*

# GENDERED RESISTANCE

Women, Slavery,
and the Legacy
of Margaret Garner

EDITED BY MARY E. FREDERICKSON
AND DELORES M. WALTERS

FOREWORD BY DARLENE CLARK HINE

UNIVERSITY OF ILLINOIS PRESS
Urbana, Chicago, and Springfield

*A note to our readers:*

*The rendering of Black and White in uppercase versus lowercase (black and white) when referencing the two racial groups reflects each contributor's personal preference involving political, disciplinary, generational, and spiritual perspectives. In the book's common areas, we defer to contemporary usage of the lowercase for these terms.*

© 2013 by the Board of Trustees
of the University of Illinois
All rights reserved
Manufactured in the United States of America
1 2 3 4 5 C P 5 4 3 2 1
∞ This book is printed on acid-free paper.

Library of Congress Cataloging-in-Publication Data
Gendered resistance : women, slavery, and the legacy of Margaret Garner / edited by Mary E. Frederickson, Delores M. Walters ; foreword by Darlene Clark Hine.
pages    cm. — (New Black studies)
Includes bibliographical references and index.
ISBN 978-0-252-03790-0 (hardback : acid-free paper)
ISBN 978-0-252-07942-9 (paper : acid-free paper)
ISBN 978-0-252-09516-0 (ebook)
1. Women slaves—United States—Social conditions. 2. Slaves—United States—Social conditions. 3. Fugitive slaves—United States—History. 4. Government, Resistance to—United States—History. 5. Garner, Margaret, 1834–1858—Influence. 6. Slavery in literature. 7. Women slaves—Social conditions. 8. Women slaves—Violence against. 9. Sex crimes.
I. Frederickson, Mary E. II. Walters, Delores M.
E443.G45      2013
306.3'620973—dc23      2013015944

# CONTENTS

# FIGURES

# GENDERED RESISTANCE NOW!

For decades I have been haunted by Margaret Garner. In the 1980s while heading the Black Women in the Middle West Archival Creation Project, I sought documents to shed light on the lives and experiences of all black women during the slavery era. This quest led me to a newspaper clipping about Margaret Garner's futile effort to escape from inherited perpetual slavery in order to build a free life with her children in Cincinnati, Ohio. Her dreams of freedom quickly turned into a nightmare of unimaginable horror. When recapture seemed imminent and inescapable, Garner, rather than consign her baby girl to a life of perpetual bondage, rape, and exploitation, cut her daughter's throat. Garner's story reflects the complex intersection of race, mixed race, gender, social status, oppression, and resistance. I recall Garner's dilemma whenever I read headlines and hear breaking news accounts of the persistence of national and international twenty-first-century gendered violence. The exploitation of, violence against, and the commodification of vulnerable women and children is an ongoing reality that raises the question of what collection or spectrum of forces operate in any society to make violence against women appear to be normal, easy to rationalize, yet impossible to eradicate. Just as it is imperative that scholars and social justice activists collect testimonies and recover and analyze the literary texts and historical accounts of gendered violence, it is equally imperative that we stimulate conversation, encourage education, generate resources, and maintain resolve at every level to resist and to abolish all forms of slavery, rape, and human degradation.

*Gendered Resistance* is an important and timely anthology of original essays admirably edited by Mary E. Frederickson and Delores M. Walters; the collection troubles the easy assumptions about enslaved women's lack of power or their ability to negotiate their experiences with exploitation such as may have been the case with Sally Hemings or Harriet Jacobs. This richly textured anthology complicates our understanding of Black women's historical and contemporary lives and experiences, and it is a significant addition to canonical texts in Black

Women's Studies, African American Studies, and Women and Gender Studies. The probing, challenging scholarship displayed in the individual chapters will inspire further research and stimulate conversations about the complex interplay between resistance and adaptation, resilience, and survival. The illuminating and provocative essays certainly will ignite debate and simultaneously equip activists in public-sphere communities and movements with a more nuanced understanding of sexual abuse and exploitation, and of the political, cultural, and economic forces that subjugate women and girls in this era of globalization.

The contributors to *Gendered Resistance* draw upon a broad range of experiences and perspectives about women's historical, social, and cultural resistance to violence, rape, and exploitation from the slavery era to the contemporary period. They explore questions about enslaved women's abilities and opportunities to manipulate space for themselves within an overarching system of power imbalance. These essays make significant contributions to contemporary conversations and social justice struggles against the persistence of gendered violence. The scholarly analysis, when complemented by poignant testimonies, enables readers to understand that with regard to violence against women, the growth in human trafficking, and the exploitation of children, there may not be as much difference between the nineteenth century and our own times as we imagine. Clearly, we need to raise our voices, mobilize national and international resources in new ways in order to empower women, forge strong community alliances, raise the consciousness of all about the detrimental effects of denying physical safety, education, healthcare, and counseling to women.

The authors persuasively argue that there remains much of value to be learned from the past. They suggest that it is important to bring more sophisticated perspectives and methodologies in order to acquire more nuanced understandings of the experiences of nineteenth-century Black women. I applaud the editors and authors of *Gendered Resistance*. They have refocused our attention on the lives and struggles of Black women who were, in some instances, able to appropriate a measure of freedom within blackness and thus mediate their apparent powerlessness. I pray that the feminist wisdom of these enslaved Black women, and our memory of Margaret Garner, will continue to inspire and facilitate our ongoing struggles for self-ownership, empowerment, and the right to live and to achieve our full human potential.

Darlene Clark Hine

# PREFACE

This anthology of women's opposition to slavery and violence in historical, contemporary, and global contexts began as a symposium titled Gendered Resistance, co-sponsored by Miami University and the National Underground Railroad Freedom Center in Cincinnati in October 2005, organized by Mary E. Frederickson, faculty member in the Department of History at Miami University, and Delores M. Walters, a cultural anthropologist then on the faculty of Northern Kentucky University and a community research specialist for the Freedom Center. Over the course of three exciting days, scholars and artists presented their work on slavery and resistance to an eager audience of students and faculty from across the region in the form of presentations, performances, and exhibitions. All of this took place within several hundred yards of where Margaret Garner, a twenty-two-year-old enslaved Kentucky woman and her family crossed the Ohio River on a freezing January night in 1856 in a desperate attempt to gain their freedom. Perhaps more than any other American slave narrative, the story of Margaret Garner, who slit the throat of her two-year-old daughter to save her from being returned to slavery, reveals the horror of slavery and the consequences of sexual violence. Despite the notoriety, complexity, and duration of Garner's trial held in Cincinnati during the 1850 Fugitive Slave Law era, her story was largely forgotten until Toni Morrison's Pulitzer Prize–winning novel *Beloved* was published in 1987, followed by Oprah Winfrey's film adaptation of the book in 1998. Recognition of Garner's role as the inspiration of Morrison's novel was broadened by the 2005 premiere of an opera titled *Margaret Garner* with a libretto by Morrison, commissioned by the Cincinnati Opera in collaboration with the Michigan Opera Theatre and the Opera Company of Philadelphia in honor of the first anniversary of the opening of the National Underground Railroad Freedom Center in Cincinnati.

The story of Margaret Garner served as the focal point of the Gendered Resistance symposium, and her experience provides this collection with a foundation from which to discuss women's resistance in both historical and contemporary contexts. As these chapters will amply demonstrate, Margaret Garner and the society and culture of which she was a part continue to remain relevant across time and place. Much is still to be learned about and from such brave resistance, and women throughout the world can take strength from similar narratives of the refusal of women to submit to systems that physically, legally, emotionally, and spiritually deny their humanity. Indeed, such stories must be recovered and told again and again, the message conveyed by the Asante Adinkra symbol of the sankofa bird that returns to the past to collect what is needed to go forward. Stories of return to the moral universe that slavery created include Octavia Butler's *Kindred* (1979), the 1993 film *Sankofa*, and Saidya Hartman's *Lose Your Mother* (2007). These works of historical imagination not only illuminate slavery's tragic legacies; the difficult choices women face; and the ways that race, slavery, and gender continue to shape the lives of women and men, but they also contain the seeds of change, the possibility of healing, and the hope of transformation.

The Gendered Resistance Symposium addressed a persistent need for opportunities to highlight women's roles in the movements against sexual slavery and economic subjugation. To broaden our understanding of gendered resistance across multiple spatial and temporal domains, a wide spectrum of scholars and thinkers were invited to participate. First the symposium and then the development and writing of *Gendered Resistance* has challenged all of us, editors and contributors alike, to find our authentic voices as scholars, artists, and women. Our goal in this volume, co-edited by a black anthropologist (Walters) and a white historian (Frederickson), has been to present multiple perspectives on enslaved women's lives and their resistance to bondage in various geographic and historical contexts while validating the voices of black women and other women of color and the stories they tell.

The chapters included in *Gendered Resistance* pay close attention to the history of American slavery and to the larger meanings of the historical and cultural representations of black women in the United States and around the world. Each chapter takes the story of Margaret Garner, as seen from historical, contemporary, and global perspectives, as a theoretical and empirical starting point. The book seeks to understand the multiple ways in which women and men respond to subjugation and sexual violence in historical and contemporary worlds. It attempts to incorporate a variety of approaches to telling these stories without misrepresenting or minimizing them, employing the methods of history, anthropology, and artistic imagination to encourage an interdisciplinary conversation about gendered resistance.

For social historians and anthropologists, scholarship has evolved over the past four decades to acknowledge more fully the centrality of race, gender, and other categories of identity in interpretations of lived experience. Historians and anthropologists working in the field of African American history have uncovered new sources—from written documents to court records to long-hidden burials—that have in turn generated new interpretations that challenge our understanding of historical memory and the powerful hold that the past can exert on the present. At the same time, the arts and literature have offered alternative ways to reveal the unrecorded history of Americans of African descent. Lowery Stokes Sims, guest curator for the 2006 New York Historical Society exhibit exploring the influence of slavery through contemporary art, notes that although most often historians "think of art as illustrating history," it is also true that "the changes in art mark history."[1] Those working in the visual arts, dance, music, and literature have long produced representations probing the history of slavery, powerfully revealing the historical contradictions that underpin the ideals of liberty and freedom. Nineteenth-century writers such as Frances E. W. Harper used poetry and fiction to excavate the fault lines between slavery and freedom; for Harper, as Kristine Yohe argues in this volume, "literary transcendence" and "literal resistance" went hand in hand as she divided her life between dual commitments to writing about the past and working politically to change the future. In the twentieth century, Toni Morrison, in the words of the Nobel Prize committee, has given the world "novels characterized by visionary force and poetic import," giving new life "to an essential aspect of American reality" as she confronts "the unspeakable things unspoken" about the African American presence in American literature and in the American past.[2]

Seeing the unspeakable also defines the work of contemporary African American artists in the tradition of Carolyn Mazloomi, Faith Ringgold, and Carrie Mae Weems, who individually and collectively have created new ways to make visible long-hidden aspects of the past—enslavement, rape, trauma, and what bell hooks has called "the diasporic landscapes of longing"—in an outpouring of works in new media, from Mazloomi's work as a quilt artist and curator, discussed in this volume, to Ringgold's paintings and intricate story quilts, to Weems's photographs.[3] Contemporary artist Jonathan Green, a South Carolinian with Gullah origins, portrays Margaret Garner as a powerful, transformative figure with a story deeply rooted in the history of slavery and oppression, one that, as contributor Veta Tucker writes, "looks ahead with searching, haunting eyes that suggest this woman knows much more than she is supposed to."[4] The image on the front cover, which was used by the Cincinnati Opera to represent Margaret Garner, symbolizes a multiplicity of oppressed women whose faces are absent from historical accounts and is reminiscent of an other-worldly quality revealed spectacularly in the extremely creative New York City Opera version of *Margaret Garner*, the story of a woman who transcended victimhood and whose spirit survives as a legacy of her strength. In another work by Green, titled "Passages," the artist depicts Margaret Garner's purpose, strength, energy, and drive. She is seen from the back, and because we cannot see her face, she represents all women who have overcome enslavement, abuse, and oppression. In sharp contrast to the brutality of slavery, this Margaret Garner is beckoned to escape to another life in which, as Green writes, memory gives way to "a sense of place, space, dignity and privacy." The vivid colors and flowing dress render Margaret Garner, as *Gendered Resistance* contributor Raquel de Souza has written, "between worlds," evoking "the spiritual journey of so many others who lost their lives before, during, and after the Middle Passage."[5]

Although most Americans tend to think of resistance to the oppression of enslavement as a nineteenth-century phenomenon, several of the contributors to this collection remind us that the parameters of global slavery continue to expand. Activist groups in the United States and around the world are fighting to end trafficking and contemporary slavery in the spirit of a modern-day Underground Railroad. The number of national, international, and grassroots groups organized to fight present-day slavery has increased dramatically in the past decade in response to an exponential increase in human trafficking that disproportionately affects women and girls eager to find well-paid jobs as domestic servants, waitresses, or factory workers. These groups, including the United Nations, Human Rights Watch, Free the Slaves, the Global Fund for Women, the International Women's Human Rights Movement, and hundreds more, consciously pay witness to contemporary human trafficking and enslavement by recording survivor testimony, collecting data, lobbying for legislative reform, and generating public outrage.[6] In this context, the act of witnessing, from either a secular or religious orientation, involves affirming the experience of the other through historical documentation, political action, and cultural expression in literature, art, music, or drama. As scholar Nthabiseng Motsemme argues, we need to rely on the "work of the imagination to reconfigure our social worlds."[7]

In the chapters that follow, Delores Walters sets the stage for the rest of this volume in her introductory essay on the experience of Margaret Garner, whose life and experience redefined enslavement and freedom in the nineteenth century and has such strong implications for the present. The remaining chapters of *Gendered Resistance* are divided into two sections. The chapters in Part I, "Historical and Cultural Perspectives on Gendered Resistance," complement historical investigation with an ethnographic approach to consider various forms of resistance, some reminiscent of Margaret Garner's defiance and rebellion, others in which an expression of love was called into play. One of the central questions addressed in this section is how these historical actors saw their resistance—as an instinctual reaction aimed at survival, as a calculated act with the same objective, or as something entirely different. When we examine closely the human conditions that these women were resisting, a set of common obstacles emerges: lack of access to family, the denial of motherhood, and the inability to direct one's own life.

In Part II, "Global Slavery, Healing, and New Visions in the Twenty-First Century," links between past and present are explored in cultural and historical studies that provide a valuable window into the manipulation of gender, racial, and sexual identities to achieve certain ends. The chapters in this section continue to display the extensive range of women's opposition to subjugation and dehumanization—as strategists, insurgents, violent and nonviolent protesters, and those possessed by spirits, all of whom are conscious to varying degrees of the long-term implications of their acts of gendered resistance. They also include several artists' views of the relationship between their art and the memory of the enslavement of women of color and their resistance to being held in bondage, in both historical and modern-day contexts, and seek to understand how artists attempt to change the world through their music, storytelling, dancing, filmmaking, and poetry.

In short, *Gendered Resistance* exemplifies and illuminates the broad scope of women's resistance in multiple contexts by including relevant theoretical perspectives and historical sources about women's resistance and survival, compelling stories and analyses complemented by personalized reflections that intersect with current resistance struggles and realities. The chapters in *Gendered Resistance* affirm that as we witness and work to reconcile the past, we must also rely on "the work of the imagination" to see new visions for the future.[8]

*        *        *

At Miami University, we thank the History Department for support from the McClellan Fund, the College of Arts and Science for a grant from the Altman Fund, and Mary Jane Berman and Dorothy Falke from the Center for American and World Cultures for their expert assistance in organizing the Gendered Resistance Symposium. We want to acknowledge griot Vanessa Johnson, who mesmerized our lunchtime audience with her performance based on historical documents: letters, court rulings, newspaper accounts, and oral histories. We thank anthropologist and poet Irma McClaurin for delivering an inspiring keynote address on "ReVisioning a World without Violence against Women." We are grateful to the National Underground Railroad Freedom Center and then-Director Spencer Crew for hosting part of the symposium. In addition, we wish to acknowledge the Center for the Study of Race and Ethnicity in America at Brown University and its director, Evelyn Hu-DeHart, for providing Delores Walters with a research affiliation during the writing and editing of *Gendered Resistance*. The James Weldon Johnson Institute for the Study of Race and Difference at Emory University, where Mary Frederickson was a Visiting Scholar in 2012–13, was the perfect research environment in which to shape the final version of the manuscript. A special thank you to Carol Andersone, Tyrone Forman, Calinda Lee, Dorcas Ford Jones, and the wonderful group of scholars they brought together. We are grateful to Darlene Clark Hine, whose enthusiastic response to reading our manuscript was the spark that brought this work to life. Larin McLaughlin of the University of Illinois Press has been a superb editor whose input and support has made the publication process a collaborative one. Working with assistant editor Dawn Durante and copyeditor Julie Gay also has been a pleasure. We value the critical comments and keen editorial eye of Jeanne Barker-Nunn, the much-appreciated editing assistance of Najwa Adra, the artistry of Vernon Walters, the skill and hard work of Margaret Keneman in researching and processing the photographs, and the technical expertise of Anthony Clark. Diane Schneiderman, Linda Moore, David Gwynn, John Grigaitis, Peggy Callahan, Jerome Kaplan, Carolyn Mazloomi, Richard Weedman, Jonathan Green, and Katie Syroney generously helped us with the images for this volume. The staff of the Manuscript, Archives, and Rare Book Library (MARBL) at Emory University provided expert assistance. We thank especially Randall Burkett, Elizabeth Chase, Elizabeth Roke, and Sara Logue. Finally, we are grateful to our families and to the contributors to this anthology whose joyful camaraderie during the symposium helped sustain us through the completion of this book. As gendered resisters, their artistic, scholarly, and professional voices have validated Margaret Garner as an enduring symbol of resilience and survival.

Following a widely recognized protocol, the "equal contribution" (or EC) model, we have used an alphabetical sequence of our names to acknowledge our equal contribution as co-editors of *Gendered Resistance*. As co-editors, we each contributed to the conception, analysis, and interpretation of the work. Both editors approved all revisions and the final manuscript.

## NOTES

1. Felicia R. Lee, "The Influence of Slavery, through Contemporary Art," *New York Times*, June 13, 2006.

2. For more on Morrison's Nobel Prize, see *The Concise Oxford Companion to African American Literature*, ed. William L. Andrews, Frances Smith Foster, and Trudier Harris (New York: Oxford University Press, 2001), 295–96. See also Toni Morrison, "Unspeakable Things Unspoken: The Afro-American Presence in American Literature," Tanner Lectures on Human Values, delivered at the University of Michigan, October 7, 1988.

3. bell hooks, "Diasporic Landscapes of Longing," in *Inside the Visible*, ed. Catherine de Zegher (Cambridge, Mass.: MIT Press, 1996), 173–79. Lee, "The Influence of Slavery, through Contemporary Art." For biographical and exhibition information on Ringgold, Weems, and Mazloomi, see the African American Visual Artists Database at www.aavad.com. On Walker,

see Gwendolyn Du Bois Shaw, *Seeing the Unspeakable: The Art of Kara Walker* (Durham, N.C.: Duke University Press, 2004).

4. Green's renditions of Margaret Garner stand in sharp contrast to that of Thomas Satterwhite Noble, a nineteenth-century Kentucky artist from a white slaveholding family who emphasized deviant defiance in his representation of Margaret Garner in his 1867 painting, *The Modern Medea*, as discussed in the introductory chapter.

5. Veta Tucker to the editors, February 1, 2010; Raquel de Souza to the editors, February 5, 2010. See Jonathan Green, *Gullah Images: The Art of Jonathan Green* (Columbia: University of South Carolina Press, 1996). Quotation from Jonathan Green, "Artist's Statement," http://www.carolinaarts.com/603burroughschapin.html (accessed March 3, 2012).

6. Kevin Bales, *Ending Slavery: How We Free Today's Slaves* (Berkeley: University of California Press, 2007); David Batstone, *Not for Sale: The Return of the Global Slave Trade* (New York: HarperOne, 2007); United Nations, Human Rights Watch, *The Small Hands of Slavery: Bonded Child Labor in India* (New York: Human Rights Watch, 1996); the Global Fund for Women, "Women Hold the Solutions," 2008–2009 Annual Report, available at http://www.globalfundforwomen.org/storage/images/stories/downloads/GFW_2008-09_AR.pdf (accessed February 6, 2013); International Women's Human Rights Movement, United Nations Development Fund for Women, "Evaluation Report of the UNIFEM Programme Facilitating CEDAW Implementation in Southeast Asia" (CEDAW SEAP), 2009, available at http://www.unifem.org/materials/item_detail.php?ProductID=137 (accessed February 6, 2013).

7. Nthabiseng Motsemme, "The Mute Always Speak: On Women's Silences at the Truth and Reconciliation Commission," *Current Sociology* 52, no. 5 (2004): 909.

8. Toni Morrison, *Beloved* (New York: Random House, 1988), 315; Motsemme, "The Mute Always Speak," 909.

# GENDERED RESISTANCE

# Re(dis)covering and Recreating the Cultural Milieu of Margaret Garner

*Delores M. Walters*

Margaret Garner's act of infanticide represents the most drastic and extreme form of woman-centered resistance to the brutality of slavery. In 1856, when Garner killed her two-year-old daughter and attempted to kill her other three children rather than see them returned to slavery, her story was sensationalized in newspaper accounts that piqued the consciousness of the nation. Garner's desperate solution to "save" her children continues to capture our interest and awe. Toni Morrison's newest revival of the Garners' horrific yet heroic tale is the libretto for *Margaret Garner*. While demonstrating her distinctive, imaginative artistry, Morrison's depiction of Margaret Garner in the opera bore little resemblance to her depiction in her novel *Beloved* and diverged significantly from the historical account.

At the biennial meeting of the Toni Morrison Society, which coincided with the opera's Cincinnati premiere in July 2005, Morrison explained that there were "many Margaret Garner stories" and that her aim in the opera was to create strong female characters who would complement the powerful African American opera divas who sang the title roles.[1] Although the opera was a resounding success, it remains uncertain whether this newest artistic rendition, or indeed the story itself, will provide a pivotal entrée to a community's memory of America's painful past.

## Margaret's Story

Margaret Garner was born on June 4, 1833, on the Maplewood Farm in Richwood (Boone County), Kentucky, which was first owned by John Gaines and then by his brother, Archibald. Described as an unnamed sixteen-year-old female "mulatto" on the 1850 Slave Census, Margaret was likely a cook, nursemaid, and domestic at Maplewood. In 1849, Margaret married Robert Garner, who was enslaved on the neighboring Marshall farm that, like Maplewood, produced hogs. As a day

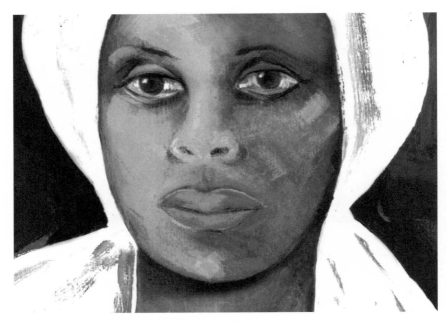

Figure I.1. Image adapted from *Nadene*, 1989, Acrylic on Masonite, 14" x 11" © Jonathan Green—Collection of Mary Mack. Courtesy of Jonathan Green and the Cincinnati Opera.

laborer, Robert was routinely rented out for various jobs, including driving hogs to market in Cincinnati. In the census of 1850, Margaret's oldest child, Tom, is listed as "Black," a strong indication that Robert was the father. Margaret's younger children, who were all light-skinned, were all born after Archibald Gaines assumed ownership of Maplewood in 1849.

On January 28, 1856, one of the coldest nights on record for Kentucky, Margaret, age twenty-two and pregnant, escaped with her four children, ages nine months to six years, her husband Robert, age twenty-one, and his parents, along with nine other enslaved people. Their meeting place was the Richwood Presbyterian Church, where Margaret was a member.[2] Because of Robert's familiarity with both Cincinnati, Ohio, and Covington, Kentucky, he likely planned the escape route. After Robert commandeered a horse-drawn sleigh and a pistol from the Marshall farm, they fled to Covington, where they abandoned the sleigh and crossed the frozen Ohio River on foot. The party of seventeen runaways split up at that point, and Margaret's group reached the home of a free cousin, Elijah Kite, in Cincinnati. The plan for Kite to obtain assistance from Quaker abolitionist Levi Coffin to get them to the next safe house on the Underground Railroad failed. Not long after the family arrived at the house, it was surrounded by Gaines and a number of deputy marshals. Resisting recapture, Robert shot and injured two of the deputies. Meanwhile, Margaret grabbed a butcher knife from the kitchen table, cut the throat of her toddler daughter, Mary, and struck the other three children. Her intent, she stated, was to prevent their return to slavery. The family was overpowered,

Figure I.2. *The Flight of the Garner Family*, Covington Flood Wall Mural by Robert Dafford, 2003. Photograph by Diane Schneiderman.

arrested, and jailed. At the coroner's inquest the next day, Margaret repeated that she was responsible for her daughter's death and that she had intended to kill all of her children and herself to avoid their being re-enslaved. She and her companions further reported being cruelly treated by their slaveholders.[3]

The Garners' failed escape attempt and its horrific outcome became front-page headlines in both pro-slavery and anti-slavery media. As the different factions revealed themselves in the press, Cincinnati became the center of the debate on slavery, although news outlets in other parts of the country carried details and commentary on the story as well. Margaret Garner had calmly and repeatedly acknowledged choosing death for her children and herself rather than a life in slavery. Yet pro-slavery headlines blared, "Stampede of Slaves: A Tale of Horror! . . . A Negro Child's Throat Cut from Ear to Ear,"[4] portraying her as a savage hysteric. The anti-slavery press was more subdued. A typical headline read, "The Fugitive Slave Case. The First Day of the Trial of the Mother and her Children."[5] Pro-slavery proponents considered Margaret's act of infanticide evidence of the savagery of Black women, thus justifying slavery, while anti-slavery activists vilified slavery itself, not its victims.

Whether Margaret would be found legally guilty or innocent depended on re-solving the case's compelling, if atypical, dilemma: whether she would be charged with the crime of murder or of theft. Since she was subject to the terms of the Fugitive Slave Law of 1850 and was also liable for murder by the state of Ohio, the case of Margaret Garner pitted a free state against the United States.[6] Given the legality of slavery, it was not surprising that a federal commissioner (judge) overruled the state's right to prosecute for murder and upheld the pro-slavery statute of 1850. Essentially, the Garners were considered property, not persons, foreshadowing the Dred Scott decision of 1857. Margaret was not tried for the murder of her child, who was not a human being under the law, nor was Robert prosecuted for wounding the deputies. The Garners were instead tried as runaway fugitives who had stolen themselves and destroyed the slaveholder's property in the process. Ultimately, slavery and its inherent racial prejudice prevailed.

Another controversial issue in the case was whether Robert and Margaret, who had previously visited the free state of Ohio, were still slaves whose escape violated the Fugitive Slave Law. The commissioner allowed Margaret to testify that she had been taken to Cincinnati as a child to act as a nursemaid. In Robert's defense, oth-ers could testify regarding his routine visits to the city as a day laborer. Margaret's statement proved uneventful and did little to change the direction of the trial. Still, granting the defense permission for her to testify was indeed exceptional in an era renowned for the silencing of Blacks in court.

On the last day of the trial, an extraordinary speech delivered by Lucy Stone, a prominent White feminist and abolitionist, electrified the courtroom with allegations that until then had remained unspoken. She alluded to the slaveholder's paternity of Margaret's children resulting from persistent rape, suggesting that the audience look at Margaret's mulatto children as "evidence":

> The faded faces of the negro children tell too plainly to what degradation the female slaves submit. Rather than give her little daughter to that life, she killed it. If in her deep maternal love she felt the impulse to send her child back to God, to save it from coming woe, who shall say she had no right to do so? That desire had its root in the deepest and holiest feelings of our nature—implanted in black and white alike by our common Father. With my own teeth would I tear open my veins, and let the earth drink my blood, rather than wear the chains of slavery. How then could I blame her for wishing her child to find freedom with God and the angels where no chains are?[7]

The press described Margaret as "a mulatto, showing from one-fourth to one-third white blood" and noted that "the child in her arms is a little girl about nine months old, and is much lighter in color than herself—light enough to show a red tinge in its cheeks" and that "the murdered child was almost white—and was a little girl of rare beauty."[8] Although Lucy Stone verbalized incriminating insinuations of sexual abuse by Gaines, those accusations were never formalized, and though she appealed to Gaines to free Margaret, she failed to convince him. Stone's speech did not change the outcome, but it did provide a stunning climax to the trial's proceedings.

The trial of the Garners became the longest, most costly, and arguably the most dramatic fugitive slave case of this era. Crowds lined the streets and jammed the courthouse.[9] Although Black spectators were barred from entering, they rallied in support outside. The Black community assisted successful runaways and comforted those who had been captured, though this was largely omitted from newspaper accounts.[10] Two weeks of controversial court hearings (typically fugitive cases were tried within hours) were followed by an additional two weeks before the commissioner rendered the predictable guilty verdict.[11] The defense attorney had tried but failed to extradite Margaret to Ohio to stand trial for the murder. He reasoned that if Margaret was tried under Ohio criminal statutes, the jury in a murder trial would sympathize with allegations that she had long been subjected to sexual abuse by Archibald Gaines.[12] Legal procedures that would have allowed Margaret to be returned to Cincinnati after the verdict was delivered also failed.[13]

Ultimately, the Garners were remanded to the custody of Gaines and eventually sold to a plantation owner in Mississippi. While en route to the slave market in Louisiana prior to the family's final destination in Mississippi, the steamboat carrying Margaret and her youngest daughter collided with another vessel, resulting in the drowning of ten-month-old Cilla. Reportedly, Margaret was relieved that another daughter would not be returned to a life of enslavement and expressed her desire for the same fate.[14] Margaret died of typhoid fever two years later, in 1858.

The story of the Garners is one of a family that remained intact despite incredible odds. Robert Garner survived the ordeal, and according to an interview with the *Cincinnati Daily Chronicle* in 1870, he served in the gunboat service of the Union Army and fought in the battle of Vicksburg.[15] After the Civil War, he lived in Cincinnati and was employed on a steamer, where he sustained a chest injury that eventually proved fatal.[16] The interviewer noted that Robert was suffering from "premature age" and that he was still in contact with his two remaining sons, Tom and Sam, who were living on a farm outside Vicksburg, Mississippi.[17] Robert Garner, listed as age forty-three on his death certificate, died in 1871.[18] Slavery threatened the longevity of both women and men as well as the sustainability of their families. By attempting to escape, Robert and Margaret defied the institution of slavery, including the possibility that they could function as a family. Margaret's last advice to Robert was "never to marry again in slavery, but to live in hope of freedom."[19]

## Who Speaks for Margaret Garner?[20]

A first-person narrative that might reveal a glimpse into Margaret Garner's inner life is not known to exist, thus much of her story remains unknown and unknowable. Who, then, should speak for Margaret Garner, and from whose perspective should slavery more generally be examined? Cases of infanticide were uncommon, according to historians, who argue that enslaved women more typically embraced motherhood. [21] Yet Black women's resistance, including infanticide and termination of unwanted pregnancies, especially in the context of sexual predation, has also been documented.[22] Still other writers point out that it is difficult to reconcile reports of mothers nurturing their children with reports that they killed or tried to abort them.[23]

Looking at various approaches to Margaret Garner's motives and her plight can assist in understanding the multiple ways in which her situation has been and continues to be viewed. These include nineteenth-century interpretations of the tragic story that persist into the present, especially anti- and pro-slavery views. Others include perceptions of Margaret Garner as a tragic heroine, while still others focus on her negotiation of selfhood within the power dynamics inherent in slavery. Despite the persistence of these perspectives, they are insufficient to explain Margaret's infanticide, her resistance to enslavement, and her apparent resolve to escape from sexual exploitation and abuse. To better understand Margaret Garner's position and the dynamics of slavery, this chapter will also examine feminist perspectives that validate the experiences of people of color and bring together the significant roles of race, gender, and class, as well as structural inequalities, negotiated realities, and personal perspectives.

*Pro-Slavery Positions (Inhumanity of the Slaves)*

At one end of the spectrum of views of slavery are the pro-slavery proponents who believed that enslaved Blacks were in need of the civilizing influence of Whites and their churches. According to this view, the failure to humanize enslaved persons would result in tragedies like Margaret Garner's infanticide. Pro-slavery activists who believed that slavery was a benign institution also viewed enslaved women's sexual relations with slaveholders as a matter of choice rather than a mandatory obligation. These adherents failed to recognize that under slavery, it was legal for forced sex to be imposed on enslaved women and girls. Such views continue to be held by some in part because too few records from subjugated females exist to corroborate that sexual abuse was commonplace.

In contemporary society, the pro-slavery perspective has been transformed into a denial of the existence and nature of the enslavement era in Southern, Northern, and border states like Kentucky. Acknowledging that vestiges of antebellum views permeate our society is the first step toward devising appropriate approaches to counterbalance them, especially in educational settings. Visits to the Maplewood Farm demonstrate that pro-slavery views remain an expressed part of the social landscape. The present owner has restored the remaining wing of the frame building where Margaret Garner was enslaved, and descendants of the slaveholding neighbors of the Gaines family, acting as docents on behalf of the owner, maintain that the Presbyterian Church in Richwood held benevolent and paternalist aspirations toward its Black members, who were seen as "equal before God."[24] While these slaveholders allowed enslaved Blacks to learn to read the Bible and provided religious instruction in accordance with their Presbyterian values, such apologists for slavery still view racially segregated seating not as the manifestation of an inequitable society but of a proper one. Similarly, while slavery was considered "morally wrong" from the Presbyterian position, the inhumane, if not brutal, consequences of failed escape attempts are not mentioned by the docents at the farm.[25] Indeed, compared to neighboring Southern states, few of those enslaved in Kentucky during the 1850s risked escaping, not because of their exemplary treatment by their enslavers, but because they feared being brutalized if caught.[26]

From this perspective, enslaved church members who refused to submit to domination, either physically or sexually, are seen as the violators rather than victims in a system predicated on violent abuses. Whether or not there was uniformity in inhumane practices, such "explanations" mainly target enslaved women rather than abusers.[27] As brutality often precipitated a slave's escape, undergraduate students from Northern Kentucky University were stunned to hear from the slaveholding descendant/docent that Margaret Garner had fled from Maplewood in order to avoid committing the sin of adultery with the slaveholder, claiming, "She would have been in moral conflict about a presumed relationship with Archibald."[28] Students understood that these comments stereotyped Margaret as a "loose" woman whose moral views and status changed following her church membership. On their visit to Maplewood, the cast of the opera *Margaret Garner*, who were less intimidated than the students, vehemently refuted the arguments made by the slaveholders' descendants as malicious characterizations of the motivations of Margaret Garner to escape.[29]

Slavery and the slave trade were essential to establishing the economy of this region, but many Americans, both Black and White, are still unable to reconcile their identities with this negative past. Outrage, surprise, and rejection characterize some Black visitors' reactions to hearing adultery presented as a motive for Margaret's escape, but others are far more complacent. Slavery in the Ohio-Kentucky borderlands is still often deemed by Whites as having been more humane than that practiced in the Deep South, as if such rationale justified it. Contemporary Ohio Valley residents whose ancestors considered ownership of other human beings the norm prefer to downplay the evils of slavery, especially the sexual violation of enslaved Black women. They view enslaved persons who rebelled or attempted to escape as uncontrolled or uncontrollable and the ownership of Black Africans for economic, sexual, or reproductive gain as acceptable. While a one-sided depiction of a family's quest for freedom continues to prevail at the Richwood site, this biased view is rarely contested in public. In a notable exception, a 2005 editorial in the *Cincinnati Enquirer* prior to the opening of the *Margaret Garner* opera stated, "Enslaved women like Garner were the property of their masters and didn't have the power to say 'no.' They were rape victims."[30]

### *Anti-Slavery (Inhumanity of Slavery): The Role of the Slave Mother*

At the other end of the spectrum are the anti-slavery proponents who espouse that it was the system of slavery itself that was inhumane, making equally violent, inhumane choices inevitable. The behavior construed as "animalistic" by pro-slavery advocates was perceived by abolitionists as definitive proof that the agony of slavery could even compel a mother to kill her child. To anti-slavery activists like Lucy Stone, the lethal measures taken by Margaret were in response to her sexual victimization. In *Modern Medea*, Steven Weisenburger agrees, hypothesizing that Margaret's motivation for the escape and infanticide are likely explained by her sexual violation, probably by Archibald Gaines.[31]

Although Weisenburger provides only circumstantial evidence, he suggests that the slaveholder Gaines was the father of Margaret's three youngest children, based on their light skin color, while her husband Robert likely fathered the darker-skinned oldest son. The author points to the co-occurrence of Margaret's pregnancies with the arrival of Archibald Gaines in Richwood and also with his wife Elizabeth Gaines's pregnancies. It was common for a free White woman to refuse sexual relations with her husband during pregnancy while ignoring her husband's forays into the quarters of the enslaved.[32] Finally, Gaines's extreme grief upon encountering the murdered toddler was telling of a personal relationship to little Mary, according to Weisenburger.[33] Mark Reinhardt, however, refutes this hypothesis, attributing paternity to Gaines by demonstrating weaknesses in Weisenburger's argument that Robert had limited access to his wife over long periods and noting that children of varying skin tones are possible whether or not Gaines was the father.[34] He also questions the most substantial reason given for Margaret's desperate acts: that she became the victim of sexual exploitation and abuse at the hands of the slaveholder, Gaines. Sexual bondage doubtlessly would explain the family's escape under the most forbidding circumstances, but, as other chapters in this volume address, enslavement does not rule out the possibility of a "consensual" sexual relationship with an oppressor or economic superior.

Lucy Stone's allegations of longstanding sexual abuse, though unofficial, nevertheless were quite spectacular in an era when neither Black nor White women had effective control over their reproductive lives. However, for a White woman to be denied moral authority and protective custody over her own children was inconceivable. Disjointed parenting was a concept reserved for Black mothers and their variably colored offspring.[35] For enslaved Black women the right of motherhood was a contradiction of institutional slavery.

In today's society, a child's skin color may be a significant determinant of a mother's behavior in educating and protecting her offspring, especially if the skin color of mother and child differ. In a recent story, a phenotypically Black man was told by his White mother while he was growing up that his "blackness" was due to an incurable skin disease that made his skin dark.[36] This allowed the mother to avoid admitting her sexual liaison with a Black man that produced a Black (or mixed-race) child. Race consciousness and contemporary racial dynamics appeared to be a factor in this contemporary situation involving a mother of a biracial child. Margaret Garner had removed her daughter from the threat of sexual violation or vulnerability when she refused to forfeit her role as protector/mother, even if this meant killing her child to save her. In the end, however, despite continuing differences on how to understand the lethal measures that Margaret chose, her own perspective, while critical, is largely missing from the equation.

## Tragic Heroine: The "Modern Medea" Viewpoint

Margaret's desperate solution to enslavement was also subject to mythological interpretations in her time and in the years that followed. Thomas Satterwhite Noble's painting *Margaret Garner*, also known as *The Modern Medea*, exemplifies a "tragic heroine" viewpoint that falls between the pro- and anti-slavery categories. Noble, a White Kentucky painter from a slaveholding family, was a teenager at the time of the escape and infanticide. His painting is the only nineteenth-century image known to exist of Margaret Garner.[37]

THE MODERN MEDEA—THE STORY OF MARGARET GARNER.—Photographed by Brady, from a Painting by Thomas Noble.—[See Page 316.]

Figure I.3. *The Modern Medea. The story of Margaret Garner.* Photographed by Brady, from a painting by Thomas Satterwhite Noble. Engraving published in *Harper's Weekly,* May 18, 1867, 308. Courtesy of Manuscripts, Archives, and Rare Books Library (MARBL), Emory University.

Officially, slavery had become a dormant issue in 1867 when Noble produced the painting portraying a defiant, proud Margaret confronting the slave catchers after the murder. Her hands point toward the dead individuals at the men's feet as if to suggest that slavery rather than she is responsible for her violent, desperate act.[38] The outstretched hands are "both a gesture of defiance and of desperation," according to Leslie Furth, who also maintains that "Noble cast Garner as a hero in a civic conflict."[39] In accordance with an anti-slavery position, the outraged Margaret portrayed in the painting was driven to take measures that were unavoidable. Yet, unlike the shocked but human countenances of the male deputies, she is also depicted as less than human. Her wild-eyed demeanor suggests that slavery was needed to control her savage instincts.[40] The painting thus dramatizes the pro-slavery view that Margaret was uncontrolled, while also positing that she acted out of scathing defiance in accordance with Euripides' myth.[41] A literal translation from the era of the Greek tragedies to the enslavement era in the United States would present Margaret's motive for killing her children, like that of Euripides's Medea, as retaliation by a willful, jilted lover. Thus, if one accepts Weisenburger's premise of the slaveholder's paternity, then a rebellious Margaret undoubtedly knew that by killing her child, she was killing not only the master's property, but also his (unacknowledged) progeny.[42]

Avoided in the painting is the reality that mixed-race individuals typically owed their existence to exploitative and/or violent sexual unions. Neither Margaret nor the mannish-looking children lying lifeless on the floor of the canvas are depicted as mulatto or "almost White" in keeping with the newspaper accounts at the time. There appears no hint that Margaret's children were fathered by her own or another White enslaver. Thus the painting ultimately denies any suggestion that her escape and subsequent infanticide were the consequence of ongoing sexual relations, likely forced, to which she had been subjected. For Noble, Margaret remains an uncontrollable "other," a racial and social inferior, an "infuriated negress" whose sensationalized depiction is similar to the pro-slavery press accounts just over a decade earlier.[43]

The artist's ambivalence about the evils of slavery predominate in the painting, while Margaret's own motivations are obscured. He rejects the freedom-seeking motive proclaimed by Margaret for her acts of resistance. Rather, Margaret is presented as a victim of her time, a woman subjugated within a system whose abuses are never acknowledged, her rebellious stance attributable to an uncivil act of retribution, against individuals who have "wronged" her—not against a brutal system. The extent to which Margaret acted out of scathing defiance as represented in the painting is debatable, according to modern scholars. Her stated reason for the murder was to free her children from bondage. Whether or not other conscious or subconscious motivations entered into her decision, we ultimately fail to hear Margaret's voice in the painting.

Thus, the "tragic heroine" viewpoint complies with both the pro-slavery position, which inferred that Margaret's attack on her children was evidence that she was not human, and the anti-slavery stance, which held that, being human, Margaret had few other options. Pro- and anti-slavery forces debated the institution of slavery, especially its impact on enslaved individuals, during and after the Garners' failed escape attempt and infanticide. The event therefore became an opportunity to manifest the private history of a woman's life in the public sphere. In certain ways, as Weisenburger asserts, Margaret had become an icon whose motives could be debated.[44]

## Negotiated Reality between Enslaved and Enslaver

Unlimited access to enslaved women through rape or coercion by White slave-holders, their sons, and associates was routine. Just as Blacks were not persons under the law, Black women could not be raped. Furthermore, resistance to the sexual demands of slaveholders often meant physical punishment and sometimes death. Nonetheless, enslaved Black women sometimes used the legal system and in exceptional cases even won a judgment against their attackers. Instances in which enslaved women successfully fended off their attackers have also been documented.[45] In these exceptional cases, women who were quick witted and likely outraged managed to prevail. More frequently, women chose life over death by acquiescing to, or negotiating the terms of their acceptance of, slaveholders' insistence on sexual relations. Especially when confronted by men intent on using force, an obvious power differential existed between the enslaver and the woman he held in bondage. The enslaved woman's perilous situation was in direct conflict with the power of her enslaver.

At the center of historic situations involving the threat of rape is the question whether the idea of a negotiated reality could in fact be applied to certain aspects of plantation life. The degree to which enslaved Black women negotiated multiple aspects of their everyday lives was not without certain limits, whether they exerted control over their labor or, to a lesser extent, over their sexual availability and reproduction. While most Black women could not prevent the abuses of their children within the system of their enslavement, historians have examined instances in which a negotiated reality might apply to mothers obtaining freedom for their offspring.[46] Most infamous perhaps is the bargain struck by the enslaved Sally Hemings, who in exchange for sexual access for her enslaver, Thomas Jefferson, obtained a better life for herself and her children.[47] However, can a woman be construed as exhibiting agency, even as a victim of rape, when faced with a choice about her own survival? This question underlies Martha McCaughey's argument that "women can't choose agency *over* victimization. Instead, women's victimization and agency must be understood as operating simultaneously in women's lives."[48] Thus, was Margaret Garner able to obtain any assurances of leniency for herself and her children by giving in to the sexual demands of the slaveholder, or was it rape amounting to longstanding sexual abuse, as has already been suggested? Furthermore, given the violent underpinnings of slavery, is it possible to distinguish between rape and consent? Aware of the impending reality of sexual abuse inherent in such an oppressive system, Margaret apparently ceased any further attempts to negotiate the well-being of her family and resorted to infanticide. As enslaved parents who attempted to escape, Margaret and her husband appear to have reached a limit in their tolerance of sexual predation.

Black women had little power in avoiding or preventing their sexual exploitation during slavery and afterward—a possible conclusion drawn from the story of Essie Mae Washington-Williams, who belatedly revealed that her father was the late Strom Thurmond of South Carolina. Washington-Williams's mother, Cassie Butler, was a sixteen-year-old African American house servant, and Thurmond was in his early twenties when Essie Mae was born. Thurmond, who was until recently the longest-serving United States senator, practiced segregationist bigotry in public and sexual license with his Black maid in private. Yet Washington-Williams waited until her father's death in 2003 at the age of a hundred, when she herself was seventy-eight, to go public—too late to expose Thurmond's hypocrisy during his lifetime.

Washington-Williams, whose life spanned both the Jim Crow and Civil Rights eras, vehemently rejected her father's intense racist polemics but rationalized it as politicking.[49] By choosing to keep silent, Washington-Williams reaped an undeniable benefit: she avoided a life of poverty, if not a "tragic" one, by accepting Thurman's financial assistance in educating herself and her children.[50] Despite a lifelong desire to be acknowledged as Thurmond's daughter, she also "didn't want *my* white blood to become an issue that might interfere with my education."[51] The return on her investment in silence perhaps was less of a calculation to free her offspring than that of the protagonist in Mary Frederickson's chapter, "A Mother's Arithmetic." Nevertheless, Washington-Williams secured the desired education for her children that she and others undoubtedly would interpret as a freedom strategy, in contemporary terms.

After more than five decades of silence and modest efforts to resist deeply entrenched racial barriers, the dutiful daughter revealed her secret. According to her memoir, "Strom Thurmond detested scandal. Mr. Straight Arrow, he detested the mere suggestion of impropriety."[52] Father and daughter distanced themselves from full disclosure of their interracial ties for all or most of their lives, respectively. How Washington-Williams would characterize the illicit sexual transgression that resulted in her birth is unclear. Indeed, she believes that her father cared for her and her mother, but that the existence of such love was socially forbidden.[53] Ultimately, however, as in the painting of Garner, Washington-Williams's mother, Cassie Butler, remains mute on her relationship with Strom Thurman, specifically about the circumstances under which Essie Mae was conceived.

## Black Feminist Perspectives

Regardless of whether we today can fully access the thoughts that led to her acts of resistance, Margaret Garner's refusal to capitulate to the injustices of slavery was based on a rational assessment of her situation. Indeed, Black women's reactions against gender violence—whether threatened or realized—were based first on critiquing and then on transforming systems of oppression. Thus, the stories of women such as Margaret Garner cannot adequately be understood without also understanding the racial and gender dynamics that fundamentally impacted their lives.

Focusing on the interplay between individual narrative and social structure (intersectional analysis) and on the textual depiction of self and other (Black feminist anthropological perspectives) can provide relevant theoretical lenses through which to approach such an understanding. These interdisciplinary, activist approaches therefore provide a useful framework for comprehending the myriad ways in which Black women have responded to violence and violation. Both theoretical perspectives allow Black women to speak from their experiences, and both place gender, race, and class at the center of the analysis of women's lives. As a result, they reveal the complex identities of individuals who interpret and negotiate the power differentials in their societies.

Since historical lives may provide important messages for contemporary ones, it is also important to apply these two theories to historical as well as contemporary contexts. Ultimately, both theories have the potential of placing voices from the past into dialogue with voices in the present. This is especially important in unraveling stories that largely remain unresolved, as is the case for Margaret Garner. Doing so may also eventually eliminate the distortions that still obscure the representation of Black women's lives.

Assessment of female slave narratives from a Black feminist anthropological perspective allows scholars to translate lived experience within and beyond particular historical contexts. Through *Incidents in the Life of a Slave Girl*, in which Harriet Jacobs chronicles her strategies for avoiding, derailing, and ultimately escaping from the rapacious slaveholder in whose house she labored, we can witness the fortitude of Margaret Garner and other enslaved women. In a similar vein, Frances Ellen Watkins Harper's poetry reflects the social contexts of Black women's lives. In both women's works, the private domain is presented in the public, political sphere. Harper's poem "The Slave Mother: A Tale of the Ohio" reveals a tragic choice that her Garneresque character must face, and, as Carla Peterson points out, also indirectly portrays Harper's own life.[54] These literary depictions occurring in close proximity historically allow one Black woman to convey the ethnographic substance of other enslaved women's lives. In doing so, a self-reflective approach legitimizes both the researcher and the researched. In *Black Feminist Anthropology*, Irma McClaurin terms the use of personal experience to analyze research subjects *autoethnographic*.[55]

A dual-perspective theoretical lens also lends itself to explicating Black women's strategic survivals in modern and historical contexts. Thus the phenomenon of dissemblance, whereby enslaved women in the past resisted sexual subjugation by appearing to acquiesce to their oppressors' demands while also avoiding disclosure of their inner lives, continues to be used in the present.[56] A recent example: in the aftermath of Hurricane Katrina, Black women and poor women avoided being further stigmatized by choosing to circumvent full disclosure of their experience as people living in abject poverty under enslavement-era conditions in the regions most vulnerable to natural disasters and most neglected by the Bush administration's inadequate response to the crisis. Using coping strategies from the past, women with the least access to the means of recovery in the disaster zone maintained their silence, particularly regarding the sexual abuse to which their race and gender made them susceptible.[57] Parallel lived experiences can therefore help illuminate the largely unspoken story of Margaret Garner and render it more accessible for contemporary witnessing.

Viewed historically, intersectional analysis also allows a community to reinstate its long-forgotten memory of its resistance movements and the individuals associated with them. During her time, Margaret Garner was viewed as nonhuman under the law and as a lesser human by many pro-slavery Whites. If the legacy of the Garners at the Richwood site is to be presented as a learning opportunity for present-day scholarly and nonacademic communities, it must also be offered with an approach inclusive of various views on enslavement.

An intersectional analysis allows one to examine slavery both as a flawed system and one in which those oppressed within it have an opposing voice. To challenge distorted characterizations of Black women is to ensure that stereotypes are not perpetuated and that the presence of African Americans in the area is not dismissed or overlooked. Voices ignored in the past because of the imbalance of power in the slaveocracy should not remain unheard in the present. Ultimately, establishing a bridge between different viewpoints promises to help resolve problems of race relations that still confound residents in the region.

## The Role of Fictionalized Depictions of Black Women's Experiences

The dehumanizing violence of slavery, especially the social and sexual degradation to which Black women were subjected, is often bypassed in discussions of slavery and resistance. Few slave narratives exist that detail the sexual exploitation experienced by enslaved Black women. Yet the lives of enslaved women generally and Margaret Garner specifically can be understood not only through existing factual narratives such as that of Harriet Jacobs's horrific ordeal but also through such fictional venues as the opera *Margaret Garner*, which acknowledged a reality that is rarely revealed in the public arena. Yet what role can fiction or fictionalized versions of history play in revealing the racial, sexual, and gender dynamic of such horrendous tales as that of the Garners? How valid is a postmodern approach that eschews a completely scientific, objective, religious or philosophical explanation to Black historical/cultural narratives? What stands to be lost or gained in the retelling?

The *Margaret Garner* opera served to stimulate an open exchange among audiences and among undergraduates regarding slavery, women's resistance, and the country's conflicted history. Community and campus-based programs prior to the opera's opening in Cincinnati invigorated discussions on freedom, justice, women's resistance to sexual abuse, and the impact of enslavement on race relations. Since participants in these programs were eager to learn more about the actual story, the dialogues became a vehicle for disclosing the history behind the opera and abating concerns about historical inaccuracies. *Margaret Garner* opened to considerable acclaim.[58] Framing historical lessons within contemporary contexts through the arts and literature may therefore provide a potent pedagogical strategy for promoting discussion aimed at understanding today's perplexing race and gender issues.

The production team for *Margaret Garner* sought to encourage a healing interracial dialogue similar to the late playwright August Wilson's intention to foster social change through works recounting the African American experience within U.S. history. Such a goal presents a formidable challenge to both artist and audience. Slavery and resistance to bondage are topics not always easily accepted either by scholarly or popular audiences, especially as many consider the topic less applicable to the country as a whole. The tremendous appeal of the *Margaret Garner* opera in Cincinnati, therefore, was significant. Excitement over the opera's opening in Cincinnati, where it sold out for all three nights, mirrored the anticipation that had accompanied the opening of the National Underground Railroad Freedom Center one year earlier. Indeed, the opera was intended to celebrate the first anniversary of the Freedom Center and to build momentum toward racial healing in the city. Thus, its creators envisioned that the opera's fictionalized account would prompt members of a diverse community to remember its history and engage in honest dialogue with one another.

Music Hall, where the opera was performed, is situated in the Black neighborhood called Over-the-Rhine in Cincinnati. Nearby, the Freedom Center sits on the banks of the Ohio River, the crossing point for many runaways escaping bondage farther south. Given the location of the three opera companies that commissioned the opera—Detroit, Cincinnati, and Philadelphia—promoting a forum for interracial exchange was an appropriate goal.

The three opera companies chose promotional images based on their perceptions of their audiences' receptivity to this heart-wrenching dramatization of the enslavement era. Cincinnati's use of the haunting image by artist Jonathan Green (reproduced on the cover of this volume) evokes perhaps the starkest visual reminder of the historic events portrayed in the opera. Green's image is of a woman whose eyes transfix the viewer with her penetrating gaze, suggesting perhaps that Margaret Garner chose survival of the spirit over survival of the flesh.[59] While Detroit (2005) and Chicago (2008) adopted a romanticized image of Margaret as a young mother, Charlotte (2006) and Philadelphia (2006) chose abstract images rather than a reconstructed portrait. Significantly, none chose Thomas Satterwhite Noble's depiction of the vengeful mother/destroyer (see Figure I.3). The difference in marketing strategies reflects calculated projections regarding the opera's relevance and impact on today's audiences. Whether the images chosen were pertinent to the opera's success was not determined, but as in Cincinnati, *Margaret Garner* sold out in all or most of the other venues where the opera was performed. At the New York City Opera, disappointed patrons who failed to obtain tickets were turned away.

For audience and cast alike, *Margaret Garner* provided an opportunity to learn about the historical journey of African Americans. "Doing the opera for me is like going back in history and discovering what really happened," said Angela Brown, who sang the role of Margaret's mother-in-law, Cilla, in the Cincinnati and Philadelphia productions.[60] During the Philadelphia run, some audience members, particularly older White opera-goers, departed at the intermission following Margaret's rape by the slaveholder at the end of the first act. It appears that, for them, the opera was a bit too real. More typically, however, others identified with Margaret's tenacity, placing themselves in the unthinkable horror of having to make Margaret's decision. The opera singers felt that the historical narrative and its manifestation as opera, fiction, and history resonated deeply with who they are. For instance, Denyce Graves, a new mother herself who sang the title role in the three cities in which the opera was co-commissioned, remarked, "This was a story of my people, something that made it very personal, as a woman, as an African-American, as an American. It was me on so many different levels."[61] Graves further noted that she believed that Margaret was "just an ordinary woman trying to protect her children in an extraordinary moment, and extraordinary time."[62]

## The Relevance of Margaret Garner's Story for Today

The story of Margaret Garner symbolizes the impossible choices that were forced upon African Americans burdened by the institution of slavery. It is a compelling story that even so had been largely lost among Blacks and Whites alike, even in the region where it occurred. Although the Garners in Kentucky lived less than twenty miles from freedom within the free state of Ohio, Cincinnati was not at the time a city where Blacks could live freely—a predicament that many Black residents still find themselves in today. Nevertheless, the story provides a vivid reminder of mutual support within and among families in Black communities living under meager conditions reminiscent of more recent times such as the mid-1960s.[63]

For Whites as well as Blacks, recognition of the role of African Americans and, increasingly, other peoples of color in building Northern Kentucky communities is a necessary precondition for a healthy dialogue about race relations. Otherwise, we risk the perpetuation of incidents such as the cross burning on the front lawn of a Black family's home in Boone County by White teenage youths in the summer of 2004. Evidently, these youths felt safe (and justified) to flagrantly display their racial hatred, since they had boasted about the deed to their friends. They, as many others in the state, were ignorant of such basic facts as that Blacks represented almost 25 percent of the population in some Northern Kentucky counties during Margaret Garner's lifetime from the 1830s to the 1850s.[64] Based on assumptions drawn from their observations of a sparse Black population in the mid-2000s, they apparently concluded that the existence and contributions of Black people to the economic growth of the region had been nil.[65] As a result of Blacks' erasure from social historical memory, to at least some Whites they had become despised "interlopers" and subject to continuing acts of vicious hatred by those who may themselves feel oppressed.

If the historical case of the Garners can inform the present, we need to acknowledge also the effect of interracial sex on the composition of families in the region. By obliterating the Garner story from public memory and restricting access to recorded and material culture, the community is deprived of its interracial heritage. Essentially, interracial sexual relations, whether violent or consensual, produced a long line of heirs.[66] Finally, Margaret Garner's story is also relevant to present-day women's resistance to intimate partner violence. Whether or not women agree with Margaret's choice, they understand the dilemma faced by women living under the constant threat of violence from partners, lovers, and husbands. The theme of women and violence is a continuing reality in the United States and the world.

Frances E. W. Harper, Harriet Jacobs, and Toni Morrison visualized themselves as witnesses and disseminators of information about their own lives that transcended their immediate communities. Likewise, research, teaching, and community dialogue focused on Margaret Garner also has the potential to enlighten learners within and beyond the local environs. An analysis of this woman's courage and resilience within feminist and intersectional frameworks allows her extraordinary story to reveal its lesson across the barriers of time and place.

## NOTES

Thanks to Kris Yohe for her editing assistance on an early version of my chapter.

1. Personal communication with the author, July 2005.

2. Richwood Presbyterian Church record, Session Book 11, dated March 1855, indicates that "Margaret a woman of color" was received into the church and her baptism ordered to

be administered. Most likely this was Margaret Garner, whose membership was recorded the year before the escape attempt.

3. *Cincinnati Gazette*, January 30, 1856.

4. *Cincinnati Enquirer*, January 29, 1856.

5. *Cincinnati Daily Gazette*, February 11, 1856.

6. Newspapers served to summarize court proceedings in lieu of court transcripts, which were destroyed in a fire. For that reason, Steven Weisenburger's detailed analysis in *Modern Medea: A Family Story of Slavery and Child-Murder from the Old South* (New York: Hill and Wang, 1998) depends almost entirely on newspaper accounts of the trial rather than on court transcripts. According to Mark Reinhardt, "The era's newspapers provide a reasonable substitute." See *Who Speaks for Margaret Garner? The True Story That Inspired Toni Morrison's* Beloved (Minneapolis: University of Minnesota Press, 2010), 60.

7. *Cincinnati Daily Gazette,* February 14, 1856.

8. *Cincinnati Daily Gazette*, February 11, 1856.

9. Reports describe thousands of spectators and tell that hundreds of armed guards escorted the shackled parents and their family, at a cost of more than $21,000. See Julius Yanuck, "The Fugitive Slave Case," *Mississippi Valley Historical Review* 40, no.1 (1953): 47–66.

10. This point is discussed by Reinhardt in *Who Speaks for Margaret Garner?*, 18–19. Other enslaved Blacks took the opportunity during the authorities' preoccupation with the trial to make good their own escape.

11. Commissioners earned five dollars for a not-guilty verdict and ten dollars for a guilty one. See Reinhardt, *Who Speaks for Margaret Garner?*, 23.

12. Years later, the prosecuting attorney agreed, revealing that in speaking to Margaret right after she was jailed, "[his] own feelings were intensely enlisted on her behalf," and that although it was his "duty to prosecute her for the offense," he doubted "whether any jury in admiring the heroic spirit of the mother who could kill herself and her offspring rather than suffer the degradation of slavery" would convict Margaret of murder (Salmon P. Chase Papers: microfilm edition, reel 30). Also see Weisenburger, *Modern Medea*, 117, 238.

13. The newly elected Ohio governor, Salmon Chase, had delayed signing the required requisition papers sent to Kentucky Governor Charles Morehead.

14. According to Weisenburger, witnesses said that Margaret "displayed frantic joy when told that her child was drowned" (*Modern Medea*, 225–26, as reported in the *Cincinnati Gazette*, March 11, 1856). Other news sources that reported on the incident are cited in Reinhardt, *Who Speaks for Margaret Garner?*, 133–36.

15. "A Reminiscence of Slavery," *Cincinnati Daily Chronicle*, March 11, 1870, 4.

16. At the time of the interview, which took place in the law offices of Colonel F. M. Moore, Robert Garner was filing a lawsuit against the crew of the steamer for negligence resulting in his ribs being fractured. *Cincinnati Daily Chronicle*, March 11, 1870.

17. Ibid.

18. The Ohio Department of Health (Division of Vital Statistics), death certificate, dated April 20, 1871, gives the cause of death as "consumption."

19. *Cincinnati Daily Chronicle*, March 11, 1870.

20. Reinhardt asks the same question in assembling the relevant primary documents in the case and providing an invaluable reference on the Margaret Garner story.

21. Marie Jenkins Schwartz, *Birthing a Slave: Motherhood and Medicine in the Antebellum South* (Cambridge, Mass.: Harvard University Press, 2006), 208–10; Brenda E. Stevenson, "Gender Convention, Ideals, and Identity among Antebellum Virginia Slave Women," in *More than Chattel: Black Women and Slavery in the Americas*, ed. David Barry Gaspar and Darlene Clark Hine (Bloomington: Indiana University Press, 1996), 175.

22. Darlene Clark Hine and Kathleen Thompson, *The History of Black Women in America: A Shining Thread of Hope* (New York: Broadway, 1998), 98–100. See also Darlene Clark Hine, "Female Slave Resistance: The Economics of Sex," in *Western Journal of Black Studies* 3 (Summer, 1979): 123–27; "Infanticide," in *Encyclopedia of African American History*, vol. 1, ed. Leslie M. Alexander and Walter C. Rucker (Santa Barbara, Calif.: ABC-CLIO, 2010), 212. Finally, most freedom seekers in Kentucky were of mixed race or mulatto, according to J. Blaine Hudson, *Fugitive Slaves and the Underground Railroad in the Kentucky Borderland* (Jefferson, N.C.: McFarland, 2002), 40.

23. See Wilma King, "'Suffer with Them till Death': Slave Women and Their Children in Nineteenth-Century America," in Gaspar and Hine, *More than Chattel*, 160.

24. See Ruth Wade Cox Brunings, "Slavery and the Tragic Story of Two Families—Gaines and Garner," in *Northern Kentucky Heritage* 12, no. 1 (2004): 42–43.

25. Ibid.

26. Ibid.; see also Hudson, *Fugitive Slaves*, 51–57.

27. For example, Richwood Presbyterian Church records indicate that an enslaved woman, Hannah, was reprimanded for "insubordination and cursing," according to Weisenburger, *Modern Medea*, 52, 296n69.

28. Brunings, "Slavery and the Tragic Story of Two Families," 39.

29. Reported in the *Cincinnati Enquirer*, July 12, 2005.

30. Editorial, "Garner Story Has Much to Teach," *Cincinnati Enquirer*, July 12, 2005. Newspaper perspectives on the problem of slavery have evolved as well. The *Cincinnati Daily Enquirer*, which was a pro-slavery newspaper at the time of the Garners' trial, demonstrates its anti-slavery position in publishing this statement.

31. Weisenburger, *Modern Medea*, 75–6.

32. Ibid., 44–48.

33. Ibid., 75–76.

34. Reinhardt, *Who Speaks for Margaret Garner?*, 14–15.

35. Dorothy E. Roberts, *Killing the Black Body: Race, Reproduction, and the Meaning of Liberty* (New York: Pantheon, 1997), 39.

36. Jeff Kunerth, *Providence Journal*, September 27, 2005.

37. The painting is on permanent display in the From Slavery to Freedom Gallery at the National Underground Railroad Freedom Center in Cincinnati.

38. Leslie Furth, "'The Modern Medea' and Race Matters: Thomas Satterwhite Noble's *Margaret Garner*," *American Art* (Summer, 1998): 39.

39. Ibid.

40. See chapter 9 for the "crazed look" analogy applied to Garner in a contemporary context of mental distress.

41. According to Jo-Ann Morgan in "Thomas Satterwhite Noble's Mulattos: From Barefoot Madonna to Maggie the Ripper" (*Journal of American Studies* 41 [2007]: 1, 113), the caption "Modern Medea" may have been influenced by Euripides's Greek tragic drama, *Medea*, which was touring at the time Noble's painting was reproduced in *Harper's Weekly* (May 18, 1867).

42. Weisenburger, *Modern Medea*, 78.

43. See Reinhardt, *Who Speaks for Margaret Garner?*, 55, for a reprint of excerpts from the *Cincinnati Columbian*, January 29, 1856.

44. Ibid., 247.

45. Melton A. McLaurin, *Celia, a Slave* (New York: Avon, 1993). Also, see the story of the enslaved cook Sukie Abbott who fought off her attacker by scalding "his hind parts" with a pot of hot soap, resulting in the cessation of his attempts to rape other women on his plantation; Brenda E. Stevenson, "Gender Convention, Ideals and Identity among Antebellum Virginia Slave Women," in Gaspar and Hine, *More than Chattel*, 172.

46. Stevenson (ibid., 176) discusses the difficulty of avoiding the dire consequences of separations from their children.

47. Consent rather than force appears to define the thirty-eight-year Hemings-Jefferson liaison, despite the power differential between a woman in her early teens held in bondage by a prominent statesman in his forties. Annette Gordon-Reed, *Thomas Jefferson and Sally Hemings: An American Controversy* (Charlottesville: University Press of Virginia, 1997), 167. Chapters in the present volume herewith also explore living arrangements established by women in subordinate positions to White male slaveholders.

48. Martha McCaughey, *Real Knockouts: The Physical Feminism of Women's Self-Defense* (New York: New York University Press, 1997), xii.

49. Interview with Essie Mae Washington-Williams, NPR, February 1, 2005, available at http://www.npr.org/templates/story/story.php?storyId=4473680 (accessed February 5, 2013).

50. Thurmond secured a commission in the Navy that allowed one of Washington-Williams's sons to complete his medical degree; Essie Mae Washington-Williams, *Dear Senator: A Memoir by the Daughter of Strom Thurmond* (New York: HarperCollins, 2005), 198.

51. Washington-Williams, *Dear Senator*, 111.

52. Ibid., 207.

53. Ibid.,148. See also, Joseph Crespino, *Strom Thurmond's America*, (New York: Hill and Wang, 2012), 32–33, 306–9.

54. Harper's poetry conveys a sense of abandonment and loss, as discussed by Carla L. Peterson, *Doers of the Word: African-American Women Speakers and Writers in the North (1830–1880)* (New York: Oxford University Press, 1995), 127–28.

55. Irma McClaurin, ed., *Black Feminist Anthropology: Theory, Politics, Praxis, and Poetics* (New Brunswick, N.J.: Rutgers University Press, 2001), 49–73.

56. This concept is discussed by Darlene Clark Hine, "Rape and the Inner Lives of Black Women in the Middle West: Preliminary Thoughts on the Culture of Dissemblance," *Signs: Journal of Women in Culture and Society* 14, no. 4 (1989): 912–20.

57. On the other hand, while Harriford and Thompson recognize the continuity of strategic approaches used by women of color, past and present, they also point out that these

women did not necessarily rely on dissemblance to advocate for adequate housing, for example. See Diane Harriford and Becky Thompson, "'Say It Loud, I'm Black and I'm Proud': Organizing Since Katrina," in *Fast Capitalism* 4, no. 1 (2008), available at http://www.uta .edu/huma/agger/fastcapitalism/4_1/harrifordthompson.html (accessed March 2, 2012). Also see chapter 9 herewith for McDaniels-Wilson's detailed discussion of dissemblance in both contemporary and historical contexts.

58. Such concerns were especially expressed by members of the Cincinnati Opera's *Margaret Garner* Opera Steering Committee, which successfully introduced the opera to both traditional and nontraditional audiences.

59. Thanks to Kris Yohe for this representation of Garner's choices.

60. "Opera: 'Margaret Garner' Comes to Life," *Cincinnati Enquirer*, September 10, 2004.

61. Tracie Luck, who was the understudy for Graves, fully embraced the role as a superb Margaret Garner, and Lisa Daltirus, who was also spectacular, sang the role of Cilla in the New York production.

62. "Graves Makes 'Garner' Her Baby: Singing the Slave's Story Is Personal for Opera Star," *Cincinnati Enquirer*, July 14, 2005.

63. See, for example, the discussion of a poor community's use of non-kinship networks for mutual support in *All Our Kin: Strategies for Survival in a Black Community* (New York: Harper and Row, 1974).

64. See Hudson, *Fugitive Slaves*, 14.

65. Kentucky's Black population declined before and after the Civil War as freedom seekers and the newly free sought less hostile environments in which to live. Blacks in Boone County numbered less than 3 percent of the population in 2008. See Boone County Census Records, http://quickfacts.census.gov.proxy.lib.muohio.edu/qfd/states/21/21015.html (accessed February 6, 2013).

66. To date, no descendants of the Garners have been identified, although Stephanie Stokes Oliver explores intriguing coincidences in her family's genealogy with that of Margaret Garner; see "The Search for My Beloved Margaret Garner," *Essence* 36, no. 10 (2006): 172.

# PART I

# HISTORICAL AND CULTURAL PERSPECTIVES ON GENDERED RESISTANCE

# CHAPTER 1

# A Mother's Arithmetic

## Elizabeth Clark Gaines's Journey from Slavery to Freedom

*Mary E. Frederickson*

In 1991, after the publication of *Beloved*, Toni Morrison addressed an audience of a thousand historians at the Organization of American Historians meeting in Louisville, Kentucky. After a stirring introduction by Darlene Clark Hine, the crowded conference ballroom grew quiet as Morrison spoke of the importance of remembering those who "brought you over," those who made it possible "to get to the other side." She had taken the process of making sense of the past to an entirely new level in *Beloved*, a novel that pivots on the tension between "keeping the past at bay" and the act of remembering.[1] Leveraging history with the power of fiction, Morrison transformed Margaret Garner, the enslaved Kentucky woman who escaped with her husband and children across the Ohio River from Covington, Kentucky, to Cincinnati, Ohio, on a freezing January night in 1856, into Sethe, who kneads memory like bread dough, turning it over and pushing it back, over and back, again and again.

Elizabeth Clark Gaines, the protagonist of the story told in this chapter, traversed the same "River Jordan" forty years before Margaret Garner's treacherous passage. Crossing the Ohio River from Covington to Cincinnati in 1817, Gaines was a manumitted slave whose history has been hidden in archives, wills, census records, city directories, court documents, newspaper accounts, and notes from an interview conducted with her grandson Peter H. Clark in June 18, 1919.[2] This history is a story of emancipation, not of a dramatic escape on the Underground Railroad nor of whips, chains, or barking dogs on the chase. In contrast to Garner, there were no trials, no speeches, no editorials, no publicity of any kind. Elizabeth Clark Gaines calculated her way out of slavery, following a route that took decades and led to Gaines's freedom and the manumission of her children. Their emancipation was her proudest legacy. Records of the manumission of slave mothers and their mixed-race children are not rare in American archives, suggesting that Gaines's story, as remarkable as it is, is more common than we think.[3]

Elizabeth Clark Gaines's story speaks directly to three questions of major concern to historians, anthropologists, and feminist scholars. First, what do the experiences of enslaved women in the United States tell us about sexual servitude? Second, how useful and reliable is oral history in reconstructing a history of gendered resistance? And finally, what do stories about enslaved mothers and their children tell us about resistance and the meaning of freedom? Margaret Garner's life offers one historical template; the life of Elizabeth Clark Gaines provides another. In sharp contrast to Margaret Garner's brilliant flash of resistance that was ultimately unsuccessful, Elizabeth Gaines's calculated, manipulative, and persistent route to freedom unfolded with no public notice. No one has written about her life. Court documents recording her name, including her manumission papers, remained buried in the archives for almost two hundred years, leaving her thoroughly "disremembered." The interview with her grandson held the key to this reconstruction of Elizabeth Clark Gaines's story. At age ninety, he spoke about his family history in eloquent detail. His account of names, places, relationships, and dates, stretching from eighteenth-century Virginia to nineteenth-century Kentucky and Ohio, began with his once-enslaved, mixed-race grandmother and his white slaveholding grandfather. Her life history, the forms of resistance she employed, and the trajectories of her children's lives bring to life a multifaceted way of negotiating enslavement and emancipation that stretched across a lifetime.[4]

The hero of this story went by three different names: born a slave named Betty in 1783, she took the name Elizabeth Clark at the time of her manumission at age thirty-one in 1814; five years later, in 1819, she changed her name to Elizabeth Clark Gaines when she married a "free man of color" named Isom Gaines. Betty lived as an enslaved woman who, according to her grandson Peter, bore five children fathered by a white slave owner named Clarke. Four of these children lived to adulthood—Peter Clark's father Michael; his sisters, Elisa and Evalina; and his brother, Elliott. One of Betty's five children apparently died in infancy. Elizabeth Clark survived as a "free woman of color" who built an independent life for herself; after age thirty-six, as a legally married woman, Elizabeth Clark Gaines gave birth to three more sons, fathered by Isom Gaines. Her seven children, four of whom were born in slavery, became influential leaders, active church members, significant abolitionists, and accomplished businessmen.[5] Their children became teachers and homemakers whose children attended public schools, went to college, and trained as physicians and musicians. They inherited a world that first took shape in their great-grandmother's imagination.

At each stage of her life, Elizabeth Clark Gaines, née Betty, plumbed the resources available to her—family, church, literacy, white allies, and the law—to navigate her way to freedom. In the process, legal battles ensued, first with the man who enslaved her for twenty-four years, and then with his eldest son. Elizabeth

Clark Gaines used the law to free herself and her four children. Her success met with hard resistance, both in Kentucky, where signed papers concerning enslavement meant nothing if a slave master refused to honor them, and in Cincinnati, where, as Elizabeth Clark Gaines's grandson Peter later put it, "Nowhere has the prejudice against colored people been more cruelly manifested."[6]

## Betty

Betty was born in 1783, in eastern Virginia's Hanover County. Evidence of her birth appears in a ledger meticulously kept by a young white man named John Clarke. Her mother, Lucy, was said to be a "mulatto;" her father, a "Black." Her parents had worked as slaves for William Clarke, a wealthy man who ran a thriving import business and inn. When William Clarke died intestate, shortly before Betty's birth, his son "John Clarke" was appointed executor of his father's complicated legal affairs, a process that eventually took twelve years. Betty's brother Edmond was born in 1789; her sister Sarah, in late 1793. Each time, expenses paid "To negro Rachel" for "laying Lucy" were carefully recorded in the Clarke book of expenditures.[7]

Betty's immediate family was able to stay together during the twelve years that John Clarke managed his father's estate, but that changed abruptly in 1793, when he divided his father's slaves among the heirs. Betty's mother, Lucy, and her brother and sister, Edmund and Sarah, went to John Clarke as part of the settlement; "a girl Betty," then age ten, went to William's daughter, Mildred Clarke Crutchfield; and Betty's father, Peter, was sent to William's daughter, Ellender. The probate of their master's estate sundered Betty's family, forcing them to live on three different Hanover County plantations. Betty, made to live apart from her parents and siblings, was separated from her mother for the first time.[8] Betty's mother, Lucy, worked in John Clarke's household, who as a son of Hanover County, had followed the dictates of custom and practice for the ruling elite in that part of eighteenth-century Virginia. He had made a proper marriage to Sally Smith, a young woman his own age from the same social class, and during the years that Lucy was pregnant with Betty and her two siblings, John Clarke and his wife also had three children: Elizabeth was born around 1788, Harriet in 1792, and William in 1794. Shortly after William's birth, Sally died, leaving her young husband with three children under the age of seven.[9] Betty's mother, Lucy, whose children were about the same ages, would have been one of the enslaved women Clarke depended on after his wife's death.

In 1795, when Betty was thirteen, John Clarke bought her from his sister, Mildred Crutchfield. This sale, quite possibly negotiated because of Lucy's influence, reunited Betty with her mother and her siblings Edmond and Sarah. Shortly afterward, John Clarke left Virginia with a number of other white Virginia families heading West. John Clarke took Betty and her mother, sister, and brother with him. Betty's father, Peter, was left behind, although a number of other Clarke slaves were selected to go. The population of Kentucky increased nearly three hundred percent in the 1790s, and Betty became part of this huge migration led by men like John Clarke, the white sons of Virginia's elite, seeking more affordable land that could be planted in tobacco, cotton, and corn and worked by slaves. After traveling over four hundred miles from Hanover County to Kentucky, John Clarke and his entourage settled first in Lexington, Kentucky.[10]

The onset of sexual activity for Betty occurred during or soon after the trip west. She conceived a child during this time and gave birth to a son, Michael, in Lexington in 1797. The oral history given by Betty's grandson Peter H. Clark tells us that his father Michael was the first of Betty's children fathered by "him." Betty was fourteen at the time of Michael's birth; John Clarke was thirty-seven. By the time her son turned two, in 1799, John Clarke had resettled Betty and her family on a two-hundred-acre farm on "Paddy's Run," outside of Cynthiana, Kentucky, about thirty miles from Lexington. According to Peter Clark's interview, over the next eight years, Betty, who Clarke later referred to as "my negro woman, Betty," gave birth to four more mixed-race children—three daughters, one of whom died in infancy, and another son—fathered by her white slave owner. The household on Paddy's Run consisted of John Clarke and his three children from his marriage to Sally Smith, who were ages ten, six, and four when Michael was born, and some twenty other enslaved men, women, and children of various ages. For more than two decades, Betty lived as John Clarke's enslaved concubine, as such "wives" were called in Hanover County, Virginia. Widowed at age thirty-five, he never remarried.[11]

John Clarke and Betty do not appear to have been "notorious in the neighborhood," as historian Joshua D. Rothman suggests people considered some mixed-race couples living together in the Early Republic society of Virginia.[12] To the contrary, the society of Harrison County, Kentucky, seems to have accepted the household structure at the Clarke farm on Paddy's Run. Clarke bought his land from Richard and Mary Timberlake, former neighbors in Virginia, who had come to Kentucky in 1790. Samuel Broadwell, a founder of the Methodist Episcopal Church on Paddy's Run, was a witness to Clarke's will. At Paddy's Run, Betty, together with her mother, Lucy, and her sister, Sarah, took care of Betty's children—two sons, Michael and Elliott, and two daughters, Elisa and Evalina—and John Clarke's three older children, left motherless when Sallly Smith died. By 1810, John Clarke's oldest children, Harriet and Elizabeth, had married Kentucky men and settled into lives of their own. Harriet wed Augustine C. Respess, who later established a business in Mason County, Kentucky. Elizabeth married James Kelley, a merchant in nearby Paris, Kentucky, who later settled in Cynthiana.[13] The youngest white child on the farm, William S. Clarke, grew to maturity knowing that he would inherit land and slaves from his father. In sharp contrast, the fate of Betty's children, the mixed-race half-sisters and half-brothers of Harriet, Elizabeth, and William, weighed heavily on their mother's mind.

Betty lived in a world structured to keep her and her children enslaved. As historian and legal scholar Annette Gordon-Reed has written in *The Hemingses of Monticello* about Sally Hemings's mother, Elizabeth, "Slavery, white supremacy, and male dominance—indeed, practically every feature of Virginian society—combined to keep her down [and] law formed the foundation of this system." Betty's life in central Kentucky, in a society modeled after that of eastern Virginia, was much the same, particularly in legal terms. As in Virginia, the law shaped Betty's oppression and John Clarke's privilege, determined their relationship, and, as Gordon-Reed put it, "set ironclad limits" on Betty's capacity to determine her fate and that of her children.[14]

While the power of the legal system to perpetuate the bonds of slavery was essentially the same in Virginia and Kentucky, differences in literacy laws, geography, and evangelicalism meant that life at Paddy's Run was not the same as life in Hanover County. Specifically, Kentucky never enacted the same literacy laws as Virginia, which meant that Betty and her children could legally learn to read and write. The way in which her sons subsequently functioned in Cincinnati as businessmen who used the legal system and wrote their own wills proves that they were literate.[15] Moreover, the farm where Betty lived on Paddy's Run was less than seventy miles from the Ohio state line, which until passage of the Fugitive Slave Act in 1850 marked the boundary between slavery and freedom. Traffic along the Paris-Cynthiana Pike passed close to Paddy's Run on the way to Cincinnati, the largest market in the area for agricultural goods and livestock. Slaves from the area around the Paddy's Run farm regularly transported crops and livestock north along this route, putting them in close proximity to the site of early abolitionist activity in the Ohio River valley. But while differences in the legal system and the geographical landscape of antebellum Kentucky opened a wedge in the ironclad slave system that shaped Betty's life, evangelicalism proved to be the strongest cultural force that Betty used to transform her life, both while enslaved and later as a free woman of color.

To say that evangelicalism thrived in rural Kentucky during the years that Betty lived at Paddy's Run is an understatement. Her move to this part of Kentucky in 1799 coincided with a period of unprecedented religious fervor in the region. On the line between Harrison and Bourbon Counties, Paddy's Run sat near the epicenter of what historian John Boles has called the "Great Revival" in the antebellum South, a phenomenon of religious awakening so spectacular that word spread all along the Eastern Seaboard and further revivals "ignited" throughout the region. The revival spirit began in southern Kentucky in 1798, and then spread north to

Lexington, Paris, and Cynthiana. In July 1801, a revival at Indian Creek in Harrison County, a couple of miles from the Paddy's Run farm, drew ten thousand people, male and female, free and slave. Methodist ministers like Samuel Broadwell of Paddy's Run joined dozens of other pastors from Presbyterian and Baptist congregations to minister to the crowds.[16]

A few weeks later, with much advance publicity, a gathering almost twice as large met at Cane Ridge, five miles from Paddy's Run. Preaching day and night, the ministers could hardly contain the emotion and zeal of those who attended. One attendee wrote later, "This was the largest meeting of any I have ever seen. It continued from Friday until Wednesday." He described that those who attended as "of all ages, from 8 years and upwards; male and female; rich and poor; the blacks; and of every denomination." Emotions ran high as "sermons hymns, hosannas, weeping filled the air." Ministers warned of the Judgment Day to come and the opportunity for salvation at hand. People fell to the ground in religious ecstasy and exhaustion as a never-ending series of sermons, hymns, and prayers produced exhaustion and near prostration, clamor and confusion, and hundreds of new converts.[17]

This religious fervor had long-lasting effects in in the Cynthiana-Paris area. In the wake of the Great Revival, slave preachers held secretly organized religious meetings in Bourbon County that, according to slave preacher Elisha Green, slave patrollers sometimes disrupted. After Cane Ridge, an increasing number of enslaved women and men signed membership rosters at white churches, and ministers baptized a larger number of slave children. Some of the first African American congregations were organized in this area, including one in Lexington and another in Paris, less than ten miles from Paddy's Run, where Elisha Green became minister. There and elsewhere both races came together "under the sacred canopy of evangelical Protestantism," as John Boles puts it, and religion reshaped slavery in Kentucky by imposing a set of moral constraints on an immoral system. Potentially subversive, religion offered slaves a sense of self-respect and an expansion of what some have called "psychic living space" within slavery. Opportunities to learn to read and write increased, and as Boles argues, churches were "perhaps the only place in southern society where bond and free so nearly met as equals." For enslaved women like Betty, identification with the Children of Israel who suffered as God's chosen people and eventually left Egypt for the promised land of Canaan offered a powerful antidote to the degradation of enslavement.[18]

## A Mother's Arithmetic

Betty's life changed dramatically in the summer of 1814, when John Clarke grew desperately ill, and she began to calculate the odds of gaining freedom for herself and her children. Wills and deeds written in Kentucky could reinforce the laws of slavery from one generation to the next or, conversely, dissolve the bonds of property that held women like Betty in perpetual servitude. In that regard, in the legal calculus of slavery, age worked in Betty's favor because she was twenty-three years younger than John Clarke. She could count on his dying before her and that the terms of his will would determine her fate and that of her children. Clarke had the power to shape her life after his death, as he could free her and her children or tighten the grip of slavery. Their future would turn on his last will and testament.

Legally defined as property, chattel, or real estate, enslaved men, women, and children were passed down from one generation to the next, the same as land, furniture, and jewelry. Because of the difference in age between Betty and John Clarke, and perhaps because of their long sexual relationship, release from the bonds of slavery at the time of his death offered Betty the best chance of obtaining her freedom and manumitting Michael, Elisa, Evelina, and Elliott.

Kentucky slave masters not infrequently used their wills to free particular slaves, often a "negro woman" like Betty or the children they had fathered out of wedlock. This happened with enough frequency that Betty would have known about this legal route out of slavery. She was thirty-one years old as John Clarke lay dying in the farmhouse on Paddy's Run. She may have used those days when he was bedridden to negotiate her freedom, to convince him to manumit her four living enslaved children. She may have talked to him quietly, reminding him of an earlier promise he had made to free her and her children, or perhaps she took advantage of his vulnerability, threatening to let him die of thirst or lie in his own waste if he did not comply with her appeal for freedom. Regardless, she knew the legal reality of his power over her. Whatever transpired between John Clarke and Betty on those stifling summer afternoons, we know that in early July 1814, John Clarke contacted his attorney, Benjamin Mills, from Lexington, to discuss preparing a will. Mills came to Paddy's Run on July 15 when, close to death, Clarke mustered enough strength to sign the document with a wobbly "X."[19]

Within days after Benjamin Mills's visit, John Clarke died, his will carefully written, properly signed, and legally notarized. Dying with his affairs in order may have been particularly important to Clarke because of the difficult twelve years he had spent settling his father's affairs in Virginia. Probated in August 1814, the document signed by John Clarke divided his property of land and slaves among his three oldest children, those borne by his wife Sally Smith, the young Virginia woman who had died in childbirth twenty years earlier. The executors of John Clarke's estate were his twenty-year-old son, William S. Clark, and his sons-in-law, James Kelley and Augustine Respess. Clarke, a relatively modest landholder of four hundred acres at the time of his death, willed two hundred acres to his son and a hundred acres to each of his sons-in-law.[20]

The twenty-six enslaved women, men, and children who lived on the Paddy's Run farm made up the bulk of Clarke's considerable wealth. Clarke divided his

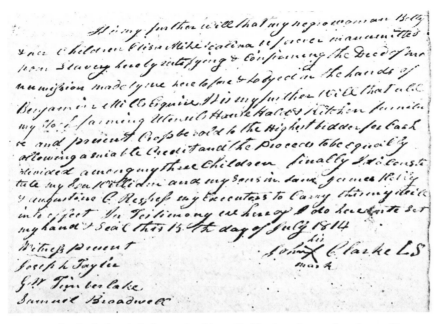

Figure 1.1. "Will of John Clarke," 1814, Cynthiana, Ky. Harrison County Courthouse, Kentucky Will Book A, p. 245. Photograph by Linda Parker Moore.

slaves among his son and two daughters and instructed "all other property to be sold and divided equally between my three children." But John Clarke's will did not end with this traditional division of property. His testament continued: "It is my further will that my negro woman Betty and her children Elisa, Mike and E[v]alina be forever manumitted confirming the deed of manumission heretofore lodged in the hands of Benjamin Mills Esq." With two strokes from the pen of a dying man, Betty gained her freedom and that of Michael, age sixteen, Elisa, age fourteen, and Evalina, age eight.

As John Clarke's lawyer, Benjamin Mills, a Presbyterian elder connected with the Cane Ridge Church, read the will, Betty must have devoured each word as soon as it left the lawyer's mouth. John Clarke acknowledged his relationship with Betty with the words, "my negro woman," at the same time he denied his paternity and role in the creation of Betty's family by referring to Michael, Eliza, and Evelina as "her children." Moreover, the phrase "and her children Elisa, Mike and E[v]alina" would have simultaneously reverberated for Betty with relief and then confusion as she realized that Elliott, her fourth child, age seven, had not been included. Before she could react, the words she had been waiting to hear would have reached her ears: "*be forever manumitted.*" Time stopped as she became a free woman. Then Mills read the legal ending: "confirming the deed of manumission heretofore lodged in the hands of Benjamin Mills, Esq."[21] The papers were in the lawyer's hands, and Betty's mind went back to Elliott. One slave child left out of the will. Had she miscalculated John Clarke's agreement, made before he crossed the lines of that wobbly X? He was to manumit her and "her children," but he had not said which children, or how many of her four children he would free. Leaving Elliott out of the will appeared to have been a calculated move by John Clarke, signed and sealed. From beyond the grave, he used the law to keep Elliott enslaved and Betty ensnared, if not enslaved, at Paddy's Run. He clearly did not intend to give her all that she wanted. He had won, in the very moment of her emancipation.

At age ten, Betty had been separated from her mother, father, sister, and brother when John Clark had settled his father's Virginia estate in 1793. Clarke followed this odious pattern again in Kentucky in 1814, when Betty and three of her children were manumitted but Elliott remained enslaved. Had Elliott been manumitted, Betty and her children could have left Paddy's Run after the will was read. As it was, Betty remained in Kentucky for two more years, her life continuing much as it had before as she worked for John Clarke's son, William S. Clarke, then twenty years old, the child she had cared for since he was a baby. Betty had long held a special position among the twenty-six Clarke slaves by virtue of her relationship to John Clarke. In 1814, her status may have increased even more after she became, according to legal principle, "a free woman." Her children, including Elliott, were William's half-siblings. The relationship between Betty and William S. Clark was clearly complicated. She had cared for him as he grew up, but slavery made a mockery of their connection.

After John Clarke's death and Betty's manumission, she became involved in a psychological battle with William S. Clarke that would go on for fifteen years. Betty used whatever domestic or emotional power she had over William to try to free her son Elliott, and her perseverance paid off. In 1815, a year after his father's death, William signed his brother Elliot's manumission papers. However, like his father before him, what he gave with one hand, he took away with the other. In this case, Elliot's freedom was held tantalizingly in front of Betty when William wrote, "I, William S. Clark [sic], . . . for divers causes & considerations do manumit and set free the negro boy slave named Elliott," and then, seeming to taunt Betty in the cruelest way imaginable, continued, "after sd. Boy slave . . . shall arrive at the age of twenty-one years" if he "behaves himself and pleases me."[22] A more effective means of control could not have been devised. Anything Elliott, a child of seven, or Betty or her emancipated children, Michael, Elisa, and Evalina, did that displeased William over the next twelve years would endanger Elliott's chances of obtaining his freedom when he turned twenty-one in 1827.

Yet, without Betty or her family doing anything, William had plenty of reasons to be "displeased." His father's will left him a diminished farm—half of the land and two-thirds of the slaves had gone to John Clarke's sons-in-law, Augustine Respass and James Kelley. William had received the remaining two hundred acres and eight adult slaves. Furthermore, although he ran the farm, he was master of neither Betty nor her free children. The year after William signed the papers promising Elliott's eventual manumission, he became engaged to marry Eliza Robinson, the daughter of a farmer and tavern keeper from Grant County, Kentucky.[23] A short time later, on August 28, 1816, Betty received a promissory note from William S. Clarke, in lieu of two years' back wages, that read, "Due Betty a negro woman formerly owned by my father $65 for value received to be returned in silver with legal interest from the date until paid."[24] At this point, Betty and her two daughters, Elisa and Evalina, left Paddy's Run and traveled the sixty-five miles northwest from Paddy's Run to Cincinnati with their deeds of manumission and Betty's promissory note in hand.

We will never know precisely why Betty left Kentucky in the early fall of 1816. Remaining in a slave state as a "free woman of color" came with considerably risk—Betty could easily have faced the auction block, a severe beating, or sexual violation. The line between slavery and freedom remained blurred for emancipated women and men, who were required to register annually, pay a fee, and carry "free papers" to prove their status as free persons of color. Women like Betty could face arrest for numerous vague violations, including keeping a disorderly house or attending meetings with slaves. Perhaps Betty's active participation at church had gotten her into trouble. Or perhaps William's bride had no intention of living at Paddy's Run with the woman John Clarke had named "my negro woman" in his will, the woman who had run the Clarke household for as long as her groom-to-be could remember. Betty had lived on that farm for more than two decades with her mother, two siblings, John Clarke's three children, and the four children of her own whom he had fathered. Her ties at Paddy's Run ran deep, but as Betty prepared to leave, her connection to her son, Elliott, now nine years old and the slave of his white half-brother William, caused the deepest anguish.

To protect Elliott once she left for Cincinnati, Betty decided to take the risk of also leaving her son Michael in Kentucky. By then he was a nineteen-year-old "free person of color" who, to comply with state law, had to have a white male guardian until age twenty-one. To put this arrangement in place, Betty sought help from Elizabeth Clarke Kelley, the white daughter of her former owner who lived in Cynthiana, about five miles from Paddy's Run. Kelley's husband, James Kelley, had inherited eight of his father-in-law's slaves, including Betty's brother Edmond. Unlike her brother William Clarke, Elizabeth Kelley seemed willing to help Betty and her family step into their new lives as free individuals. She asked her husband to become Michael's guardian, and James Kelley agreed.[25] The two women had grown up together, with Betty only a few years older, and they shared memories that stretched back to Virginia.

## Elizabeth Clark

After she arrived in Cincinnati, Betty filed her manumission papers and those of Elisa and Evalina at the courthouse in Cincinnati, as required by law, and came into her own as a free woman, shedding the name *Betty* like an old skin.[26] She adopted the surname of her former owner but dropped the "e" in Clarke, and from 1816 on, she used the name Elizabeth Clark. We know little about Elizabeth Clark's first two years in Cincinnati, a rapidly growing city on the banks of the Ohio River that stood as a beacon for Southern blacks, legally manumitted and fugitive alike. When Betty arrived in Cincinnati, she was one of fewer than four hundred African Americans in the city, out of a total population of about nine thousand. Seventy percent of these men, women, and children had come from the South with little money and a pressing need for cash wages and homes. Betty's promissory note from William S. Clarke, for instance, could not buy food for her children. The poverty among African Americans in the city meant that by 1820, only sixty-six independent black households had been established; 44 percent of African Americans were counted as part of the white households where they worked as live-in domestic workers.[27]

During this period, Cincinnati, in sharp contrast to other Ohio cities, rigidly enforced a series of "black laws," passed in 1804 and 1807, that made it difficult for African Americans to obtain work and impossible for them to apply for public assistance through the city's "poor fund." When Betty and her daughters crossed the Ohio River, they entered a city that denied African Americans the right to vote, testify in court, attend a public school, or receive services in a hospital or orphanage. Betty came north just as Cincinnati began an unprecedented period of growth for both its black and white populations, but just before the boom began; a crippling depression hit the city in 1819, making life for African Americans even more precarious. Despite these obstacles, the black community in the city grew by some 450 percent over the next decade, to 2,250 in 1829, primarily through the continued migration of Southern blacks out of the slave states of the South. The white population also grew rapidly during these years, but at a slower rate. Blacks made up 9 percent of the city's total population of 24,148 in 1829, a figure that made many white Cincinnatians uneasy about more fugitive slaves settling in the city.[28]

As the migration of Southern blacks into Ohio continued, racial discrimination became a cornerstone of the city's social and economic structure, and Cincinnati increasingly gained the reputation of being a Southern city in a Northern state. Nonetheless, Elizabeth Clark made a life for herself in the city, supporting her daughters and most likely sending them to one of the small private schools for

African American children in the section of the city known as "Little Africa." Opportunities to worship in black congregations led by African American ministers increased during the two years that Elizabeth Clark lived as a "free woman of color."[29] To her, the city must have resembled the "promised land of Canaan" that she first envisioned during the turn-of-the-century evangelical revivals that had transformed the lives of so many Kentuckians, slave and free alike, in the area surrounding Paddy's Run.

## Elizabeth Clark Gaines

On December 12, 1819, two years after Betty arrived in Cincinnati, she married a man named Isom Gaines, a free black man of property described by her grandson, Peter Clark, as "a full-blooded negro." At this point, she added her husband's surname to her own and legally became Elizabeth Clark Gaines. We know little of Isom Gaines's life before he married Elizabeth Clark, but as one of fewer than two hundred free black men in the city, his status as a property owner distinguished him. He had the same surname as the white Gaines family who had settled twenty miles south of Cincinnati at Gaines Crossing, Kentucky, in 1797, although we do not know if he had ever been enslaved there. Betty's enslaved family members had come with John Clarke from Hanover County, Virginia, and Abner Gaines had emigrated with his slaves from nearby Augusta County at the same time. Settling within forty-five miles of each other in Kentucky, these families became part of a north-central Virginia diaspora in north-central Kentucky. While still at Paddy's Run, Betty may have met Isom as he traveled south along the Cincinnati-Lexington stagecoach line that Abner Gaines established; they may have met at one of the huge revivals near Paddy's Run that brought together thousands of blacks and whites from the surrounding counties. Regardless, once they became free people of color living in Cincinnati, Elizabeth Clark and Isom Gaines found each other, married, and together built a life on the solid foundation of family bonds, church devotion, and community loyalty.

Elizabeth and Isom purchased a house on the south side of Sixth Street between Broadway and Culvert, six blocks from the Ohio River. The couple prospered, despite the legal system in Cincinnati that restricted so many liberties for "free persons of color, mulatto and black." Their first child was born on November 6, 1821, and they named him John Isom Gaines. Names carry weight, and the fact that Elizabeth Clark Gaines gave her first child, fathered by Isom Gaines, the same first name as her former master raises a question about the parameters of the relationship she had with John Clarke and her feelings about the life they shared for twenty years. Elizabeth and Isom eventually had two more sons.[30]

As their children grew up, Elizabeth and Isom lived at the center of a tightly connected family. Elizabeth's son Michael, whom she had left behind in Kentucky as a "free man of color" at age nineteen, joined the rest of the family in Cincinnati in 1823, the year his brother Elliott turned sixteen. Michael trained as a barber, one of the few lucrative trades open to African Americans in the city, and ran a thriving shop in a building he owned on Broadway near Second Street. Michael married and eventually had five children. Elizabeth's eldest daughter, Elisa, married John Woodson, a carpenter and builder of considerable reputation, and settled in the house next door to Elizabeth and Isom. Evalina, six years younger than her sister, lived with Elizabeth and Isom until she married a carpenter named Peter Harbison and moved into a house on Sixth Street. Members of the Clark-Gaines family participated actively at the newly built Bethel A.M.E. Church that opened in 1824, almost directly across Sixth Street from Elizabeth and Isom's home. The church became the center of abolitionist activism in the African American community, and Elizabeth's son, John Isom Gaines, and her son-in-law, John Woodson, both took part in the growing Underground Railroad movement in Cincinnati in the 1820s.[31]

Given the increasingly harsh economic and political discrimination that African Americans faced in Cincinnati in the 1820s, Elizabeth and Isom forged a remarkable life for themselves and their children. Nevertheless, the shadow of Elliott's continued enslavement under the control of William S. Clarke remained a constant concern for twelve long years. In 1828, Elliott turned twenty-one, and following the terms of the agreement that Betty had negotiated, William Clarke handed over her son's manumission papers. Elliott crossed the Ohio and joined the rest of the family on Sixth Street. He trained as a barber, like his older brother Michael, and soon got a job at one of the hotels in the city.[32] Fourteen years after John Clarke signed his will with that wobbly "X," Betty and her four children were all finally "manumitted from slavery."

Despite her relief that William S. Clarke had honored his promise to free Elliott, Elizabeth Gaines never forgot the debt that Clarke had owed to her for thirteen years. She had not dared to enforce it while Elliott remained enslaved, but in 1829, one year after Elliott's emancipation took effect, Elizabeth Clark Gaines sued William S. Clarke in the Harrison County, Kentucky, Circuit Court. Her lawyer, prominent Kentucky lawyer John Trimble, filed for payment on February 28, 1829. In bringing this suit, Elizabeth Clark Gaines again turned to one of John Clarke's daughters for assistance. Harriet Clarke Respess, like her sister Elizabeth Kelley, was willing to help "Betty," now known as Elizabeth Clark Gaines, to sue her brother, William S. Clarke, who also held an unpaid debt to Harriet's husband, Augustine Respess.[33] One can only imagine the complex family dynamics involved as Harriet, like her sister Elizabeth, demonstrated that her allegiance to "Betty" outweighed the loyalty she had toward her younger brother.

As a "free woman of color," Elizabeth Clark Gaines faced the considerable risk of being apprehended and returned to slavery if she crossed back into Kentucky. So in lieu of attending the court proceedings in person, Elizabeth arranged for Respess to represent her in court in the case of "Betty, a free woman of Color vs. Wm Clarke." The officers of the court issued a summons for William Clarke to appear in court on March 11, 1829. Trimble, Elizabeth's lawyer, presented the promissory note William Clarke had given to Betty on August 28, 1816, just before she left Paddy's Run for Cincinnati. An additional statement signed "Betty a woman of color by J. Trimble, attorney" was affixed to the bottom of the note, which read, "Yet the said Debt remains unpaid wherefore she prays Judgement for her Debt and Damages for the detention of the same together with her costs." The son of Betty's former owner failed to appear in court on March 11, 1829, and the judge awarded "Betty, a free woman of color," the $65 plus thirteen years of 6 percent interest and $5.71 in court costs, a total of $135.50 ($3,277.28 in 2010 currency).[34]

After Betty and her children left Paddy's Run, William S. Clarke's fortunes had taken a turn for the worse. He and his wife Eliza Robinson had seven children, and the family went deeper into debt with each passing year. To pay court judgments on his debts, William sold some of the Paddy's Run slaves, which had made Elizabeth Clark Gaines's enslaved son Elliott's future increasingly uncertain. William also mortgaged and then sold the land he inherited from his father. Soon after the suit brought by Elizabeth Clark Gaines and Augustine Respess, William S. Clarke began to move from one Kentucky county to another to stay ahead of summons-serving sheriffs, his life revolving around lawsuits and bankruptcies. There is no record that Clarke ever paid the court-mandated debt to Elizabeth Clark Gaines. But even had he paid her back wages for two years of unpaid labor after she became a "free woman of color," that debt did not begin to repay what Betty's family had endured across four generations of enslavement and sexual violation, belied by relationship. Moreover, William S. Clarke's "detention" of the "Debt and Damages" he owed to Betty paled in comparison to his keeping her son Elliott in custody from age nine until age twenty-one.

Remarkably skilled at using the resources available to her, Elizabeth Clark Gaines had leveraged the power of the law at least four times to gain her freedom and that of her children. This was not a simple process, but one that involved multiple calculations over many years, the services of skilled lawyers, the cooperation of the Kentucky Circuit Court, and assistance from the married daughters of her former owner and their husbands. Elizabeth Clark Gaines's continued connection to Elizabeth Clarke Kelley and Harriet Clarke Respess and their husbands, James Kelley and Augustine Respess, transcended the formidable barriers of enslavement and race and speak to the personal bonds between Betty, Elizabeth, and Harriet that had been forged as they grew up in Virginia and at Paddy's Run. These relationships underscore Betty's keen ability to use the assets at her disposal, to negotiate, and to wait—precisely as long as necessary—to achieve a specific goal.

The timing of the Elizabeth Clark Gaines's court case against William S. Clarke had turned on Elliott's release from enslavement and his safe passage to Cincinnati. However, she had decided to recover what would have been a sizeable amount of money in the spring of 1829 in the midst of rapidly intensifying racial tensions in the city of Cincinnati. Fears of impending racial violence led many African Americans throughout the city to make plans to relocate, to leave Cincinnati for points north in the state of Ohio, or, alternatively, to join a group of African American emigrationists determined to establish an all-black colony in Canada. As "Betty, a free woman of color" filed her suit against William S. Clark, the city's First Ward, where Elizabeth and Isom lived, became the focus of a concerted effort on the part of white citizens to force African Americans out of the neighborhood. A petition to the Cincinnati City Council targeted the danger of fire from the "all-board houses in that neighborhood tenanted by negroes." The council, which included several active members of the American Colonization Society, responded that it would be impossible to "drive the black population from the city in the summary way of pulling down the houses over their heads." Rather, they supported what they saw as the more benevolent strategy of helping African Americans return to Africa.[35]

In the spring of 1829, white Cincinnatians voted en masse for public officials who pledged to strictly enforce the 1807 Ohio black law requiring "all black and mulatto persons" in Cincinnati to post a bond (usually set at $500) or be forcibly removed from the city. Even before the spring election, as historian Nikki Taylor has argued, African American emigrationists in Cincinnati had moved ahead with plans to purchase land in Canada and establish an all-black colony that would be economically self-sufficient and culturally independent. By the summer of 1829, the group had made steady progress, locating land and negotiating its purchase. The emigrationists worked as quickly as possible to put their plans into motion, but even before they finalized the land purchase, white mob violence erupted in the city. The forced eviction of African Americans from the city reached a fevered pitch between August 15 and August 22. Newspapers reported that "the houses of the Blacks were attacked and demolished, and the inmates beat and driven through the streets till beyond the limits of the corporation." Meanwhile, as Taylor writes, "mobs of two to three hundred whites, armed with stones, demolished black buildings, homes, and shops." Police offered no protection from this racial terror, and during that week, between eleven hundred and fifteen hundred African Americans left Cincinnati, some to join the emigrationists heading for Canada, others to take refuge in rural communities outside the city.[36]

Elizabeth's family—the Gaineses, the Clarks, and the Woodsons—managed to remain in Cincinnati as part of a seriously diminished population of African Americans. As the years passed, Ohio's discriminatory racial laws continued to erode the hard-won freedom of free blacks within the state. Throughout this period, Elizabeth Clark Gaines's children and grandchildren worked tirelessly for the abolition of slavery and as part of the Underground Railroad system transporting slaves across the Ohio River and on to Canada. Her sons participated in the Ohio black conventions, beginning in the 1830s, and worked continuously for the repudiation of Ohio's discriminatory black laws. Her son John Isom Gaines, a powerful orator and fluent writer known for the pride he took in his dark skin and African ancestry, spearheaded the campaign to establish schools for African American children in Cincinnati. Like his mother, John knew how to use the law to his advantage. When the city of Cincinnati refused to fund black schools under a new Ohio state law, he helped to instigate a successful suit against the city.[37]

Just as ongoing racial oppression and violence shaped the lives of Elizabeth Clark Gaines and her children, the cholera epidemics that plagued Cincinnati killed a disproportionate number of African Americans, including Elizabeth's husband Isom. In 1832, the *Daily Gazette* ran a daily column labeled "CHOLERA," which listed those who had died in the previous twenty-four hours. Isom Gaines fought for his life for two weeks after he became ill, but he died on October 21 along with twenty-two other men, women, and children.[38]

As a widow, Elizabeth Gaines headed her own household until at least 1840, staying in the home on Sixth Street where she and Isom had lived since 1819. Her daughter Evalina's family continued to live next door, and three more of her children and six grandchildren lived nearby. In 1841, Cincinnati witnessed another, even bloodier racial riot. Whites set up a canon in the street and fired at African Americans, who were themselves armed with guns. The epicenter of the mayhem and destruction was at Broadway and Sixth, a half a block from the Gaines's home.[39]

## The Poisoned Shirt of Memory

Elizabeth Clark Gaines's first grandchild was born on March 29, 1829, in Cincinnati, just two weeks after Elizabeth sued William S. Clarke in the Kentucky Circuit Court, and six months before the exodus of half of the city's African American population. Elizabeth's son Michael, who had stayed behind in Kentucky to protect his enslaved younger brother Elliott, named this child Peter, perhaps after Betty's father, left behind in Virginia when the family migrated to Kentucky in 1795. Peter Clark became a well-known Ohio educator and orator, following in the footsteps of his uncle, John Isom Gaines.[40] He gave hundreds of speeches throughout Ohio and the nation on numerous topics, including slavery, education, citizenship, workers' rights, and politics. He rarely referred to his personal life or family history, but the speech he delivered at the Emancipation Day Celebration in Dayton on the afternoon of September 22, 1873, proved an exception. When Clark addressed the audience of more than three thousand, his words rang with passion:

> I do not forget the prejudice of the American people; I could not if I would. I am sore from sole to crown with its blows. It stood by the bedside of my mother and intensified her pain as she bore me. It darkens with its shadow the graves of my father and mother. It has hindered every step I have taken in life. It poisons the food I eat, the water I drink and the air I breathe. It dims the sunshine of my days, and deepens the darkness of my nights. It hampers me in every relation of life, in business, in politics, in religion, as a father or as a husband. It haunts me walking or riding, waking or sleeping. It came to the altar with my bride, and now that my children are attaining their majority, and are looking eagerly with their youthful eyes for a career, it stands by them and casts its infernal curse upon them. Hercules could have as easily forgotten the poisoned shirt which scorched his flesh, as I can forget the prejudice of the American people.

Peter Clark drove home the impact of the devastating, long-term effects of the prejudice of the American people by using metaphorical examples from his own family. On another level, Clark's reference to the "poisoned shirt" of Hercules reveals one of the most important metaphors of his life—his heritage from his paternal grandparents, a male slave owner and his female slave. Peter Clark's enslaved grandmother, Betty, like the mistress of Zeus, gave birth to Clark's father Michael, who, like Hercules, wore a poisoned shirt of tainted blood symbolizing a misfortune from which there is no escape. The poisoned shirt that burned Hercules's flesh to the bone stands as a powerful symbol of the toxic memory of slavery and its aftermath. Throughout Peter Clark's life, the history of his white grandfather's double relation of master and father haunted him as surely as the "prejudice of the American people" restricted his actions.

On June 18, 1919, Elizabeth Clark Gaines's grandson agreed to an interview with William Breckenridge, the head of the Missouri Historical Society. At age ninety, Peter Clark talked about his family in eloquent detail, telling a powerful story of slavery and freedom, of race and ethnicity. Clark's oral history led straight back to Betty, his once-enslaved, mixed-race grandmother. The hope inherent in his grandmother's story of obtaining her freedom and creating a life beyond slavery countered the poisoned shirt of memory that led to Peter Clark's despair about his white slaveholding grandfather. Peter Clark had earlier hinted at this history in his address at the Dayton Emancipation Day Celebration, when his reference to Hercules revealed a history that "spoke better than it knew." His careful admonition, "I do not forget," and his willingness to speak, at age ninety, of the details of his family history made it possible to follow the threads of Clark's family lineage closely enough to find Betty and piece together the story of her life.[41]

Betty's experience coming to Cincinnati in 1816 was the antithesis of Margaret Garner's. The circumstances of these two women could not have been more different. Elizabeth Clark Gaines came to Ohio in 1816 as a "free woman of color." She used the law to protect herself and her family. She and her children survived the horrors of enslavement and eventually thrived in a world of their own making.[42] In sharp contrast, Margaret Garner, the subject of so much notoriety at the time of her escape in 1856 and a great deal of literary and historical attention since, escaped slavery on the run. The legal system in place by the 1850s worked against her at every turn, particularly after the passage and enforcement of the Fugitive Slave Law. The possibility of escape for enslaved women was exponentially more difficult in 1856 than it had been in 1816, when Betty crossed the Ohio River. Slavery killed Margaret Garner's family as surely as city, state, and national authorities accused her of killing her child.

The lives of Margaret Garner and Elizabeth Clark Gaines unfolded in historical contexts as distinct as the trajectories of their lives. Yet, these two women shared a common history of enslavement and sexual violation at the hands of white male oppressors who regarded them more as property than as human beings. They both worked to protect the lives of their children, albeit in disparate ways. They each sought something better for themselves and their families and took enormous risks to achieve something that they could only envision as a possibility. The lives of these two women illustrate powerfully that remembering and disremembering is a long-term process. Their histories show how the narratives of trauma and triumph that pass from one generation to the next form the core of our identities as individuals, families, communities, and citizens. The phases of a life—from birth to death—are not separate and distinct, nor are they defined by the historical categories of black, white, slave, free, single, or married. As the experience of Elizabeth Clark Gaines illustrates, a history of gendered resistance can begin with the reconstruction of an individual woman's story, across time and place, but as Margaret Garner's life teaches us, the process of witnessing women's freedom strategies has no end.

NOTES

My thanks to Susan Hathaway Boydston and Delores M. Walters for their invaluable critiques of an earlier version of this chapter.

1. Toni Morrison, Organization of American Historians, Louisville, Kentucky, 1991; Toni Morrison, *Beloved* (New York: Random House, 1988), 42.

2. William Clark Breckenridge interview with Peter H. Clark, June 18, 1919, William Clark Breckenridge Papers, Missouri Historical Society Library.

3. For examples, see John Hope Franklin, *The Free Negro in North Carolina, 1790–1860* (Chapel Hill: University of North Carolina Press, 1995), and Thomas D. Morris, *Southern Slavery and the Law, 1619–1860* (Chapel Hill: University of North Carolina Press, 1999).

4. Clark Interview, June 18, 1919. William Breckenridge's notes from the interview read in part: "His father was Michael Clark . . . Michael Clark's father was called Major Billy Clark. Betty, his slave, was the child of a mulatto and a Black and was born at Charlottes-ville, Va. She was the mother of 3 daughters and 2 sons by him. Her son Michael was born at Lexington, Ky. The rest of her children were born at Cynthiana, Ky. . . . Betty, soon after coming to Cincinnati, married a full blooded Negro named Isom Gaines. And had by him a son John Isom Gaines." There is no record of John Clarke ever being called "Major Billy." This nickname most likely was ascribed to John Clarke's son, William S. Clarke. More important, Breckinridge's notes include: "When Major Billy went West, he took his family to Cincinnati and gave to Bettie and to each of his children DEEDS OF MANUMISSION." Over the years, Peter Clark's family built on this story, developing an oral tradition that Peter Clark's grandfather was the explorer William Clark, of Lewis and Clark fame. A short biographical article published by Dovie King Clark in *The Negro History Bulletin* in May 1942, which enjoyed widespread acceptance and amazing durability, picked up this family legend. The author was a distant relative of Peter Clark's by marriage and a student at Gaines High School while he was principal. In her short article, she described Clark's genealogy this way:

> His family history dates back to the year 1804 [*sic*], when President Thomas Jefferson commissioned his [Clark's] grandfather, William Clark, with Captain Meriwether Lewis to explore the newly acquired Pacific Northwest territory in what is now known as the Lewis and Clark Expedition.
>
> William Clark was a bold and adventurous young white man. His wife and children were colored, and when about to go upon this expedition, fearing he might not return and that his family might be enslaved, he moved them from the south to Cincinnati with enough money for their support during his absence. One child was Michael Clark, who became a respected citizen of Cincinnati, and Peter, the subject of our sketch, was Michael's first born.

Scholars have cited Dovie King Clark's work for decades. In 1977, Philip S. Foner said of Clark, "His grandfather was the 'Clark' of the Lewis and Clark expedition." In a 1982 article, Paul McStallworth asserted that Peter Clark "was the grandson of William Clark of the famous Lewis and Clark Expedition." In a 1988 essay, Clark biographer David Gerber wrote that "Clark's father, Michael, was the natural son of Major William Clark, who achieved fame accompanying Meriwether Lewis." He repeated the story in 1999, this time with the caveat, "The oral tradition of Peter Clark's family contends that. . . ." Based on Dovie Clark's article, over the years Peter Clark's identity became inextricably bound to William Clark the explorer. For many years, largely because of this short biography, interest in Peter H. Clark focused more on his purported association with William Clark, the explorer, than on his own work and public success as an abolitionist, educator, and politician. Dovie King Clark's article also includes numerous errors. For example, Peter Clark's wife, Frances, attended Oberlin, not Clark; Clark was fired from his position in Cincinnati for an action that was a source of great pride; he and Frances moved to St. Louis in 1888, and it was only in 1902, after Frances's death, that Ernestine moved to St. Louis with her four daughters to take care of her father. These are errors she would probably not have made had she received her information from Peter H. Clark.

5. Elizabeth Clark Gaines's son Elliott Clark was an extremely successful businessman, noted in 1870 as owning $12,000 worth of real estate. "Elliott Clark," 1870 U.S. Manuscript Census, Cincinnati, Ohio, 1st Ward. John Isom Gaines was not only a successful business owner and educator but also a highly respected abolitionist orator, writer, and leader in Ohio and national organizations. See John M. Langston, "Eulogy on the Life and Character of John I. Gaines," *The Liberator*, April 27, 1860. Peter Clark's daughter, Consuelo Clark-Stewart, was an honors graduate of Boston University School of Medicine in 1884 and the first African American woman licensed to practice medicine in Ohio.

6. Peter H. Clark, "Black Brigade of Cincinnati: Being a Report of Its Labors and a Muster Roll of Members; Together with Various Orders, Speeches, etc. Relating to It," Ohio Historical Society Archives, Library Pamphlet Collection, Columbus, Ohio, 3.

7. Eugenia G. and Preston G. Glazebrook, Virginia Migrations, Hanover County: Volume I, 1723–1850 (Baltimore, Md: Genealogical Publishing, 2000 [Richmond, 1943]), 23–26. Donald, Scott & Co. vs. Clarke admir., Nov. 1805, in Federal Records, Unrestored, U.S. Circuit Court, box 65, Library of Virginia; and John Murdoch & Co. vs. Admir. & als, Nov. 7, 1807, in Federal Records, Unrestored, U.S. Circuit Court, box 7, Library of Virginia. The accounts show that the estate paid for "laying Lucy" (in other words, providing a midwife) in April 1784 (name of baby not given); in January 1789 (baby's name given as Edmond); and in 1794 (baby's name not given). Inasmuch as the expenditures were not always entered in a timely manner, each of these events could have occurred weeks or months prior to the expense entry date. That is quite likely the case with Betty's birth in late 1783 and Sarah's birth in late 1793. Later census records confirm their birthdates more precisely. For an excellent discussion of the lives of black and white women in the neighboring King William Parish, see Joan Rezner Gundersen, "The Double Bonds of Race and Sex," *Journal of Southern History* 52, no. 3 (August, 1986), 351–72. There Gunderson also includes detailed material on slave births and naming practices.

8. Betty, Edmond, and Sarah appear in John Clarke's will, locating them in Kentucky. Lucy does not, indicating that she probably died before 1814. Betty was given to Mildred Crutchfield when William Clarke's estate was distributed to his children. No bill of sale for John Clarke's acquisition of Betty from his sister Mildred Crutchfield has been located. "Will of John Clarke," Harrison County, Kentucky Will Book A, 245.

9. Julia Spencer Ardery, *The Duncans of Bourbon County, Kentucky* (Lexington: privately published, 1943), 17–18. Henrico County Deeds 1750–1767, pp. 99, 111–12. Betty M. Harris, "Untangling Some Obadiah and Luke Smiths," *Tidewater Virginia Families: A Magazine of History and Genealogy* 4 (February/March 1999). Mary Munden Smith (1747–1833) was the mother of Sarah (Sally) Smith (1769–1794), the wife of John Clarke.

10. Fayette County Tax List for 1797 and Harrison county Tax List for 1799. John Clarke is listed in the 1797 Fayette County Tax List and in the 1799 Harrison County Tax List.

11. Bourbon County Deeds, Book D, 204–5. The deed was signed on June 19, 1797. Slave

narratives frequently recount the sexual exploitation of enslaved slave women by their owners. See Marion Wilson Starling, *The Slave Narrative: Its Place in American History* (Washington, D.C.: Howard University Press, 1988). Harriet A. Jacobs, *Incidents in the Life of a Slave Girl, Written by Herself*, ed. Jean Fagan Yellin (Cambridge, Mass.: Harvard University Press, 1987 [1861]) contains one of the most detailed first-person accounts by an American slave woman of sustained sexual exploitation. Jacobs was repeatedly harassed over a seven-year period by Dr. Norcom, the father of her mistress. See Christina Accomando, "'The Laws Were Laid Down to Me Anew': Harriet Jacobs and the Reframing of Legal Fictions" *African American Review* 32, no. 2 (1998): 229–45.

12. For an excellent new analysis of these relationships, see Joshua D. Rothman, *Notorious in the Neighborhood: Sex and Families across the Color Line in Virginia, 1787–1861* (Chapel Hill: University of North Carolina Press, 2003). Numerous historians have written about married white slave owners having long-term sexual relationships with their black female slaves. See Deborah Gray White, *Ar'n't I a Woman: Female Slaves in the Antebellum South* (New York: Norton, 1985); Jacquelyn Jones, *Labor of Love, Labor of Sorrow: Black Women, Work and the Family from Slavery to the Present* (New York: Vintage, 1986); Elizabeth Fox Genovese, *Within the Plantation Household: Black and White Women of the Old South* (Chapel Hill: University of North Carolina Press, 1988); and Brenda Stevenson, *Life in Black and White: Family and Community in the Slave South* (New York: Oxford University Press, 1996). On the most well-known of these couples, see Annette Gordon-Reed, *Thomas Jefferson and Sally Hemings: An American Controversy* (Charlottesville: University of Virginia Press, 1998) and Jan Lewis, Peter S. Onuf, and Jane E. Lewis, eds., *Sally Hemings and Thomas Jefferson: History, Memory, and Civic Culture* (Charlottesville: University of Virginia Press, 1999). See also Edward Ball, *Slaves in the Family* (New York: Farrar Straus & Giroux, 1998) and Edward Ball, *The Sweet Hell Inside: A Family History* (New York: Morrow, 2001).

13. Will of John Clarke, Harrison County, Kentucky Will Book A, p. 245. His legatees, besides William S., were daughters Elizabeth (ca. 1788), the wife of James Kelley (m. 1805), and Harriett (b. 1792), the wife of Augustine C. Respass (m. 1809). Respass frequently used Austin as his first name. In the Bourbon County, Kentucky, Deed Book D, p. 204, is a deed for the first two hundred acres Clarke purchased from Timberlake. The 1809 Harrison County Tax List shows Clarke owned four hundred acres acquired from Richard Timberlake. Bourbon County Kentucky Marriage Records, book 2, pp. 21 and 42.

14. Annette Gordon-Reed, *The Hemingses of Monticello: An American Family* (New York: Norton), 82.

15. Junius P. Rodrigues, *Slavery in the United States: A Social, Political, and Historical Encyclopedia*, vol. 2 (Santa Barbara, Calif.: ABC-CLIO), 172. Will of Michael Clark in Hamilton County Will Book 5, pp. 87–89; John Isom Gaines (b. November 6, 1821) became a leading figure in Cincinnati, renowned for his work in establishing schools for African American children. He was also a highly respected abolitionist orator and writer.

16. John Boles, *The Great Revival* (Lexington: University of Kentucky Press), 36–39; John Boles, *Religion in Antebellum Kentucky* (Lexington: University of Kentucky Press), 26.

17. Boles, *Religion in Antebellum Kentucky*, 26.

18. Quotations, in order, from Boles, *Religion in Antebellum Kentucky*, 7, 95–99, and 85.

19. "Will of John Clarke," Harrison County, Kentucky Will Book A, p. 245. See Peter Onuf, "Every Generation Is an 'Independent Nation': Colonization, Miscegenation, and the Fate of Jefferson's Children," *William and Mary Quarterly* 57, no. 1 (2000): 153–70.

20. "Will of John Clarke."

21. "Will of John Clarke." On Benjamin Mills, see *Biographical Encyclopedia of Kentucky* (Cincinnati: J. M. Armstrong, 1878) and Rev. Robert Stuart Sanders, *Presbyterianism in Paris and Bourbon County, Kentucky, 1786–1961* (Louisville, Ky.: Dunne, 1961).

22. William S. Clark(e), Manumission of Elliott, May 22, 1815, Harrison County, Kentucky Deed Book 4, 346.

23. Harrison County, Kentucky Marriage Bonds and Marriages, 1814–1827, Bond #1205, October 10, 1817. The marriage of William S. Clarke and Eliza Robinson was not recorded. Harrison County, Kentucky Court Record Book C.

24. A copy of the promissory note is in the packet for the case "Free Betty v. William S. Clarke" in Harrison County Kentucky Circuit Court, February 28, 1829. On hiring practices in nearby Bourbon County, Kentucky, see Keith C. Barton, "'Good Cooks and Washers': Slave Hiring, Domestic Labor, and the Market in Bourbon County, Kentucky," *Journal of American History* 84, no. 2 (1997): 436–60.

25. A July [1816?] court order states that "Michael a boy of Color being admitted by the court Chose James Kelley for his guardian. . . ." Inasmuch as only free persons were admitted by the court, and James Kelley was John Clarke's white son-in-law, this "boy" was almost certainly Michael Clark. Harrison County, Kentucky Court Record Book C, 356.

26. Disastrous fires in 1849 and 1884 destroyed huge quantities of Hamilton County's early records. While a great many of the lost records were reconstructed over the years, the deeds of manumission are not among them. Only a handful still exists.

27. See Nikki Taylor, "Reconsidering the 'Forced' Exodus of 1829: Free Black Emigration from Cincinnati, Ohio, to Wilberforce, Canada," *Journal of African American History* 87 (Summer 2002): 283–302, especially 285–86. Richard C. Wade, "The Negro in Cincinnati, 1800–1830," *Journal of Negro History* 39, no. 1 (1954): 43–57, includes an excellent review of the 1829 enforcement of the black laws that drove more than half of Cincinnati's African American population to Canada. Leonard Richards, *Gentlemen of Property and Standing: Anti-Abolition Mobs in Jacksonian America* (New York: Oxford University Press, 1970), 92–100, 122–30. On the susceptibility of all black families in the Kentucky/Ohio borderland to the "long reach of slavery," see Joan E. Cashin, "Black Families in the Old Northwest," *Journal of the Early Republic* 15, no. 3 (1995): 461–62, and Joe Trotter Jr., *River Jordan: African American Urban Life in the Ohio Valley* (Lexington: University Press of Kentucky, 1998).

28. Taylor, "Reconsidering," 285. Richard C. Wade, "The Negro in Cincinnati, 1800–1830," *Journal of Negro History* 39, no. 1 (1954): 43–57, includes an excellent review of the 1829 enforcement of the black laws that drove more than half of Cincinnati's African American population to Canada. See also Leonard Richards, *Gentlemen of Property and Standing: Anti-Abolition Mobs in Jacksonian America* (New York: Oxford University Press, 1970), 92–100, 122–30. The 1841 riot is well described in the *Cincinnati Daily Gazette*, September 6, 1841; see also William Cheek and Aimee Lee Cheek, "John Mercer Langston and the Cincinnati Riot of 1841," in *Race and the City: Work, Community and Protest in Cincinnati,*

*1820–1970*, ed. Henry Louis Taylor (Urbana: University of Illinois Press, 1993), 29–69. On the susceptibility of all black families in the Kentucky/Ohio borderland to the "long reach of slavery," see Joan E. Cashin, "Black Families in the Old Northwest," 461–62, and Trotter, *River Jordan*.

29. Lewis Perry, *Boats against the Current* (Lanham, Md.: Rowan and Littlefield, 1993), 112.

30. Restored Hamilton County, Ohio, Marriages 1889–1849, 98. Isom Gaines's name is spelled "Isam Gains" in the marriage record. His first name is also found as Isum and Isham, but Isom is the most common spelling and the only one used by his son, John Isom Gaines (b. November 6, 1821).

31. Will of Michael Clark, Restored Hamilton County, Ohio. Marriages 1808–1840, 318. On Underground Railroad connections between Kentucky and Ohio, see J. Blaine Hudson, *Fugitive Slaves and the Underground Railroad in the Kentucky Borderland* (Jefferson, N.C.: McFarland, 2002), and Wilbur H. Siebert, *The Underground Railroad from Slavery to Freedom* (New York: Macmillan, 1898).

32. "Elliott Clark," 1870 U.S. Manuscript Census, Cincinnati, Ohio, 1st Ward. William S. Clark(e), Manumission of Elliott; "Elliott Clark," 1870 U.S. Manuscript Census, Cincinnati, Ohio, 1st Ward. Elliott died in Cincinnati in 1874.

33. Harrison County Circuit Court Bundle #4653, Free Betty v. Clarke, filed February 28, 1829. The documents in the case include William S. Clarke's signed and sealed promissory note; a $100 surety bond for Betty signed by Augustine Respass; the plea for payment of the note issued to the court for Betty by Respass's lawyer, John Trimble, on February 29, 1829; and the decision in favor of Betty issued by Judge John H. Duncan on March 11, 1829, with Clarke's absence from the court duly noted. Respass won a judgment against Clarke at the same session of the court for payment of a past due debt of $1,351.12.

34. Ibid.

35. Taylor, "Reconsidering," 287.

36. Ibid., 291.

37. On John Isom Gaines, see Taylor, *Race and the City*, 58–59.

38. See the column listing cholera deaths, *Cincinnati Gazette*, October 23, 1832. In the 1840 U.S. Census, 1st Ward, Elizabeth Gaines, with three children, and John Woodson, with four children, are listed consecutively. Michael Clark, with four children, is listed separately.

39. See William Cheek and Aimee Lee Cheek, "John Mercer Langston and the Cincinnati Riot of 1841," in Taylor, *Race and the City*, 29–69. Procter and Gamble tore down Elizabeth Clark Gaines's Cincinnati house, on Sixth Street between Broadway and Culvert, and the A.M.E. Church where she and her children worshiped, when the company cleared the site for office buildings in the late 1940s. In 2004, the National Underground Railroad Museum and Freedom Center was built along the Cincinnati riverfront, less than a mile from where Elizabeth and Isom Gaines raised their children and hid from white mobs during the 1829 riot.

40. On Peter H. Clark, see Mary E. Frederickson and Walter Herz, "A Matter of Respect: The Religious Journey of Peter H. Clark," *A.M.E. Church Review* (April 2002), 27–28.

41. Breckenridge interview with Peter H. Clark. Clark's Dayton speech was published in the *Cincinnati Commercial*, September 23, 1873. The phrase "speaks better than it knows"

is from Susan Hathaway Boydston, "One True Thing: Speaking Truer than It Knows," *PSYART: A Journal for Psychological Study of the Arts* (November 2002): 2. Boydston's perceptive critique of Anna Quindlen's novel *One True Thing* and the film on which it is based uses the phrase to describe Freud's Wiederkehr des Verdrangten, or the "return of the repressed," arguing that in Quindlen's work there are two plot lines, "with the subplot contradicting (and deconstructing) in important ways, the intentions of the main plot."

42. By the 1880s, Elizabeth Clark Gaines's descendants were regularly the topic of almost every column on "Our Colored Citizens," published weekly in the *Cincinnati Commercial Gazette*. Without question, Betty's family did well, distinguishing themselves in professions ranging from business to medicine to education and the arts, as well as in politics and religious life, unto the fourth and fifth generations.

# CHAPTER 2

# COERCED BUT NOT SUBDUED

## The Gendered Resistance
## of Women Escaping Slavery

*Cheryl Janifer LaRoche*

> Oh woman, woman! Upon you I call; for upon your exertions almost
> entirely depends whether the rising generation shall be anything more
> than we have been or not.
>
> —Maria W. Stewart, "An Address Delivered before the Afric-American
>   Female Intelligence Society of Boston" (1832)

### Ten Dollars Reward.

RAN AWAY from the subscriber, on the 10th instant, a negro woman named LUCY, aged about 30 years, very black, and walks lame in consequence of having been frost bitten — She formerly belonged to Jonathan Avery, and is well known in Wilmington and its vicinity. All persons are forewarned from harboring or carrying her away, as the law will be rigidly enforced ——The above reward will be paid on her delivery to me, or the Jailor in Wilmington.

**JOHN M. VAN CLEEF.**

ʼAugust 14                                                    tf

Figure 2.1. "Ten Dollars Reward." Runaway slave advertisement
published in *Cape Fear Recorder* [Wilmington, N.C.], April 12, 1825.
Courtesy of the *North Carolina Runaway Slave Advertisements Project*,
a collaboration between the University of North Carolina at Greens-
boro and North Carolina Agricultural and Technical State University.

Margaret Garner's story of resistance and escape from slavery is emblematic of the experiences of enslaved women who fled the multiple and gendered oppressions of the slave regime. From the earliest days of slavery to the end of the Civil War, women escaped bondage while attempting to maintain a firm grip on both their families and the hope of liberty. Women displayed uncommon courage, determination, steadfastness, and even ruthlessness in seeking to deliver themselves, their children, and their families out of bondage. For the most part, however, an analysis of women's collective experiences of escape has been difficult to document. Margaret Garner's story, combined with other narratives of black women's escape from slavery, provides a composite view of women participating in the cause of their own liberation. Although overlapping and competing factors shaped women's motivations and strategies in freeing themselves from slavery, this chapter focuses on the gendered resistance of women's efforts to maintain family ties even as they aborted their pregnancies, resorted to infanticide, or abandoned children and family in their quest to escape captivity and to embrace the consequences of freedom. As cultural works such as *Beloved* and the *Margaret Garner* opera and other forms of artistic expression attest, these women's stories resonate with powerful contemporary value, reflecting how the present reshapes our interpretation and understanding of what Walter Johnson calls a history "shaped by the conditions of [its] own production."[1]

Margaret Garner haunts us still. As a mother, as an enslaved woman, as a wife—by every gendered measure—her story is troubling. Yet her life, her desperation, her extreme actions cry out for notice among a group of women who rarely claim scholarly attention: women willing to escape slavery. For several years, I have been thinking about and researching such women and confronting what historian Joseph C. Miller identifies as the "failure of scholars of slavery to include the numerous women enslaved in instances they have studied."[2] Each time I encountered their stories in scholars' accounts, they were counterbalanced by obligatory yet perfunctory disclaimers such as "young men ran away in greater numbers" or, more generally, "women were less likely to run away because they had often begun to raise families."[3] Undeterred, I noted the substantial number of cases spread among multiple contexts, singular in nature, anecdotal, poorly documented, and randomly scattered throughout dissimilar sources. Powerful accounts of women's resolute pursuit of freedom lay submerged in sources beyond runaway slave advertisements. Much of Margaret Garner's story has been derived from interviews and from newspaper descriptions of her sensational trial. Embedded in, or tangential to, larger narratives of escape, women's various efforts to transcend bondage were incidental to the letters and diaries, biographical accounts, and legal proceedings historians often used to support arguments premised on analysis of the slave as male, on male escapes, or on factors that prevented women from fleeing slavery.[4]

Using the framework of Margaret Garner's story to analyze escape patterns of enslaved women provides access to fundamental unexamined presumptions involving women's strategies of resistance. Toni Morrison drew her inspiration for the character of Sethe in *Beloved* from the dramatic escape of Garner and her family from a Kentucky plantation with seven other relatives. As the escape plan collapsed, leaving the family trapped and under siege by pursuers outside Cincinnati, Margaret Garner declared that she would kill herself and her four children before she would return to slavery and submit to unremitting bondage. Seizing a butcher knife, she cut the throat of her "nearly white" two-year-old daughter Mary. Wholly bent on keeping her children out of slavery, Garner attempted to take the lives of the other three children as well as her own. After fighting "with the ferocity of tigers," the family was overpowered by an armed posse of eleven slave catchers and Margaret was later put on trial.[5]

In this chapter, I focus principally but not exclusively on one among several motives for escape: the concern for family, which provoked Margaret Garner. She escaped, after all, with seven of her relatives. The actions of freedom-seeking women emerge from the moral and psychological morass of slavery and the social activism it engendered. Although the constraints that kept women mired in captivity are well documented, their strategies in overcoming seemingly insurmountable obstacles to freedom are not. The Garner family faced all the formidable obstacles that women faced: limited mobility, little knowledge of geography, and concern for loved ones, further complicated by the encumbrances of escaping with young children. Although historians have identified these apprehensions as primary motivating factors for *not* escaping slavery, Garner's story demonstrates that enslaved women fled while managing family attachments in complex, innovative ways.

To secure freedom, women often devised measured solutions that went beyond the bold actions of their male counterparts.[6] Black women used the chaos of the American Revolution, the War of 1812, and the Civil War to forge alternative and expanded paths to self-liberation. They effected emancipation through the courts, escaped with and to family members, or reunited with relatives once freedom was realized.[7] Whenever possible, women escaped within groups or relied on networks. When the opportunity presented itself, they often purchased their freedom or the freedom of loved ones and combined these purchases with escape strategies.[8]

Women confronted oppression and invented solutions, disguising themselves and defying gender norms when necessary. By subverting nineteenth-century race and gender conventions, for example, Ellen Craft, an enslaved black woman, disguised herself as a white man; with the help of abolitionists, fifteen-year-old Anna Marie Weems, dressed as a boy, "perfected herself in the art of wearing pantaloons," learned the rhythm, gait, and demeanor of a young lad, duped her captors, and make good her escape.[9]

Figure 2.2. "Anna Maria Weems escaping in male attire," n.d. Anonymous photograph published in *The Underground Railroad: A Record of Facts, Authentic Narratives, Letters . . .*, William Still (1872). Courtesy of Manuscripts, Archives and Rare Books Division, Schomburg Center for Research in Black Culture, New York Public Library, Astor, Lenox and Tilden Foundations.

Women who escape tread new ground literally and metaphorically, the middle ground between slavery and freedom. Certainly, travel, the transcendent journey as both metaphor and reality, is a legitimate part of the escape experience, an aspect of self-discovery beyond the narrow confines of slavery.[10] According to Joseph C. Miller, "Women born into slavery in the Americas by the late eighteenth century had only the constrained world of the plantations where they had been born available as options."[11] Yet, historian Nell Painter warns of "the temptation to equate slave society to southern society and specifically to plantation settings."[12] Beyond plantations, women escaped from presidents, statesmen, and ministers; they flew from cities and towns, North and South; they fled poverty, luxury, benevolence, and malevolence alike. Women fled from every conceivable context where slavery was present. In 1796, seamstress Ona Judge left Philadelphia by ship

Figure 2.3. *Ellen Craft*, n.d. Engraving by J. Andrews & S. A. Schoff, from a daguerreotype by Hales. From *Portraits of American Abolitionists*. Courtesy of Massachusetts Historical Society, Boston, Mass.

for New Hampshire, escaping from the first house used as the executive mansion. In her wake, she left her owner Martha Washington and the nation's first president, George Washington, fuming and complaining of her ingratitude.[13] In removing themselves from slavery, women necessarily found new experiences in asserting selfhood in the patriarchal world, both black and white.[14]

Enslaved women such as Garner were forced to confront what Linda Krumholz terms their "incompatible roles as a slave and as a mother."[15] Ultimately, maternal rites were not theirs to enjoy. Historian Wilma King, however, has recounted that enslaved women also undermined slavery by subverting reproduction in refusing to conceive children, aborting them, or, most famously, as exemplified by Margaret Garner, resorting to infanticide. Enslaved black women used abortion and infanticide to sabotage the perpetuation of slavery through economic and sexual exploitation of their female reproductive potential, depriving future generations of an enslaved workforce composed of their children.[16]

Physical escapes from slavery marked the most obvious form of resistance, yet gendered escapes of varying duration took multiple forms; whether on foot, by carriage, or boat, circumstances of escape varied widely, whether women fled alone, with children, or with family. At times, deliverance was brief and the respite short; at other times, permanent liberation was the penultimate reward. Equal consideration is given to mode of transportation. Defining unrealized escape attempts as failures diminishes the agency and the boldness implicit in the decision to leave. For our purposes here, escaping and demonstrating an unyielding attitude toward enslavement and a willingness to resist captivity for a chance at freedom deserves as much attention as the outcome of the ultimate mission of liberation. Such a paradigm represents a departure from the success model that privileges the narrative of triumphal escape over the failure of recapture. This is particularly important for the gendered escape strategies of women. In the end, after all, the Garners spent a scant twelve hours chasing freedom. But although Margaret Garner was remanded into slavery, her short-lived escape made a lasting impression on history.[17]

From the earliest days of slavery through the American Revolution and throughout the Civil War, women escaped slavery while attempting to maintain a firm grip on both their families and the hope of liberty.[18] Within the United States, the lives of Margaret Garner and Harriet Tubman, two very different women widely associated with escape and the Underground Railroad, lay at opposite ends of the spectrum in the quest for liberation. Their life experiences are indicative of the numerous liberation strategies and the divergent roles women actively undertook. The escape of Margaret Garner with her extended family required forethought, planning, and organization, while Harriet Tubman escaped alone, finding help along the way.

## Historical Memory and Recovery

Increasingly, historians are recognizing the viability of historical recovery and the ability of individual and collective memory to challenge historical unconsciousness.[19] Beyond informing historical awareness, the saga of black women in slavery, as Krumholz notes, inspires artists and writers "to tap the resources of memory and imagination as tools of strength and healing."[20] For African American women, memory often has had to do the work of history. As Hortense J. Spillers put it, the "incestuous, interracial genealogy" of the enslaved women's experiences in the United States, the moral implications of legal rulings, and the overarching humanity in the face of inhumane treatment render stories such as Margaret Garner's a necessary act of recovery for understanding the ethical and racial foundations of the nation. These stories speak to aspects of a collective past that hold present-day meaning.[21]

Female subjects brought to the fore in this chapter were problematic historical figures whose narratives of subjectivity, according to Miller, carry "three different categories of exclusion": slavery, race, and gender.[22] Stories of sexual misuse and violence, physical abuse, and the crippling effects of slavery on motherhood historicize the profound nature of such gendered experiences. The complicated racialized social location and liminal status of enslaved black women in American society expose troubling paradoxes within a democratic nation. As historian Darlene Clark Hine has argued, "Black women's history compels the individual to come to grips more completely with all of the components of identity. Through the study of black women it becomes increasingly obvious how historians shape, make, or construct history, and why we omit, ignore, and sometimes distort the lives of people on the margins."[23] Large numbers of enslaved women escaped and, more important, *attempted* to escape bondage, often at great cost to themselves and others. As historians acknowledge and analyze the depth of this reality, the profundity of the moral, legal, social, and psychological effects of such resistance cannot be ignored. This chapter recovers from the historical void some of the histories and memories of black women who resisted enslavement, actively or passively, successfully or disastrously. The process of excavating these stories, their meaning, and their relevance in the present is the work of the *Gendered Resistance* project.

## Historiographical Arguments

In *Essence of Liberty*, historian Wilma King notes that "the advent of a 'new' history following the social, economic and political upheaval of the 1960s resulted in shifting greater attention to women's history, past and present."[24] Into the 1970s and 1980s, scholars showed a deeper interest in the lives of enslaved women, and there has been a resurgence of interest since the 1990s. The literature on enslaved women has expanded considerably in the past ten years, across a range of academic disciplines. One of the most influential works, *Women and Slavery*, applies a focused, analytically gendered consideration of women held in slavery with substantial attention to "the subtler ways in which women have cannily assessed and expertly exploited even situations as theoretically oppressive as enslavement to create dynamic spaces of their own."[25] Deborah Gray White began this work more than a quarter-century ago in *Ar'n't I a Woman?*, which focuses entirely on the experiences of enslaved women. One review of this seminal text claims that it articulates the "relationship between resistance, activism, and power" while "centering on violence, sexuality, and the body."[26] In the introduction to the 1999 revised edition, White saw much to celebrate: "new source material on black women has been unearthed," historians are using these materials in inventive ways, and history books on African American women have continued to multiply. Thavolia Glymph extends this analysis in *Out of the House of Bondage: The*

*Transformation of the Plantation Household* by exploring the systematic violence by white women against enslaved women and delineating the political dimensions of their day-to-day interactions.[27]

The voices of women who fled bondage emerge most clearly through their own words captured in slave narratives. Jean Fagan Yellin drew from *Incidents in the Life of a Slave Girl*, one of the most famous escape narratives, to expose the sexual abuse of enslaved women. In *Harriet Jacobs: A Life*, Yellin puts the life and times of Harriet Jacobs in context and explores the sexual exploitation she encountered, the seven years Jacobs spent hiding in her grandmother's attic, her escape, and her subsequent life in freedom.[28]

Harriet Tubman ensured her own legacy by narrating one of the most important slave narratives of the nineteenth century, *Harriet Tubman: The Moses of Her People*. After sixty years of inattention by historians, five recent books have focused on Tubman's life. Her narrative provides the lens through which subsequent biographers have reconstructed her life. Kate Clifford Larson's biography, *Bound for the Promised Land: Harriet Tubman, Portrait of an American Hero*, relies on new sources to add different dimensions to Tubman's life and the escapes she engineered. In *Harriet Tubman: Myth, Memory, and History*, Milton Sernett concentrates on separating the legend from the woman, and Jean Humez provides valuable primary source documents that further enhance our ability to understand Tubman as a counterintuitive female hero in *Harriet Tubman: The Life and the Life Stories*.[29]

Several works bring greater specificity to well-known stories of escapes that involved women. Recent works highlight the varied strategies and conditions of escape that freedom-seeking women endured. Two authors have focused on the escape attempt aboard the schooner *The Pearl*. The Edmondson Sisters were among the seventy-six escapees from Washington, D.C., who took part in an aborted getaway aboard the ship. Similarly, in *In the Shadow of the Civil War: Passmore Williamson and the Rescue of Jane Johnson*, Nat Brandt vividly narrates the story of the escape of Jane Johnson and her children and of Passmore Williamson, who came to her aid. This harrowing story reveals the complexities confronting women attempting to escape powerful owners. Bryan Prince expands on and adds detail to the family life and escape of Anna Maria Weems in *A Shadow on the Household: One Enslaved Family's Incredible Struggle for Freedom* (see figure 2.2). For this deeper look at the Weems family, Prince draws from one of the most famous narratives of escape, recounted in William Still's *Underground Railroad*.[30]

Women rarely escaped alone. Family members, often their husbands, joined with wives, mothers, sisters, and loved ones for deliverance from bondage. The narrative of Ellen and William Craft, *Running a Thousand Miles for Freedom; or, The Escape of William and Ellen Craft from Slavery*, gave nineteenth-century readers the details of the couple's shrewd escape, revealing one of the more clever ruses invented by escapees to beat back the forces of slavery. The pair disguised the fair-skinned Ellen Craft as an ailing white man who was being escorted north for medical treatment by his slave, William Craft (see figure 2.3). In *I've Got a Home in Glory Land: A Lost Tale of the Underground Railroad*, Karolyn Smardz Frost introduces another couple and a new story into the genre. Thornton and Lucy Blackburn, husband and wife, fled slavery in Kentucky and, using the Underground Railroad, arrived safely in Toronto, Canada.

Journalist Betty De Ramus takes a different approach in *Forbidden Fruit: Love Stories from the Underground Railroad*, telling stories of love and dedication, of women and couples motivated to escape slavery in order to keep families, relationships, and marriages intact. Most relevant for this chapter, Steven Weisenburger focuses on the story of one woman and delivers an in-depth analysis of the life of Margaret Garner and her escape with her family in *Modern Medea*, the first nonfiction account to grapple with this unsettling and moving story. In *Who Speaks for Margaret Garner?* Mark Reinhardt deciphers the legal and public opinions and attitudes surrounding the famous case.[31]

Beyond such narratives, detailed focus on women and escape from slavery has been rare. *Runaway Slaves: Rebels on the Plantation* by John Hope Franklin and Loren Schweninger remains the definitive general work on escape from slavery. Since Franklin and Schweninger neither investigate nor theorize the distinctive gendered aspects of female escapes, a text that reconstructs the lives and experiences of women who escaped from slavery is long overdue. Although the narratives of Harriet Tubman and Harriet Jacobs, for example, provide insight into the accomplishments of women who fled unaccompanied by family, a survey monograph addressing women's escape from slavery has yet to be written.[32]

Young, unmarried men of supposed superior intellect and skill, often between the ages of sixteen and twenty-two, dominate descriptions of the typical person escaping slavery. As Franklin and Schweninger note, young men "were more willing to defy overseers" or slaveholders "if they felt aggrieved. Once away from the plantation, young men could better defend themselves and were willing to resist recapture . . . men offered 'fierce resistance.'"[33] Yet despite their fewer numbers, I contend that women such as Harriet Tubman or Eliza Harris also displayed uncommon courage, "fierce resistance," determination, and steadfastness in delivering themselves, their children, and their families out of the hell of bondage.

Although this work focuses on the United States, Margaret Garner and other women who escaped with their children and families also represent women who repeated their own forms of gendered resistance in Cuba, Surinam, or Jamaica. The same may be said for Brazil and locales throughout the diaspora.[34] Women were with Zombie in Palmeres, a "Quilombo" or early hinterland settlement of

Brazilian maroons. In three quantitative studies of maroonage in Saint Dominguez, women represented 22 percent, 10 percent, and 13 percent of the runaways. Between 1807 and 1834, women constituted 37 percent of the runaways in Barbados.[35] In her 1988 study of *Slave Women in Caribbean Society, 1650–1838*, Barbara Bush found that escaping female slaves in Jamaica took their children with them far more frequently than did men. Similar to women in the United States, the Jamaican women were more likely to seek kin and family. When the Windwood Maroons revolted in Jamaica between 1730 and 1740, their female leader, Nanny, sheltered women and children who came under her protection in "Girls' Town" or "Women's Town."[36] Women in the French colonies who sought to free themselves or their children or to keep their family members from being sold may well have used their sexuality as a tool of liberation against their male slaveholders, a form of resistance rarely available to enslaved men. Historians have tended to extend the more generic male confrontational model of slave resistance to female slaves without carefully exploring the different options open to women as female slaves under the control of men.[37]

## Misleading Interpretations of Runaway Ads

Stephanie Camp, assuming that few new sources will come to light, urged innovative interpretation of existing evidence.[38] More recent works on women and slavery rely on diaries, letters, and reminiscences. Legal compilations, collections of slave narratives, and testimonies also make available a more fully realized understanding of women's escape than is available from newspaper advertisements alone, although the prevailing scholarship based on newspaper advertisements provides some baseline percentages.[39] It is through these advertisements that many female escapes come to notoriety. Between 1763 and 1790, almost a third of the runaway advertisements for escapees in Georgia newspapers announced the escape of enslaved women, with the majority of those 273 runaway women fleeing without children.[40] Franklin and Schweninger conclude in *Runaway Slaves* that female escapees accounted for 19 percent of runaways. In *Stolen Childhood*, Wilma King studied advertisements in the Richmond (Virginia) *Enquirer* and found that between 1804 and 1824, 15 percent of the Virginia runaways were females, and 2 percent were children.[41]

Elizabeth Fox-Genovese raises an important concern inherent in relying solely on runaway slave advertisements for analytical purposes, which is that the advertisements misrepresent "perhaps to a great degree" the proportion of women escapees to men. As she argues, slaveholders were less likely to advertise for women, whom they may have considered less valuable or whom they may have thought were away temporarily visiting family or kin and more likely to return volun tarily.[42] Since the advertisements are a major source from which historians have derived statistics and demographics, reliance on them skews the data and biases our perceptions, making it appear as though few women attempted escape when in fact fewer women may have appeared in advertisements due in part to their strategy of temporary escapes. As historian Peter Wood admonishes, advertisements "represent little more than the top of an ill-defined iceberg."[43]

Permanent escape was less the objective for many female slaves than visiting relatives and friends, an obtainable short-term, gendered solution often referred to as "lying out." Women fled temporarily to visit family, to avoid work or punishment, or for some form of relief from the constant demands of the "mean and servile labor" of slavery. This form of resistance, also referred to as truancy, involved temporary flight to gain momentary autonomy while still being held in bondage—an experience common to substantial numbers of women. According to one scholar, more than four-fifths of all female escapees in South Carolina were said to be visiting relatives, while just one in ten set a determined goal of permanent freedom.[44]

Here, the experience of Jane Moore is instructive. After repeated beatings, she escaped along with her son, William, who had attempted to help her during her latest beating. The pair hid in the nearby woods for several months, relying on Moore's daughters for food and to dress their mother's wounds. The daughters erroneously signaled that it was safe to return when that was not the case, forcing mother and son to flee again. Ultimately, the slave community demanded their safe return and an end to the beatings.[45]

Because women often remained nearby, close to family and relatives, when they did leave, not only were enslavers less motivated to advertise for their return, but they also viewed such behavior as less serious. When analyzed as "little more than truancy," this form of escape obscures the subversive nature of the act. According to historian Gerald Mullin, "Planters accepted the fact that absenteeism, particularly in the evening hours, was scarcely controllable," which implies that slaveholders' acquiescence to the actions of the fleeing women lessened the subversive nature of this particularly gendered form of resistance.[46] Thavolia Glymph found female slave resistance was often dismissed as a problem of behavior, which minimized the perceived potential threat. Camouflaging outright resistance in the language of "recalcitrant behavior" proved less disturbing to slaveholders.[47]

One such slave, Maria, who had cost her enslaver the lofty sum of $1,500, repaid him by running away. Her "fondness for *running out nights*" was unaffected when slaveholder Tryphena Fox attempted to lock her in. After climbing out a window, Maria remained undetected in the neighborhood for six months, despite an intensive manhunt.[48] The fact that most escapees maintained their liberty for only a few days prompted Peter Kolchin to argue that "slave flight did not significantly cut into the profitability of antebellum southern slavery." According to Kolchin, "runaway slaves constituted an annoyance . . . to masters," [49] and the role women would have played as a subset of that "annoyance" would have been miniscule. Relying on similar arguments, historians conflate the lower percentages for women fleeing slavery with a lack of significance, leaving the experiences of female fugitives marginalized, under-theorized, and frequently ignored.

Yet permanent escape from slavery was also a goal for many enslaved women, and "lying out" could be an instructive first step toward freedom. Women counted among those who not only escaped but who repeatedly ran away. Colonies looked for ways to thwart persistent escape attempts. As early as 1643, Virginia's General Assembly passed laws that established penalties for runaway slaves. A Virginia Fugitive Law authorized enslavers to brand an "R" on the face of runaway slaves, leaving an everlasting mark on persistent escapees by branding their faces as an indicator of repeated attempts. Yet neither multiple escape attempts nor the brandings subsided. An advertisement for Annas, an escapee in Virginia, which appeared once in the cold winter of 1768, described her as a five-feet-tall, "thick, well made . . . very white Mulatto" who carried the marks of slavery on her person. If she could not be identified by the "several cuts on the back part of her neck, and a scar upon her left side," then she surely would have had difficulty concealing from her would-be captors the "E" branded on her right cheek and an "R" branded on the left—the initials of her enslaver, Edward Rutland.[50]

The *Charleston Courier* carried an advertisement offering a twenty-dollar reward for apprehending a slave named Molly. Consider what slavery must have meant for this particular young woman, who appears to have attempted several escapes. According to the advertisement, this slim teenager was between the ages of sixteen and seventeen when she escaped in 1825. Her body bore the marks of her struggle: she had been "branded on her left cheek [with an] 'r,' and a piece is taken off her ear on the same side; the same letter is branded on the inside of both her legs."[51] This particular branding indicates that Molly had attempted to escape more than once during her young life. A 1691 South Carolina statute actually mandated that those who fled multiple times should be branded. For women, branding an R on the left cheek in addition to a severe whipping was the punishment for a fourth offense.[52] For another woman, Bettey, branding impelled her escape from North Carolina with her two sons in June 1838. Her enslaver, Micajah Ricks, stated in an advertisement that "a few days before she went off, I burnt her with a hot iron on the left side of her face; I tried to make the letter M."[53]

In the colonies, neither age nor location deterred women from fleeing slavery. Recently enslaved women were equally as determined. A 1734 Pennsylvania advertisement for a girl between age sixteen and eighteen indicated she was newly arrived from Africa, possibly "Whedaw," which probably refers to the historic port of Widah in West Africa, now Benin, where many Africans were sold into slavery. "N.R." had been branded on her breast, and a twenty-shilling reward was offered for her return.[54] A group of three, two men and one woman, fled from New York City in 1763. All three were newly arrived, presumably from Africa or the Caribbean. The woman retained her country marks and could be identified by the scarification on her face and the beads she wore around her arms and neck.[55]

Women harbored and sheltered their husbands and male partners, and men did the same for their wives. A 1775 North Carolina advertisement accused twenty-eight-year-old Jem of harboring his wife, Rachael. One advertiser claimed a Virginia man he enslaved was "supported and concealed . . . by several Negro women whom he calls his 'wives.'"[56] Mark, a forty-year-old preacher from Bergen County, New Jersey, escaped with his literate wife, Jenney, in 1775. Demonstrating why literacy was ever a threat to the slave regime, Jenney more than likely had altered or written the pass that ensured their freedom. Some were bilingual, such as seventeen-year-old Lens, who was able to "speak good Dutch and English and sings a good song."[57] The variety of advertisements provides a glimpse into how slaveholders viewed and described the women who fled their oppression.

Women resorted to multiple tactics to triumph over their lack of understanding of geography. In 1821, for example, a man known as Queen was indicted in Maryland for assisting an enslaved woman, Nelly, "in eloping and running away from [her master]." Queen had ensured Nelly's safety and ultimate goal "by accompanying her a considerable distance, and showing her the road by which she might escape."[58] Children also fled to find their mothers and fathers. In one incident, a "Negro girl 10 or 12 years of age," led her "nearly, or quite blind" mother out of slavery only to be apprehended in Pike County, Illinois, and remanded first to the poorhouse and then back into slavery.[59]

In most instances, however, enslaved females rarely escaped alone. Difficulties notwithstanding, group and family escapes helped women overcome their spatial illiteracy—a general lack of knowledge of the landscape resulting from limited exposure beyond the plantation or work environment to which they had been held captive. In Maryland, eighteen-year-old Leah Green, inspired by Henry Box Brown's creative escape from slavery, had herself crated and shipped by train from Baltimore's President Street Station to freedom in Philadelphia. Fear of the auction block and an impending sale south impelled sixty- or seventy-year-old Jane Davis to seek her freedom in 1857. According to William Still, "Jane, doubtless, represented thousands of old slave mothers, who, after having been worn out under the yoke, were frequently either offered for sale for a trifle, turned off to die, or compelled to eke out their existence on the most stinted allowance." [60] Having been rid of her, Jane's enslaver probably would not have bothered to advertise for her return. Attempts by women to escape were sufficiently rampant, however, that newspapers printed several different stereotypes and icons depicting female runaways to accompany their runaway slave advertisements (figure 2.1).

Beyond newspaper advertisements, alternative sources expand our statistical understanding of who was escaping and how those women accomplished—or did not accomplish—their mission of freedom. Documented examples of women's escapes derived from recent electronic sources and database compilations using multiple sources support preliminary findings that women may represent as much as 30 percent of the total number of freedom seekers, particularly under local or specific historical circumstances.[61]

## War and Chaos

The upheaval of the American Revolution fostered the earliest large-scale disruption of and threat to the slave regime. For the first time, African American women and men contemplated the irony of the rhetoric of liberty throughout the colonies that denigrated the tyrant for attempting to enslave the citizenry.[62] The idea of liberty, however, had gripped the hearts and minds of the enslaved population from the earliest days of their captivity. Prior to gradual emancipation in the North and proportionate to the enslaved population of the state, slaveholders in New York, New Jersey, Pennsylvania, and Massachusetts were as likely to have escapees as those Maryland, Virginia, Georgia, or the Carolinas. The process of bifurcating the country into the nascent categories of North and South began with the Revolutionary War.

Increasingly during the war, enslaved husbands and wives heeding the British offer of freedom attempted to escape together to Loyalist strongholds. Co-founder of the first Baptist church at Silver Bluff, Georgia, David George, and his wife, Phillis, for example, fled Savannah, eventually sailing to Charleston and then to Halifax with their three children.[63] Paralleling life after the Civil War, African Americans seized the opportunity to reunite with family and formed communities in British-controlled areas, using the chaos brought on by war to reconstitute families with both intergenerational and extra-kinship relations.[64] In the aftermath of war, the promised light of liberty faded into the reality of gradual emancipation in the North and recalcitrant slavery in the South.

Throughout the period between the American Revolution and the Civil War, mothers' concern for the well-being of their enslaved children did not wane. Famous black abolitionists such as Samuel Ringgold Ward and Henry Highland Garnet were the children of fugitive mothers. Ward's mother had fled slavery with him in her arms.[65] Garnet had been a mere nine years old when a group of eleven, including his parents, relatives, and a sibling, escaped slavery in Maryland. When the young Garnet grew exhausted and could no longer keep pace with the group, the more able carried him on their backs.[66]

For some enslaved men and women, the imminent threat of being sold south overrode familial considerations. For example, despite Mattie Jackson's father's "deep affection" for his family, he felt compelled to escape from slavery. Her mother helped him leave after she realized that he would be sold away from the family. Mattie's mother struggled to hold the family together in the face of impending sales and the disruptions of the Civil War, taking solace in the knowledge that her husband was a free man.

Two years after her husband's escape, Mattie's mother made a futile attempt to flee with her two children. Runaway slave advertisements led to their arrest, imprisonment in St. Louis, and eventual sale. Mattie would escape again during the Civil War but would, at the urging of her mother, return "home" only to be betrayed by her enslaver, who planned to sell her. The slaveholder made several efforts to sell the family before emancipation, particularly "while the proclamation was pending," when an entire family could be purchased "for a trifle." Mattie's mother finally entered into a Faustian agreement with her enslaver—he would not sell her children if she agreed not to attempt to escape. That agreement notwithstanding and despite Mattie's mother's steadfast efforts, the family was kidnapped and hijacked across the free state of Illinois to Portland, where they were transported to Louisville before their eventual separation and sale at "extravagant prices" in 1863. Undaunted, Mattie made her last successful escape attempt seven months before the Emancipation Proclamation. After seven attempts and forty-three years of bondage, Mattie's mother finally managed to escape with her son during the summer of 1865.[67]

As was true for Mattie's brother, children were a part of their parent's quest for freedom. Noted teacher and Civil War diarist Susie Baker (King Taylor) was fourteen years old in April 1862 when her uncle dragged her along with his family of seven onto a federal gunboat passing near Georgia's Fort Pulaski. Paralleling the efforts of so many captives who sought the protection of the Union soldiers, the family escaped to the Union fleet at St. Catherines Island, Georgia.

In *Closer to Freedom*, Stephanie Camp argues that by the time of the Civil War, enslaved couples had been making the decision together whether to leave or not, but that enslaved women coping with the pressures of war discarded strategies that had worked in the past. As Camp notes, "With the choice between freedom or slavery at stake, women could not afford to wait for their male relatives or friends to help them. Southern slaveholders attempted to protect their valuable 'property' by moving enslaved men to the interior away from Union troops." With the numbers of black men available to assist women fleeing slavery further diminished by the labor demands of the Union and Confederate armies alike, enslaved women improvised different responses to the shifting circumstances of war.[68] Camp delineates an important shift from antebellum patterns, in which "despite women's relative spatial illiteracy, cooperation among themselves became a vital part of their escape strategy."[69]

By July 1864, the Civil War had raged for more than two years when Lizzie, joined by her husband Stephen and their children, made the decision to escape from the low country. Leaving with one other fellow, the group was joined by eight people enslaved on four other plantations. The escapees were determined to reach either the federal fleet or the contraband camp. To the surprise of their former owner, apparently Lizzie and her family weighed the risks of discovery and recapture against the worsening conditions they faced and the prospects of family separation and, mirroring the Garner family's choices, concluded that fleeing with their family intact was the better option.[70]

## Mothers Who Left Children Behind

As Harriet Jacobs recounts in *Incidents in the Life of a Slave Girl*, as she was planning her own escape from enslavement, her grandmother entered the room and told her: "Nobody respects a mother who forsakes her children; and if you leave them, you will never have a happy moment . . . and your sufferings would be dreadful."[71] On occasion enslaved women weighed their options, rejected the prevailing societal and maternal dictates, and escaped alone, leaving family and children under the tyranny of slavery. Of course, strong ties to kin and family bound some women more tightly than others.

Harriet Jacobs is a prime example. *Incidents in the Life of a Slave Girl,* which remains the most widely read woman's slave narrative, has ensured Jacobs's place as one of the most famous of all women to have escaped slavery.[72] Jacobs fled to avoid the persistent threat of sexual abuse from her enslaver, Dr. James Norcom, a threat that began when Harriet was fifteen and continued after she bore two children by another man in an attempt to secure his protection against her owner. Her grandmother's admonition, "Stand by your own children, and suffer with them till death," embodies an almost universal understanding of the duties of motherhood.[73] In 1842, after seven years in hiding, Jacobs fled slavery, leaving her children behind in the care of their father, a white lawyer, and their great-grandmother. After fleeing north, Jacobs would later be united with her daughter in New York City.[74]

The mournful wailing following the broken bond between mother and child, painfully brought on through sale, stipulation in wills, or escape from slavery, was a constant source of despair among enslaved families. This sentiment remained so strong that voluntarily leaving children behind was supposedly an unthinkable option. William Still's brother Peter, for instance, lamented how he "had been torn away from his mother, when a little boy six years old; how, for forty years and more, he had been compelled to serve under the yoke, totally destitute as to any knowledge of his parents' whereabouts; how the intense love of liberty and desire to get back to his mother had unceasingly absorbed his mind through all these years of bondage." Peter was unable to conceive that as a result of the escape of his mother, Charity Still, and the self-purchase of her husband, his mother was forced to leave two of her four children in slavery, leaving Levin and Peter, ages eight and six, respectively, "at the mercy of the enraged owner." The children were "soon hurried off to a Southern market and sold, while their mother, for whom they were daily weeping, was they knew not where. They were too young to know that they were slaves, or to understand the nature of the afflicting separation." Unable to conceive of the possibility that their mother had abandoned them, for years the children entertained only one conceivable explanation—that they must have been kidnapped.[75]

Margaret Garner, Charity Still, and Harriet Jacobs represent a class of enslaved women who were trapped in the bowels of slavery's untenable choices. Their decisions stood in contradistinction to anti-slavery rhetoric that stressed the immorality of the forced and involuntary separation of mother and child, and the voluntary separation, desertion, or infanticide that undermined the image of the devoted slave mother.[76] In the face of such desperate actions, abolitionists found it difficult to perpetuate their indictment of the degradation and immorality of slavery. The general concern among abolitionists for family life, proper gender relations, and the moral dilemma of the enslaved mother stood at the center of the battle over slavery.[77]

## Freedom without Beloved Kin Was a Meaningless Deliverance: Harriet Tubman and Margaret Garner

For many, freedom without beloved family was a meaningless deliverance.[78] As was true for the Garner family, attachment to kin often led to group desertions, which were by far the hardest to accomplish. Harriet Tubman left her husband behind when she initially escaped alone from Maryland's Eastern Shore in 1849. She risked returning to rescue him two years later only to learn that he had remarried and would not leave. Brokenhearted, perhaps, but undaunted and not wanting to squander the opportunity, she rescued a group of enslaved men and women and brought them to Philadelphia. Tubman repeatedly returned to the Eastern Shore to liberate groups of immediate and extended family members.[79]

The gendered components of Margaret Garner's well-planned but ultimately doomed escape included fleeing with her husband, family, and children. Keeping young children quiet and calm while moving through the night confronted many an enslaved mother. The use of a sled helped Garner's husband overcome the ubiquitous problem of an effective mode of travel, particularly with young children and with such a large group. Most important, the group had family contacts in Cincinnati and a plan to connect with Underground Railroad agents.

In contrast, Harriet Tubman, one of the few well-known women conductors on the Underground Railroad, initially escaped alone after she was forced to abandon an earlier escape attempt with her two brothers. Tubman's narrative contextualizes the range of gendered responses. She managed to make contact with the Underground Railroad only after she had made her decision to flee. Leaving behind her husband and beloved family, Tubman returned time and again to extricate her relatives from the grasp of slaveholders. Her concern for family manifested itself in her first "solemn resolution" that her family should be free. Her strategies were different, but her motivations mirrored Garner's. For women such as Tubman who suffered slavery's physical abuse, if not its sexual misuse, freedom from oppression was motivation enough. Tubman delivered her family from bondage and settled them in the North. For all of Tubman's triumphs, however, her younger sister Rachel, and Rachel's children, Angerine and Ben, would remain enslaved despite Tubman's spending ten years attempting their rescue.[80] Margaret Garner, however, occupies a very different place in the national psyche. Whereas Tubman's narrative reigns as the personification of triumph over slavery, Garner's story disturbs us still as the ultimate condemnation of slavery—two different women, two extraordinary responses to oppression.

Every aspect of Garner's actions—her escape with family, her willingness to commit infanticide, and her subsequent trial—is emblematic of gendered resistance. Killing her daughter and injuring her remaining children rather than having her offspring subjected to the depravity of slavery may have seared the conscience of the nation, but the nation at large, the upholders of slavery, remained unmoved. The country would endure another nine years of slavery and a civil war before it would relinquish slavery and the inhumane treatment of African Americans. Garner's actions reflect a profound knowing—her gruesome solution paralleled the hideousness of the institution in which she and her family were trapped. Tubman's critique of slavery was equally powerful. In an interview six years after her escape, she told journalist Benjamin Drew, "I know what a dreadful condition slavery is ... I think slavery is the next thing to hell."[81]

Reflecting the desperation and horrific realities of slavery in taking her daughter's life, Garner's act of infanticide simultaneously deprived her enslaver of his property as it spared the child from a potential lifetime of enslavement, and of sexual oppression in particular. The deliberateness of Garner's actions, however, has produced a range of explanations by scholars. In *Killing the Black Body*, Dorothy Roberts locates infanticide as the most "extreme form of slave mother's resistance."[82] Wilma King locates the onus of responsibility for infant mortality at the nexus of the effects of the relentless physical demands of the enslaver and the desperation of mothers who killed their own children. Acknowledging the difficulty in reconciling "accounts of the unwavering love slave mothers had for their children with reports of infanticide," King and other scholars reason that "mothers who resorted to such drastic measures preferred to see a child die rather than survive in slavery despite conflicting emotions or the psychological costs involved."[83]

In *Killing the Black Body*, Roberts takes an example from historian and legal scholar A. Leon Higginbotham regarding how to think about infanticide. In reviewing an 1831 Missouri case of infanticide and questioning the motivations of Jane, an enslaved mother, for killing her daughter, Higginbotham reasons that perhaps "the mother felt that the taking of her daughter's life was an act of mercy compared to the cruelty she might confront," to which Roberts adds, "Death may have appeared a more humane fate for her baby than the living hell of slavery." Yet as she also observes, "Judge Higginbotham does not ask a more troubling question: What if Jane sacrificed her child as an act of defiance, one small step in bringing about slavery's demise?"[84]

Historian Jane Landers found a comparable act of desperation in St. Augustine, Spanish Florida, in 1787. After being told her children were to be sold away from her, Juana drowned her son, Juan Baptista Salom, age five, and her daughter, Isabel Anna Salom, age two, in a well and then fled. Speaking through an interpreter at her subsequent trial after her recapture, Juana revealed that she had been chained to a bed, beaten, and abused by her enslaver, Juan Salom, for not having sex with him and harassed and abused by the wife for her husband's interest in his slave. Juana had no other recourse when she decided to end the lives of her children after Salom had taunted her "to look one last time at the children which were not hers, but his."

Rather than hanging Juana, as was the custom for a capital crime, in "consideration of her enormous crime," the court meted out "lashes in the pillory and that 'the delinquent' be made to wear an iron collar for six years to satisfy her punishment and at the same time 'cleanse' the community of the evil of infanticide." The relative clemency reflected the court's opinion that the crime may have been "involuntary or impetuous on the mother's part since she was driven almost mad by the pain of leaving her children forever in the custody of a feared owner."[85]

Abolitionists and sympathetic authors consciously exploited such desperation and matriarchal plottings as a device to exercise moral suasion.[86] Indeed, the courage and extreme anxiety of enslaved women have served as inspiration for two of the nations' most compelling works of fiction, Harriet Beecher Stowe's *Uncle Tom's Cabin* and Toni Morrison's *Beloved*, and most recently for the opera *Margaret Garner*.[87] They and other writers have found literary power and pathos in the maternal struggle particular to the bond between enslaved mother and child, and the familial bonds between husband and wife.

Stowe's fictionalized account of Eliza Harris's escape drew upon the real-life heroics of an unnamed enslaved woman who, with her infant child wrapped in a shawl in her arms, leaped across the breaking ice floes of the thawing Ohio River at Ripley, Ohio. Stowe, however, eliminated the more problematic, complicating details of the escapee's story. In her quest for freedom, the enslaved mother had left her husband and other children in slavery when she fled.[88] Where Garner had been remanded to jail, subjected to a trial, and sent back into slavery, the real Eliza Harris, along with her child and other escapees, was sent by the Greenville branch of the Underground Railroad to Sandusky, Ohio, and then she crossed Lake Erie to the safety of Canada, finally relocating at Chatham, Ontario.[89]

Stowe narrated the monstrousness of the slave experience and the havoc it wrought on the enslaved family during her own time. Morrison, on the other hand, revived a story that never should have been forgotten. In *Beloved*, according to the editor of *A House Divided: The Antebellum Slavery Debates in America*, Morrison struggles to answer the question of "how the individual, the family and the community, and indeed the reader, are supposed to reconcile an act of motherhood which would value taking the life of a child over allowing the child to live as a slave?"[90] Stowe, too, obliquely probed the subject of infanticide, observing, "I do not think there is a mother among us all who clasps her child to her breast who could ever be made to feel it right that that child should be a slave; not a mother among us all who would not rather lay that child in its grave."[91]

Garner's story ranks as one of "the most tragic incidences in the history of antebellum slavery;" it has inspired numerous letters and poems acclaiming Garner's act "as one of supreme motherly love."[92] In breaking the silence around Garner's story, Morrison's validation of memory and of "rememory" reconceptualizes American history in *Beloved*. Linda Krumholz sees Morrison as constructing history through the "acts and consciousness of African-American slaves rather than through the perspective of the dominant white social classes."[93] Envisioned by Morrison as a vessel for healing, the opera *Margaret Garner* ensures that the nation continues to be haunted by not only Garner's story but also by the meaning and aftermath of slavery, and by the heroism of the women these stories represent.

*    *    *

Following in the tradition of Stowe and Morrison, *Gendered Resistance* is "part of the union of women . . . resolved to liberate the slave woman from the bondage and isolation of her silence."[94] We can never fully comprehend the multidimensional effects of coercion, physical and emotional constraints, and abuse on the female population seeking a way out of slavery. Slavery and its ever-present threat of violence and sexual abuse forced desperate decisions. Uncertain consequences of a women's quest for liberty could mean death sentences for loved ones, isolation, dislocation, and the severing of all lines of support.

The stories of these valiant women—mothers, wives, and daughters—lay bare the mighty human impulse toward freedom. As Franklin and Schweninger note in *Runaway Slaves*, "The portion of females fleeing with their offspring in the total runaway population was small, but they bore silent testimony to the indomitable spirit of those who rejected slavery."[95] In her keynote address at the Gendered Resistance Symposium, out of which this volume emerged, Irma McClaurin emphasized that women's bodies represent a people and the nation.[96] For enslaved African American women, this gendered resistance was expressed literally in their branded, exploited bodies. At times, it took as much courage to leave as to stay, to kill children as to take them along or leave them behind. These women's experiences silently counterbalance male-dominated accounts. Enslaved women slipped away, sometimes for an evening, sometimes permanently, from licentious enslavers, impending sale, and the glare of runaway advertisements. In exploiting a nation at war, they defined their own freedom. Although women occasionally escaped alone, the vast majority discussed in this chapter received aid and assistance, often (mirroring Margaret Garner's experience) escaping in family groups with their husbands, children, and relatives.

The paucity of specific sources relative to the number of enslaved women who sought freedom reveals the peripheral position to which historians have relegated their experiences. After concluding that far fewer women sought freedom than did men, most scholars have incorporated women's experiences into those of men rather than analyzing the evidence. Yet enslaved women's stories of escape reveal a previously unrecognized tenacity and intractable resistance to slavery in the face of the nation's reliance on their reproductive capacity to perpetuate and sustain its economic development.

The stories of Margaret Garner's determination that her children should be free and of Harriet Tubman's ten years of efforts to rescue her female relatives and niece and nephew from slavery tell of the strength of women's determined resistance to enslavement. We should hold Mattie's mother's experience as the reconceived image of women fleeing bondage, as her success at age forty-three, after seven attempted escapes, reflects a resolute form of resistance largely hidden in the recesses of the literature.[97]

Inherent in their roles as wife, mother, and family member, women resorted to several gendered escape strategies. Delivered into a world that left them seemingly little control over the use of their bodies or the future of their children and few choices in the conduct of their lives, freedom-seeking women nevertheless persisted and overcame myriad disadvantages.

NOTES

This research was funded in part by the Africa in the Americas Committee of the University of Maryland, College Park. Thank you to the editors of this volume for their suggestions, patient guidance, and support.

1. Walter Johnson, *Soul by Soul: Life Inside the Antebellum Slave Market* (Cambridge, Mass.: Harvard University Press, 1999), 10.

2. Joseph C. Miller, "Preface," *Women and Slavery*, vol. 2 of *The Modern Atlantic*, ed. Gwyn Campbell, Suzanne Miers, and Joseph C. Miller (Athens: Ohio University Press, 2007), xvi.

3. John Hope Franklin and Loren Schweninger, *Runaway Slaves: Rebels on the Plantation* (New York: Oxford University Press, 1999), 210–12.

4. See "Preface," "Introduction," and "Strategies of Women and the Constraints of Enslavement in the Modern Americas," in Campbell, Miers, and Miller, *Women and Slavery*; Deborah Gray White, *Ar'n't I a Woman? Female Slaves in the Plantation South*, rev. ed. (New York: Norton, 1999); Franklin, *Runaway Slaves*; Marie Schwartz, *Born in Bondage: Growing Up Enslaved in the Antebellum South* (Cambridge, Mass.: Harvard University Press, 2000), 172; Gerald W. Mullin, *Flight and Rebellion: Slave Resistance in Eighteenth-Century Virginia* (New York: Oxford University Press, 1972); Gad Heuman, ed., *Out of the House of Bondage: Runaways, Resistance and Maroonage in Africa and the New World* (Totowa, N.J.: Cass, 1986) Other works that address this topic are Wilma King, "Suffer with Them till Death," in *More than Chattel: Black Women and Slavery in the Americas*, ed. David Barry Gaspar and Darlene Clark Hine (Bloomington: Indiana University Press, 1996), 147–68;

5. Steven Weisenburger, *Modern Medea: A Family Story of Slavery and Child-Murder from the Old South* (New York: Hill and Wang, 1998), 72–75; Levi Coffin, *Reminiscences of Levi Coffin, the Reputed President of the Underground Railroad* (Cincinnati: Western Tract Society, 1876), 557–61.

6. Jean Fagan Yellin, *Harriet Jacobs: A Life* (New York: Basic Civitas, 2004); William Craft, Ellen Craft, and R. J. M. Blackett, *Running a Thousand Miles for Freedom: The Escape of William and Ellen Craft from Slavery* (Baton Rouge: Louisiana State University Press, 1999); Josiah Henson, *Autobiography of Josiah Henson: An Inspiration for Harriet Beecher Stowe's Uncle Tom* (Mineola: Dover, 1969); William Still, *The Underground Railroad* (Philadelphia: Porter and Coates, 1872; reprint edition Salem, N.H.: Ayer Company, 1992); Karolyn Smardz Frost, *I've Got a Home in Glory Land: A Lost Tale of the Underground Railroad* (New York: Farrar, Straus and Giroux, 2007); Kate Clifford Larson, *Bound for the Promised Land: Harriet Tubman, Portrait of an American Hero* (New York: Ballantine, 2004).

7. Cassandra Pybus, *Epic Journeys of Freedom: Runaway Slaves of the American Revolution and Their Global Quest for Liberty* (Boston: Beacon, 2006); Graham Russell Hodges, *The Black Loyalist Directory: African Americans in Exile after the American Revolution* (New York: Garland, 1996); Cheryl Janifer LaRoche, "Introduction," in Barbara Stephanic, *Joseph Holston: Color in Freedom: Journey along the Underground Railroad* (New York: Pomegranate, 2008).

8. Leslie A. Schwalm, *A Hard Fight for We: Women's Transition from Slavery to Freedom in South Carolina* (Champaign: University of Illinois Press, 1997); Kate E. R. Pickard and

William Henry Furness, *The Kidnapped and the Ransomed: Being the Personal Recollections of Peter Still and His Wife "Vina," after Forty Years of Slavery* (Syracuse: W. T. Hamilton; New York: Miller, Orton and Mulligan, 1856).

9. Bryan Prince, *A Shadow on the Household: One Enslaved Family's Incredible Struggle for Freedom* (Toronto: McClelland & Stewart, 2009); Still, *Underground Railroad*, 184.

10. Mary G. Mason, "Travel as Metaphor and Reality in Afro-American Women's Autobiography, 1850–1972," *Black American Literature Forum* 24, no. 2 (1990): 337–56.

11. Miller, "Preface," in Campbell, Miers, and Miller, *Women and Slavery*, xxv.

12. Nell Irwin Painter, "Soul Murder and Slavery: Toward a Fully Loaded Cost Accounting," in *U. S. History as Women's History*, ed. Linda K. Kerber, Alice Kessler-Harris, and Kathryn Kish Sklar (Chapel Hill: University of North Carolina Press, 1995), 125–46, quote at 126.

13. Rev. Benjamin Chase, "Letter to the Editor," *The Liberator,* January 1, 1847, as quoted in *Slave Testimony: Two Centuries of Letters, Speeches, Interviews, and Autobiographies*, ed. John W. Blassingame (Baton Rouge: Louisiana State University Press, 1977), 248–50; Edward Lawler Jr., "The President's House Revisited," *Pennsylvania Magazine of History and Biography* 129, no. 4 (2005): 371–410.

14. Ashley Tidey, "Limping or Flying? Psychoanalysis, Afrocentrism, and 'Song of Solomon,'" *College English* 63, no. 1 (2000): 48–70; Mason, "Travel as Metaphor."

15. Linda Krumholz, "The Ghosts of Slavery: Historical Recovery in Toni Morrison's *Beloved*," *African American Review* 26, no. 3 (1992): 396.

16. King, "Suffer with Them till Death," 159–60; Kenneth Morgan, "Slave Women and Reproduction in Jamaica, ca. 1776–1834," in Campbell, Miers, and Miller, *Women and Slavery*, 27–53; Richard Follett, "Gloomy Melancholy: Sexual Reproduction among Louisiana Slave Women, 1840–60," in Campbell, Miers, and Miller, *Women and Slavery*, 54–76.

17. Weisenburger, *Modern Medea*, 72. The goal of freedom is reflected in the majority of slave narratives. Harriet Tubman, William Wells Brown, and Frederick Douglass discuss their failed attempts against the backdrop of their ultimate success. Recapture, arrest, and failed attempts are generally reflected in court records and legal proceedings.

18. Franklin and Schweninger, *Runaway Slaves*, 210; White, *Ar'n't I a Woman?*, 70.

19. Krumholz, "The Ghosts of Slavery"; Ira Berlin, "American Slavery in History and Memory," in *Slavery, Resistance, Freedom*, ed. Gabor Boritt, Ira Berlin, and Scott Hancock (New York: Oxford University Press, 2007), 1–20; David W. Blight, *Race and Reunion: The Civil War in American Memory* (Cambridge, Mass.: Harvard University Press, 2001); David W. Blight, ed., *Passages to Freedom: The Underground Railroad in History and Memory* (New York: HarperCollins, 2006); Milton C. Sernett, *Harriet Tubman: Myth, Memory, and History* (Durham, N.C.: Duke University Press, 2007); Geoffrey Cubitt, *History and Memory, Historical Approaches* (Manchester, N.Y.: Manchester University Press, 2007).

20. Krumholz, "The Ghosts of Slavery," 396.

21. Hortense J. Spillers, "Mama's Baby, Papa's Maybe: An American Grammar Book," *Diacritics* 17, no. 2 (Summer 1987), 77; Tidey, "Limping or Flying?"; Krumholz, "The Ghosts of Slavery," 395.

22. Miller, "Preface," in Campbell, Miers, and Miller, *Women and Slavery*, xv.

23. Darlene Clark Hine, *Hine Sight: Black Women and the Re-construction of American History* (Bloomington: Indiana University Press, 1994), xxi.

24. Wilma King, *Essence of Liberty: Free Black Women during the Slave Era* (Columbia: University of Missouri Press, 2006), 1.

25. Campbell, Miers, and Miller, *Women and Slavery*.

26. Jessica Millward, "More History than Myth: African American Women's History since the Publication of *Ar'n't I a Woman?*," *Journal of Women's History* 2, no. 19 (2007): 161–67.

27. White, *Ar'n't I a Woman?*, 4; Thavolia Glymph, *Out of the House of Bondage: The Transformation of the Plantation Household* (New York: Cambridge University Press, 2008).

28. Harriet A. Jacobs, *Incidents in the Life of a Slave Girl Written by Herself* (New York: Simon and Brown, 2012); Yellin, *Harriet Jacobs*.

29. Clifford Larson, *Bound for the Promised Land*; Minton C. Sernett, *Harriet Tubman: Myth, Memory, and History* (Durham, N.C.: Duke University Press, 2007); Jean M. Humez, *Harriet Tubman: The Life and the Life Stories* (Madison: University of Wisconsin Press, 2003). Also see Catherine Clinton, *Harriet Tubman: The Road to Freedom* (New York: Little, Brown, 2004).

30. Josephine F. Pacheco, *The Pearl: A Failed Slave Escape on the Potomac* (Chapel Hill: University of North Carolina Press, 2005); Mary Kay Ricks, *Escape on the Pearl: Passage to Freedom from Washington, D.C.* (New York: Morrow, 2007); Nat and Yanna Kroyt Brandt, *In the Shadow of the Civil War: Passmore Williamson and the Rescue of Jane Johnson* (Columbia: University of South Carolina Press, 2007); Frost, *I've Got a Home in Glory Land*; Prince, *A Shadow on the Household*.

31. Betty De Ramus, *Forbidden Fruit: Love Stories from the Underground Railroad and Beyond* (New York: Atria, 2005); Weisenburger, *Modern Medea*; Mark Reinhardt, *Who Speaks for Margaret Garner? The True Story that Inspired Toni Morrison's* Beloved (Minneapolis: University of Minnesota Press, 2010).

32. Gerald Mullin in *Flight and Rebellion* may be the first twentieth-century historian to include a substantive analysis of women who fled slavery. Following the arguments outlined by Mullins, historians centered their studies on the aspects of escape from slavery that constrained the lives of the vast majority of women held in bondage. The historical analysis of women's escape from slavery developed from the observation that fewer women than men escaped, generally followed by an analysis of the reasons why women could not or would not escape: kinship ties, little to no knowledge of geography, lack of marketable skills to sustain them, and foremost, the constraints of motherhood and the logistical impossibility and hardships of escaping with young children. Debra Grey White based her statistics on female escapes on Mullin's analysis in *Flight and Rebellion* and Peter Wood's findings in *Black Majority: Negroes in Colonial South Carolina from 1670 through 1787* (Westport, Conn.: Greenwood, 1983) and argued that the responsibilities of childbearing and child care seriously limited and circumscribed the lives of enslaved women, leading to their underrepresentation in the fugitive population. In *Within the Plantation Household: Black and White Women of the Old South* (Chapel Hill: University of North Carolina Press, 1988), Elizabeth Fox-Genovese paralleled White's analysis, although Fox-Genovese demonstrated that notwithstanding their deep ties to community, many enslaved women resisted slavery through acts of "lonely defiance" (303–4). Fox-Genovese also relied on the

available statistical compilations of advertisements for runaways in *Black Majority* and *Flight and Rebellion* for her understanding of enslaved women who sought to secure their freedom. See for example, Barbara Bush, *Slave Women in Caribbean Society, 1650–1838* (Bloomington: Indiana University Press, 1990); Franklin and Schweninger, *Runaway Slaves*; Stephanie Camp, *Closer to Freedom: Enslaved Women and Everyday Resistance in the Plantation South* (Chapel Hill: University of North Carolina Press, 2004); Heuman, *Out of the House of Bondage*.

33. Franklin and Schweninger, *Runaway Slaves*, 211.

34. See, for example, Bush, *Slave Women in Caribbean Society*; "The History of Mary Prince, A West Indian Slave (Related by Herself)," in *Six Women's Slave Narratives*, ed. William L. Andrews (New York: Oxford University Press, 1988), 1–40; Gabino LaRosa Corzo, *Runaway Slave Settlements in Cuba: Resistance and Repression* (Chapel Hill: University of North Carolina Press, 2003); Pamela Scully and Diana Paton, eds., *Gender and Slave Emancipation in the Atlantic World* (Durham, N.C.: Duke University Press, 2005); Richard Price, *Maroon Societies: Rebel Slave Communities in the Americas*, 3rd ed. (Baltimore, Md.: Johns Hopkins University Press, [1979] 1996); Kenneth Bilby and Filomena Chioma Steady, "Black Women and Survival: A Maroon Case," in *The Black Woman Cross-Culturally*, ed. Filomina Chioma Steady (Rochester, Vt.: Schenkman, 1981), 457–64; Pedro Paulo A. Funari, "Maroon, Race and Gender: Palmares Material Culture and Social Arrangements," in *Historical Archaeology: Back from the Edge*, ed. Pedro Paulo A. Funari, Martin Hall, and Siân Jones (London: Routledge, 1999), 308–27.

35. Gad Heuman, "Runaway Slaves in Nineteenth-Century Barbados," in Heuman, *Out of the House of Bondage*.

36. Bush, *Slave Women in Caribbean Society*.

37. Miller, "Preface," in Campbell, Miers, and Miller, *Women and Slavery*, xxi.

38. Camp, *Closer to Freedom*.

39. Erlene Stetson, "Studying Slavery: Some Literary and Pedagogical Considerations on the Black Female Slave," in *All the Women Are White, All the Blacks Are Men, but Some of Us Are Brave: Black Women's Studies*, ed. Gloria T. Hull, Patricia Bell-Scott, and Barbara Smith (Old Westbury, N.Y.: Feminist, 1982).

40. Barbara Krauthamer, "A Particular Kind of Freedom: Black Women, Slavery, Kinship, and Freedom in the American Southeast," in Campbell, Miers, and Miller, *Women and Slavery*, 108.

41. Wilma King, *Stolen Childhood: Slave Youth in Nineteenth-Century America* (Bloomington: Indiana University Press, 1995).

42. Fox-Genovese, *Within the Plantation Household*, 304.

43. Wood, *Black Majority*, 240.

44. Heuman, *Out of the House of Bondage*.

45. Jane Moore, *Texas Narratives*, vol. 5, 134–37, as cited in Glymph, *Out of the House of Bondage*, 57.

46. Mullin, *Flight and Rebellion*, 56, 103–5.

47. Glymph, *Out of the House of Bondage*.

48. Wilma King, ed., *A Northern Woman in the Plantation South: Letters of Tryphena Blanche Holder Fox, 1856–1876* (Columbia: University of South Carolina Press, 1993), March

29, 1861, p. 115; January 29, 1862, p. 133; and n14, p. 133, as cited in Glymph, *Out of the House of Bondage*, 70.

49. Peter Kolchin, "Review of *Runaway Slaves: Rebels on the Plantation*," *Journal of the Early Republic* 20, no. 1 (2000): 163–64.

50. *Virginia Gazette*, January 28,1768, as cited in Lathan A. Windley, compiler, *Virginia and North Carolina*, vol. 1 of *Runaway Slave Advertisements: A Documentary History from the 1730s to the 1790s* (Westport, Conn.: Greenwood, 1983), 57.

51. *Charleston S.C. Courier*, [n.d.], 1825, in Lydia Maria Child and David Lee Child, *American Almanac Collection* (Library of Congress), American Anti-Slavery Society, 1840, 11.

52. "Act for the Better Ordering of Slaves," in *The Statutes at Large of South Carolina: Acts, 1787–1814*, vol. 7 (Columbia, S.C.: Johnston, 1840), 343–47.

53. *North Carolina Standard* [Raleigh], July 7, 1838.

54. *Pennsylvania Gazette*, June 27, 1734.

55. *Parker's New York Gazette; or, The Weekly Post-Boy*, July 28, 1763.

56. *Virginia Gazette*, Williamsburg, October 31, 1777.

57. *Parker's New-York Gazette; or, The Weekly Post-Boy*, June 18, 1761.

58. *Queen v. State*, 5 Thomas Harris Jr. and Reverdy Johnson, *Reports of Cases Argued and Determined in the General Court and Court of Appeals of the State of Maryland*, 232, June 1821.

59. *Pike County Free Press*, July 29, 1847.

60. Still, *The Underground Railroad*, 394.

61. See for example, Gwendolyn Midlo Hall, "The Louisiana Slave Database and the Louisiana Free Database," available at http://www.afrigeneas.com/library/louisiana (accessed February 8, 2013).

*Charleston Gazette of the State of South Carolina*, March 17, 1779.

Still, *The Underground Railroad*, 394.

Hall, "The Louisiana Slave Database"; Maryland State Archives, "Beneath the Underground Railroad: The Flight to Freedom," http://ww2.mdslavery.net; Northern Kentucky University, Institute for Freedom Studies, "Runaway Enslaved Persons Database (REPD) Project," http://www.nku.edu/~freedomchronicle/OldSiteArchive/archive/issue4;

University of Virginia, "Virginia Runaways: Runaway Slave Advertisements from 18th-Century Virginia Newspapers," http://etext.virginia.edu /subjects/runaways;

"Runaway Ads, Baltimore County MD," http://www.afrigeneas.com/library/runaway_ads /balt-intro.html; "The Geography of Slavery (Virginia and Maryland)," http://ww2.vcdh .virginia.edu/gos/explore.html; African American History Website, Radford University, "Colonial Era Runaway Slave Advertisements," http://www.runet.edu/~shepburn/web /Runaway%20Slave%20Advertisements.htm;

Colonial Williamsburg, "Transcriptions of Virginia Gazette Runaway Slave Ads," http:// www.history.org/history/teaching/runaway.cfm. (All foregoing sites accessed February 9, 2013.) See a description of the Runaway Slave Database, Appendix 7, *Runaway Slaves: Rebels on the Plantation*, 328. Percentages derived from Pen Bogart's lecture at the Borderlands Conference, Northern Kentucky University May 18, 2001, and personal communication with S. Charles Bolton, Department of History, University of Arkansas at Little Rock.

62. John Adams, "Novanglus," in Charles Francis Adams, *The Works of John Adams* (Boston: Little and Brown, 1851), vol. 4, 28.

63. David George, "An Account of the Life of Mr. David George from Sierra Leone in Africa: Given by Himself, in Conversation with Brother Rippon of London and Brother Pearce in Birmingham," *Baptist Annual Register* 1(1790–1793): 473–84.

64. John W. Pulis, ed., *Moving On: Black Loyalists in the Afro-Atlantic World* (New York: Garland, 1999), xv.

65. Samuel Ringgold Ward, *Autobiography of a Fugitive Negro: His Anti-Slavery Labours in the United States, Canada, and England* (London: Snow, 1855); Jermain Wesley Loguen, *The Rev. J. W. Loguen, as a Slave and as a Freeman; A Narrative of Real Life* (New York: Negro Universities Press, 1968).

66. Joel Schor, *Henry Highland Garnet: A Voice of Black Radicalism in the Nineteenth Century* (Westport, Conn.: Greenwood, 1977).

67. "The Story of Mattie J. Jackson," in Gates, *Six Women's Slave Narratives*, 2–42.

68. Schwalm, *A Hard Fight for We*, 89.

69. Camp, *Closer to Freedom*, 125.

70. Schwalm, *A Hard Fight for We*, 89.

71. Jacobs, *Incidents in the Life of a Slave Girl*, 91.

72. Yellin, *Harriet Jacobs*, back cover.

73. Jacobs, *Incidents in the Life of a Slave Girl*, 91.

74. Jean Fagan Yellin, "Introduction" in Jacobs, *Incidents in the Life of a Slave Girl*, xviii.

75. Still, *Underground Railroad*, 23.

76. Stephanie A. Smith, "The Tender of Memory: Restructuring Value," in *Harriet Jacobs and Incidents in the Life of a Slave Girl: New Critical Essays*, ed. Deborah M. Garfield and Rafia Zafar (New York: Cambridge University Press, 1996), 251–74; quoted at 260.

77. Mary McCartin Wearn, *Negotiating Motherhood in Nineteenth-Century American Literature* (New York: Routledge, 2008); Elbert B. Smith, "Review of *Gregarious Saints*," *Journal of the Early Republic* 3, no. 2 (1983): 233–35; Lawrence J. Friedman, *Gregarious Saints: Self and Community in Antebellum American Abolitionism, 1830–1870* (New York: Oxford University Press, 1982); Chris Dixon, ed., *Perfecting the Family: Antislavery Marriages in Nineteenth-Century America* (Amherst: University of Massachusetts Press, 1997); Weisenburger, *Modern Medea*.

78. Norrece T. Jones Jr., *Born a Child of Freedom, Yet a Slave: Mechanisms of Control and Strategies of Resistance in Antebellum Carolina* (Hanover, N.H.: Wesleyan University Press, 1990), 165.

79. Larson, *Bound for the Promised Land*.

80. Larson, *Bound for the Promised Land*.

81. Benjamin Drew, "Harriet Tubman," in *A North-Side View of Slavery: The Refugee: Or, The Narratives of Fugitive Slaves in Canada. Related by Themselves, with an Account of the History and Condition of the Colored Population of Upper Canada*, ed. Benjamin Drew. (Boston: Jewett, 1856), 30.

82. Dorothy Roberts, *Killing the Black Body: Race, Reproduction, and the Meaning of Liberty* (New York: Vintage, 1997), 48.

83. King, "Suffer with Them till Death," 160.

84. Leon A. Higginbotham Jr., "Race, Sex, Education, and Missouri Jurisprudence: *Shelley v. Kramer* in Historical Perspective," *Washington University Law Quarterly* 67 (1989): 673, 694–95, as cited in Roberts, *Killing the Black Body*, 48.

85. Jane Landers, "In Consideration of Her Enormous Crime: Rape and Infanticide in Spanish St. Augustine," in *The Devil's Lane: Sex and Race in the Early South*, ed. Catherine Clinton and Michele Gillespie (New York: Oxford University Press, 1997), 205–17.

86. Bruce Mills, "Lydia Maria Child and the Endings to Harriet Jacobs's *Incidents in the Life of a Slave Girl*, *American Literature* 64, no. 2 (1992): 266, as cited in Diane Roberts, *The Myth of Aunt Jemima: Representations of Race and Region* (New York: Routledge, 1994), 129.

87. Harriet Beecher Stowe, *Uncle Tom's Cabin* (New York: Oxford University Press, 1998); Toni Morrison, *Beloved* (New York: Knopf, 1987); *Margaret Garner, a New American Opera*: music by Richard Danielpour, libretto by Toni Morrison; co-commissioned by the Michigan Opera Theatre, Cincinnati Opera, and the Opera Company of Philadelphia. Go to www .margaretgarner.org (accessed September 21, 2012).

88. Fergus M. Bordewich, *Bound for Canaan: The Underground Railroad and the War for the Soul of America* (New York: HarperCollins, 2005).

89. Coffin, *Reminiscences*, 147–51.

90. Mason I. Lowance Jr., ed., *A House Divided: The Antebellum Slavery Debates in America, 1776–1865* (Princeton, N.J.: Princeton University Press, 2003), xlvi.

91. Harriet Beecher Stowe, "Appeal to the Women of the Free States," *The Independent*, February 23, 1854, and *Provincial Freeman* (Toronto), March 25, 1854.

92. Leslie Furth, "'The Modern Medea' and Race Matters: Thomas Satterwhite Noble's *Margaret Garner*," *American Art* 12, no. 2 (1998): 36–57; *Cincinnati Commercial* and *Cincinnati Times*, quoted in *New York Daily Times*, February 2, 1856; Weisenburger, *Modern Medea*.

93. Krumholz, "The Ghosts of Slavery," 395.

94. Cynthia Griffin Wolff, "'Margaret Garner': A Cincinnati Story," *Massachusetts Review* 32, no. 3 (1991): 417–40.

95. Franklin and Schweninger, *Runaway Slaves*.

96. Irma McClaurin, keynote address at the Gendered Resistance Conference, Miami University, Oxford, Ohio, October 6–8, 2005.

97. "The Story of Mattie J. Jackson" in Gates, *Six Women's Slave Narratives*.

# CHAPTER 3

# SECRET AGENTS

## Black Women Insurgents on Abolitionist Battlegrounds

*Veta Smith Tucker*

The confrontation over the abolition of slavery in America has been framed by historians and in the popular imagination as primarily a contest between Northern and Southern men. As a result, abolitionist resistance performed by women—black and white, enslaved and free—has not received the attention given to resistance by men. Nineteenth-century women as a group were typically viewed as passive vessels preoccupied with domestic duties, ill equipped intellectually to understand the machinery of politics, and too weak physically and emotionally to use violence to confront the power of Southern slaveholders. Seldom were black women, in particular, viewed as champions of their own or others' liberation. As recent scholars have noted, studies of resistance to enslavement by the enslaved have largely

Figure 3.1. "Harriet Tubman," full-length portrait (between ca. 1860 and 1875), H. B. Lindsley, photographer. Courtesy of Library of Congress Prints and Photographs Division, Washington, D.C.; "Mary Ellen Pleasant at age eighty-seven." Courtesy of the Bancroft Library, University of California, Berkeley; "Mary Bowser(?)," n.d. Photograph source: James A. Chambers, U.S. Army Deputy, Office of the Chief, Military Intelligence.

focused on the methods used by men, which include displays of violence, physical prowess, or intellectual decisiveness, while the crafty tactics that black women used to resist slavery have been understudied and generally mischaracterized as either impulsive or mystical.[1]

Current scholars agree that sexual abuse and reproductive exploitation were a persistent subtext of all enslaved women's lives, even if some disagreement surrounds the extent of the abuse, the methods of perpetration, and the motives for it. The personal anxieties caused by this ever-present sexual menace were powerfully disclosed by Harriet Jacobs in her 1861 autobiography, *Incidents in the Life of a Slave Girl.* Jacob's text reshaped received conceptions of relations between master and slave by framing their relations as a contest of race *and* gender.[2] The revisioning sparked by the republication of Jacobs's narrative in 1987 dislodged conventional conceptions of slavery, and the accompanying advances in feminist theory gradually stretched our understanding of slavery itself. Literary historian Jean Fagan Yellin, who awakened modern scholars' interest in Jacobs's narrative, situated Jacobs's experience within gender theory, pointing out that "in important ways *Incidents* diverges from received notions about the slave narrative" in that it "presents a heroic slave mother struggling for freedom and a home." As Yellin points out, given the clearly defined gender roles of nineteenth-century America, Jacobs presents the struggles of Linda Brent, the name of Jacobs's literary double, as the acts of a devoted mother, the most valued feminine role for the white women to whom the work is addressed.[3]

As literary historian and critic Houston Baker points out, by placing Jacobs's experience within the mercantile economics of slavery, we are able to see that "mulatto children in *Incidents in the Life of a Slave Girl* signify the master's successful sexual aggression; such offspring both increase his stock and mark his domination." From Baker's perspective, "the central relationship in [Jacobs's] narrative is between an implacable male sexual aggression and a strategically effective female resistance and retreat . . . from scenes of daily life . . . equivalent to burial alive."[4] Recent scholarship by Darlene Clark Hine, Adrienne Davis, and others has also theorized the intersections between gender and slavery to better understand enslaved black women's subjugation and their reactions to it.[5] As Davis contends, "Enslaved women were sexually exploited for a variety of purposes: pleasure, politics, punishment, as well as profit. In addition . . . slavery replenished its workforce through black women. This convergence of sexual and reproductive relations with market and political relations . . . leads Davis to name slavery a sexual political economy."[6]

Clearly, enslaved black women stood at the intersection of sex and commerce, profit and power, economics and rape. Positioned as they were, enslaved black women devised unique strategies of resistance to defy and defeat the subjugation imposed on them by both slavery and patriarchy. Their words and actions challenged the bizarre illogic of gender practices inside and outside of American slavery. In the absence of a fully articulated theory of gendered resistance, many of black women's resistance strategies have escaped detection. This chapter, therefore, seeks to increase understanding of the gendered schema at the core of enslaved black women's abolitionist resistance and the scholarly neglect it received by ex-amining the multiple and varied forms of resistance to labor and sexual abuse that four enslaved women engaged in: Mary Elizabeth Bowser, Margaret Garner, Harriet Tubman, and Mary Ellen Pleasant.

*   *   *

The Civil War activities of Mary Elizabeth Bowser illustrate the problems that hinder our understanding of black women's strategic gendered resistance. Bowser was born into slavery in 1839 in Richmond, Virginia, the property of John Van Lew.[7] After Van Lew's death in 1851, the Van Lew women freed all the family's slaves, and Van Lew's daughter, Elizabeth, sent Bowser to Philadelphia to attend school.[8] When the Civil War began, Elizabeth Van Lew, a Southern abolitionist, summoned Bowser back to Richmond and secured employment for her as a do-mestic servant in the home of the Confederate president, Jefferson Davis. While working in the Confederate White House, Bowser memorized vital information about the war effort that she surreptitiously gathered. Later in the Van Lew home, Bowser conveyed the memorized information to Elizabeth, who encoded it and passed it on to a Union spy ring in Richmond.[9] As historian Catherine Clinton explains, however, "there are only a few instances when Bowser's activities can be corroborated, and evidence about her—before, during, and after the War—remains sketchy at best."[10]

Bowser's contradictory roles as formerly enslaved domestic and spy both conceal and reveal the obscurity that cloaks black women's agency and insurgency. Bowser, a free black woman, posed as the nonliterate enslaved woman she had once been to engage in undercover activity in the enemy's headquarters. Because she was born enslaved, Bowser's personal life would not customarily be documented or recorded; therefore, biographical details of her early life are difficult to recover. Indeed, Bowser becomes historically visible only when her former mistress eman-cipated her and sent her to Philadelphia to attend school. The details of Bowser's emancipation, schooling, and marriage are the salient facts recorded about her early life. Few records have been found to confirm details about Bowser's life be-fore going to Philadelphia or after returning to Richmond.[11] The secrecy needed to disguise Bowser's true identity and to shield the spy operation from detection also served to obscure Bowser's presence in and importance to the operation.

The intentional and necessary secrecy of espionage in general presents unique difficulties for historical verification and may explain why Bowser's service to the

Union cause went unrecognized until the last decade of the twentieth century.[12] It is also possible that minimal scholarly attention has been given to Bowser and Van Lew's "secret service" because their conspiracy ridiculed the powerful men they deceived and undermined the concept of male intellectual superiority that patriarchy presumes. Indeed, disguised as her former self, a nonliterate enslaved domestic, Bowser exploited the Confederate command's faith in the stereotype not only of the loyal slave but of the intellectually vacuous slave woman. While Bowser skillfully deployed the stereotype as a screen for her intelligence, it also functioned as a shield obscuring her service to the Union cause from scholars.

\*    \*    \*

Thus, a plausible rationale for scholars' neglect of enslaved women's subversive resistance may simply be what Clinton asserts—that their subversive exploits are not easy to confirm. However, the lack of scholarly attention to the Bowser–Van Lew conspiracy and to other black women spies suggests that the reasons for this scholarly neglect may be ideological as well as practical.[13] The sensational media coverage given to another slave woman's resistance during the period—that of Margaret Garner—suggests that like her antebellum contemporaries, historians may have been more willing and perhaps even eager to construct black women as passive objects and tragic victims rather than as self-conscious agents of insurgency deliberately resisting both slavery and patriarchy.

As discussed elsewhere in this volume, Garner's bloody deed exposes many of the circumstances that could activate a slave woman's desire to commit violence. Her actions expressed a deliberate choice to seek freedom for her children and herself and, failing to achieve freedom, to seek death. If murder had been Margaret's first choice to avoid slavery, she could have committed multiple infanticide and suicide while still enslaved. Only when the possibility of freedom was completely closed to her did she commit lethal violence.

According to Steven Weisenburger, the reason Margaret's child murder received so much attention across the nation was that it constituted a "masterstroke of rebellion against the whole patriarchal system of American slavery."[14] Garner's misdeed and her justification for it demonstrate that she was fully aware of the political and economic implications of her actions. From an economic standpoint, Garner acted to remove herself and her children from their obligatory roles as enslaved laborers—her daughters, especially, from their obligatory roles as females forced to reproduce and replenish the enslaved labor pool. This was a profound insight and decision for a nonliterate, physically confined, twenty-two-year-old mother of four to grasp. Bowser's "secret service" similarly shattered racialist and sexist assumptions—particularly those asserting that women in general, and slave women in particular, were less capable than men of masterminding and performing complicated paramilitary maneuvers. Given that Margaret Garner's dramatic story was largely forgotten, "surfacing only in an odd historical footnote" until 132 years later when she was reinserted into the American imagination via Toni Morrison's novel *Beloved*,[15] it is perhaps not surprising that Bowser's secret intelligence has taken even longer to be acknowledged and recognized.

Margaret Garner's and Mary Elizabeth Bowser's heroic acts of resistance exacted revenge against the master class. Garner's violence also disturbingly mirrored the violence perpetrated upon her by the patriarchal master class. Both women's acts of resistance illuminate slavery's contradictions and enact subversions that proslavery advocates and apologists considered so radical that the subversions had to be suppressed and denied. Considered from this standpoint, many slave women's acts of resistance coalesce as direct forms of subversion. Examining their subversion within a gendered-resistance paradigm reveals enslaved women's knowledge of patriarchal oppression, their consciousness of gender exploitation, and their keen awareness of the gendered role they played in the economy of slavery.[16]

*    *    *

When examined as strategic gendered resistance, Harriet Tubman's much-better-known and well-documented rescue missions demonstrate that she possessed an understanding of patriarchal oppression and gender exploitation. Yet to uncover Tubman's knowledge and the subversive agency it fostered, we must consider some aspects of Harriet Tubman's life and exploits that have not been well publicized. Helpful in this regard are the three biographies of Tubman published in 2004 by Jean M. Humez, Kate Clifford Larson, and Catherine Clinton, each of which presented new research and fresh interpretations that explore Tubman's life in the rich historical context of slavery and the Civil War.[17] And yet, as comprehensive as they are, these new works also underscore the challenges facing all Tubman biographers: the paucity of written sources, the mythic quality and heroic emphasis in much of the literature on Tubman, and the daunting task of imagining and documenting the complex life and critical work that Tubman accomplished in her lifetime.

To this end, examining her financial struggle in the context of her relationship to John Brown provides a powerful example of the gendering of Tubman's resistance. It is not well known that after her own escape from slavery and between repeated sorties into Maryland to rescue others, Tubman suffered the same indignity of poverty as most black women fugitives. She supported herself as a cook, laundress, and scrubwoman—menial work performed primarily by black women.[18] Tubman also solicited donations from abolitionist friends to finance her missions, to support her aged parents while she carried out her missions, and to save her house from foreclosure.[19] Tubman's unequivocal support of John Brown's raid on

Harper's Ferry is also a neglected moment in most narratives of her life. When these aspects of Tubman's life are included in her heroic story, her life and exploits fit the paradigm of gendered resistance to slavery and subversion of patriarchy examined in this chapter and volume.

Tubman first met with John Brown at her home in St. Catherine's, Ontario, in April 1858. There Brown divulged his plans to create an insurrection in the vicinity of Harper's Ferry, Virginia, and he expressed his desire to have Tubman join his cadre of insurgents. At this meeting, Tubman apparently divulged to Brown the locations of her co-conspirators in the region. After the meeting, Brown spoke of Tubman with awe and admiration. In a letter to his son, Brown wrote, "He is the most of a *man*, naturally, that I *ever* met with."[20] Of course Brown intended his reference to Tubman *as a man* to be complimentary—to stress Tubman's courage and valor. It is, nevertheless, troubling that Brown seemed to find it necessary to erase Tubman's female gender and transform her into an honorary man. Clearly, Tubman's fearless exploits disrupted Brown's gender assumptions and made it difficult for the radical abolitionist to credit Tubman's heroism to her as a woman. Attempting to explain Brown's masculine reference to Tubman that earlier biographers had glossed over, Catherine Clinton argues that "Brown was an Old Testament patriarch, who condemned the second-class status of blacks but accepted women's subservient role."[21] According to Clinton, "Brown's attitudes toward the female sex were so absolute that when confronted with a blatant exception to his rigid rule, he merely ignored the fact that Tubman was a woman—'transubstantiating' her into a male. He desperately needed her, so much so that he could only view her as General Tubman, an invaluable recruit for his army."[22] Although such a reconfiguration of Tubman's gender may seem trivial, it proved costly to Tubman when Reconstruction Congressmen rejected petitions to compensate her for the four years she served the Union Army as a scout, spy, and nurse.

Tubman's bravery and unstinting efforts to serve the Union cause are clear from the description of this little-known aspect of her Civil War service offered by her biographer and contemporary, Sarah Bradford:

> She was often under fire from both armies; she led our forces through the jungle and the swamp, guided by an unseen hand. She gained the confidence of the slaves by her cheery words, and songs, and sacred hymns, and obtained from them much valuable information. She nursed our soldiers in the hospitals . . . In this way she worked, day after day, till late at night; then she went home to her little cabin, and made about fifty pies, a great quantity of ginger-bread, and two casks of root beer. These she would have some contraband sell for her through the camps, and thus she would provide her support for another day.[23]

As Bradford also noted, "Officers and *men* were paid. But this woman sacrificed everything . . . and risked her life hundreds of times for the cause of the Union without one cent of recompense."[24] In four years, Bradford wrote, Tubman drew "only 20 days rations from the Government." Yet Tubman's petitions to Congress requesting a pension were denied because there was no law that covered it, and even the efforts of her friend, Secretary of State William Seward, "seconded by other distinguished men, to get a pension for her were sneered at in Congress as absurd and quixotic."[25] Tubman's gendered valor apparently was as incomprehensible to U.S. Congressmen as it had been to John Brown and the antebellum public.

At the time of her daring rescues, public praise for Tubman was framed in masculine imagery, the popular identification of Tubman as "Moses" registering the public's inability to reconcile her deeds with her gender. Because she transgressed her expected gender role, Tubman was regarded as an aberration, bringing her notoriety as well as fame, which allowed her the male privilege of addressing the public. At the same time, however, her valorous deeds denied her the financial reward and security she had so courageously earned.

The economic uncertainties that Tubman negotiated as a self-emancipated woman in the North and the notoriety she gained for transgressing gender expectations are not particular to Tubman, however, and illustrate some of the difficulties that plagued the majority of antebellum black women. These difficulties included lack of education, menial labor at near starvation wages, public humiliation, defeminization,[26] and finally, scholarly neglect. Economic privation resulting from racial subordination made it nearly impossible for black women to adhere to accepted nineteenth-century gender roles. Therefore, antebellum black women had more latitude to participate in commerce related to economic production and in public affairs related to racial uplift.[27] Masses of enslaved and impoverished black women entered public space every day to perform menial, physically taxing labor unbecoming to a "True Woman." And because they labored physically and publicly, enslaved and poor black women were categorically denied "True Woman" status.

In addition, most nineteenth-century enslaved women were prevented from marrying legally, and thus their intimate relationships with men were considered illicit, and the children they birthed were deemed illegitimate. These perceived unladylike, unchaste, stigmatized, yet unavoidable social relations effectively degraded all black women—enslaved and free, poor and privileged—and contributed to the notion that all black women possessed inherent character defects. More important, however, this delegitimization of enslaved women's intimate relationships, denial of legal marriage, and refusal to acknowledge the paternity of their children were slavery's linchpins that legitimized sexual aggression upon enslaved black women for profit and pleasure. Enslaved black women had to outmaneuver this ever-present sexual menace or surrender to it. The fact that the women featured in this chapter resisted and frequently outmaneuvered this potentially soul-crushing menace suggests they understood it well.

A woman who entered public space to perform dangerous gender-*in*appropriate acts of heroism such as those performed by Bowser, Garner, and Tubman might earn rebuke or reward. While Garner earned rebuke and a century of neglect and Bowser was never given sufficient attention to receive either, Tubman received both rebuke and neglect. For her self-endangering bravery Tubman was lionized; for her gender transgression, she was masculinized. Although Tubman appreciated the veneration, she refused the masculinization. Quite possibly Tubman's feminine gender was accepted unequivocally only in private with her extended family and closest friends. Indeed, as Clinton has pointed out, the particulars of Tubman's employment in menial jobs reserved for underclass black women—as cook, laundress, and domestic servant—rarely appear in modern accounts of her life; quite simply, they do not fit Tubman's heroic, masculinized public image.[28]

The contradictory aspects of Tubman's social identities exerted a great deal of influence on the ways that Tubman's resistance has been scripted by biographers and historians. Most twentieth-century books about Tubman have been juvenile biographies interested primarily in her heroic accomplishments.[29] Most have reproduced the mythical nineteenth-century Tubman with very little attention to quotidian aspects of her life.[30]

Captivated by the mythical, masculinized public image created by Tubman's contemporaries, most modern biographers repeated the awe-inspiring myth and embellished it with superhuman, supernatural qualities. Ironically, the mythical qualities projected onto Tubman have also effectively obscured her role as a master strategist and tactician and her privation as an indigent woman. It may be that some of the mythical qualities her contemporaries attributed to her might have been required at the time to give the impression that Tubman acted alone to protect the identities of her extensive network of contacts and co-conspirators. Some mythical embellishments, however, may be the result of Tubman's affecting a self-effacing humility to serve her own purposes. Perhaps Tubman did not approve of the masculine image the public foisted upon her and, wishing to preserve her feminine identity, she may have unwittingly diminished her role as strategist and tactician by describing her exploits as providential miracles.[31] It is possible that Tubman characterized her role as a mere vessel used by God to garner public approval, to deflect criticism for inappropriate gender behavior, and to preserve her feminine identity.

According to Frances Smith Foster, discipleship was a familiar frame appropriated by nineteenth-century women who desired to preach: by claiming God's approval, religious women could "bypass men's authority."[32] By claiming direct communication with God concerning her missions, Tubman may have asserted not only her religious faith but also feminine humility and invoked God's approval rather than man's for her transgressive gender conduct. (It may be noted, however, that Tubman's carrying a pistol would seem to undermine her claim of complete reliance on God.[33])

Always in need of funds, Tubman often solicited donations for her missions at public appearances, and her public speeches show that she relished uniquely female devices and deceptions. Unlike several female fugitives who cross-dressed, assuming male identities to accomplish their escape, Tubman never reported having assumed a male identity while carrying out her sorties. In one public appearance, Tubman told the audience about a moment on a mission when she and three fugitives received food and shelter from a trusting, poor black family and that she showed the poor family her gratitude by "peeling off her undergarments," offering the undergarments to the family because she had no money to offer them.[34] While obviously intended to underscore her need for funds, this incident also evokes a titillating scene of a woman undressing. That Tubman circulated this story herself suggests that she intended to engage her audience by emphasizing the burlesque gender dimensions of her actions. In another story that Tubman conveyed publicly, she mocks the folly of women's dress while at the same time indicating her compliance with gender norms for women's clothing: Tubman quipped that after tripping on the hem of her skirt during her sweep through plantations along the Combahee River with Colonel James Montgomery's black soldiers during the Civil War, she would never again wear a skirt on a military expedition.[35]

Perhaps Tubman's contemporaries were unaware of an implicit desire on Tubman's part to assert her feminine gender and to point out the value of her gender to the success of her missions. Tubman's peers ignored the gendered tactics Tubman used in her exploits and missed the gender dynamic in her retellings. Tubman's contemporaries and modern biographers almost exclusively stressed her providential interpretations of her deeds. For instance, one of Tubman's most devoted Underground Railroad contacts, Thomas Garrett, recalled that he "had never met with any person of any color who had more confidence in the voice of God, as spoken direct to her soul."[36] Garrett is also responsible for circulating another story that emphasized Tubman's supernatural gifts. According to Garrett, Tubman once visited his store and announced, "God tells me you have money for me." When Garrett asked her how much money she needed, Tubman answered about twenty-three dollars. According to Clinton's version of the tale told by Garrett, "Shortly before, a letter from Eliza Wigham, secretary of the Anti-Slavery Society of Edinburgh, had arrived at Garrett's store. A Scottish gentleman moved by tales of *Moses'* heroics, donated the sum of five pounds to her cause . . . Garrett had the five pounds in hand which worked out to be twenty-four dollars."[37] To a twenty-first-century thinker, this exchange hardly qualifies as miraculous, yet Garrett cited it as proof of Tubman's gift of supernatural foresight.[38]

While Catherine Clinton's 2004 study of Tubman relied on earlier providential rationales for Tubman's successes, it also broke new ground by providing glimpses of the ingenious tactics and careful planning Tubman exercised that enabled her to accomplish her missions and camouflage her true identity and purpose. Clinton's historical analysis, together with Kate Clifford Larson's extensively researched and carefully documented biography, and Jean Humez's exquisite work to recover what she calls the "core stories" that formed the basis of the recurring legends and myths about Harriet Tubman, reconstruct Tubman's life based on new historical and cultural evidence. These works, and those by Milton C. Sernett and Beverly Lowry that followed, provide rich renditions of the historical Harriet Tubman that contradict earlier patriarchal and racist conceptions of her as a larger-than-life American icon. Moving beyond the static heroic image of Harriet Tubman, the academic scholarship of this generation of historians has introduced us to a more complex and nuanced Harriet Tubman whose actual life and work, long cloaked in legend and myth, was both more powerful and more influential than previously recognized. As an enslaved woman, freedom fighter and secret agent, spiritual seer, nurse and Union scout during the Civil War and suffragist and community activist afterward, Tubman lived a life that surpasses at every turn the iconography that has surrounded her for so long.[39]

For instance, while Tubman may have trusted God to aid her in freeing herself and others, she was also skilled at gathering and making shrewd use of human intelligence. Tubman's first flight to freedom ended in Philadelphia, a city with a long tradition of anti-slavery and Underground Railroad activism and a strong coalition of free and fugitive blacks and Quakers who could provide Tubman with detailed descriptions of Underground Railroad station locations and the names of Underground Railroad conductors and sympathizers. The legendary Philadelphia Underground Railroad agent, William Still, became one of Tubman's co-conspirators.[40] Still's experience gained from assisting and interviewing hundreds of fugitives would have provided Tubman with some of the best intelligence available.

Nor did Tubman overreach her capacity in her initial rescues, which helps explain her early success. Her early missions were made to familiar locations near her family's home in Maryland to rescue family members with whom she had communicated via letters and on whom she could depend to execute necessary arrangements in Maryland. Indeed, Tubman's third mission had a decidedly romantic purpose; she returned to rescue and reunite with her husband, only to learn that he had taken another wife. It was not until this third mission that Tubman returned with complete strangers. By then, Tubman was confident of her network, familiar with the terrain, and forced to articulate a different purpose, a religious one, for her rescues.

The timing of her missions is another significant though often overlooked dimension of Tubman's strategic planning. Tubman settled on a seasonal cycle, which consisted of infiltrating a slave community in late fall, announcing her presence and departure plans via the slave grapevine, escaping with a group in the early winter, wintering at home with family in Canada, working as a domestic in the States from spring through fall, then setting out on a new rescue mission in late fall. This seasonal regularity would enable those who desired to escape to make preparations to leave well in advance and to remain alert for Tubman's late-fall return, relying on the grapevine and the season rather than on calendar dates for her arrival.

Finally, it is clear that Tubman, like Bowser and others, also outwitted Southerners by exploiting their reliance on gender and racial stereotypes of black women. Two legendary incidents illustrate Tubman's use of the stereotype for deceptive purposes. Abolitionist Alice Stone Blackwell retold the story that Tubman used gospel music and spirituals to signal to fugitives hidden along the road, because "no one would notice what was sung by an old colored woman as she trudged along the road."[41] In another incident, in which Tubman had to pass through a town near her former Maryland home in daylight, she disguised herself as an old woman, wearing a large sunbonnet and carrying an armload of live chickens. When she recognized her former master approaching as she walked through town, she yanked the strings tied to the legs of the chickens, then pretended to tend to the squawking birds as her former master passed within inches without recognizing her.[42] Though mistaken for an elderly woman, Tubman could not have been older than thirty-five when these encounters took place.[43] These incidents illuminate both the intentionality of Tubman's "old woman" disguises and her preference for female disguises.

Tubman's self-image, social knowledge, and strategic manipulation of gender stereotypes thus come into focus when neglected fragments of her life and designs, devices, and discourse are recovered and examined through the lens of gendered resistance. They suggest that Tubman wanted to be seen and remembered as a courageous abolitionist warrior *woman*. In word and deed, Tubman contested the prevailing racist and patriarchal presumptions that black women were incapable of executing complex, covert paramilitary operations.

*    *    *

Mary Ellen Pleasant is another remarkable example of a black woman whose understudied insurgency has survived primarily in legends. Like Mary Elizabeth Bowser and Harriet Tubman, Mary Ellen Pleasant carried out her insurgency and subversion while doing domestic work. Pleasant's unconventional tactics, like those of Bowser and Tubman, confounded her contemporaries and historians alike. Consequently, histories of the abolitionist movement rarely mention her. Pleasant had requested that her grave marker be inscribed, "She was a friend of John

Brown,"[44] and perhaps her association with the infamous Brown or the strategic secrecy she deployed to protect herself from public criticism served to remove her from historical sight. In any case, some combination of historians' neglect and her own craftiness has deprived us of the intriguing events of Mary Ellen Pleasant's life, her valiant abolitionist insurgency, and her resistance to patriarchal domination.

Pleasant's case is unlike Bowser's, however, in that a great deal is known about Pleasant's life. Nevertheless, prior to the last decade of the twentieth century, Pleasant had received minimal scholarly attention. Despite her important role in the abolitionist movement, Pleasant did not earn celebrity, and today few recognize her name.

Many important details of Pleasant's life are disputed. She claims to have been born on August 19, 1814, in Philadelphia to free parents. She identified her father as Louis Alexander, a native Hawaiian, and her mother as a full-blooded Louisiana Negress. Pleasant's mother cannot be traced because Pleasant gave no additional details about her—not even her name. Contradicting her claim to free status, however, Mary Ellen seems not to have had a patronym as a child; the only surnames recorded for her were those of her respective husbands. The lack of a surname and the mystery surrounding the parents she claimed convinced many of Pleasant's contemporaries that she invented the story of free parents to hide enslaved origins.

The historically verifiable details of Mary Ellen's childhood begin at age ten or twelve when she was living on the island of Nantucket off the coast of Massachusetts. Young Mary Ellen worked as a quasi-slave or indentured servant in the household and shop of a Quaker widow, Mary Hussey. During Mary Ellen's adolescence in the 1820s, Nantucket was a prosperous whaling port dominated by some of the wealthiest early American families, many of whom were Quakers.[45] Although Mary Ellen probably learned about Quakerism from intimate contact with "Grandma" Hussey and her neighbors and customers, she did not become a Quaker, which suggests that Grandma Hussey did not consider Mary Ellen a family member. As an adult, Mary Ellen became one of the founding members of the African Baptist Church on York Street, the first black church on Nantucket Island, home to Nantucket's free black population, which was concentrated in a segregated area of the island called New Guinea. Many of the African Baptist Church's founders were entrepreneurs like whale master Absalom Boston, captain of the *Industry*, a whaler with an all-black crew.[46]

In a prominent, entrepreneurial Quaker community with access to travel and trade from many points on the Atlantic, young Mary Ellen was positioned to learn much about commerce and travel. Furthermore, due to her own status as a bondservant in a thriving black community that included many who were formerly enslaved, Mary Ellen would have understood and appreciated the fugitive's desire for freedom. Many fugitives made their way to Nantucket with the help of a Nantucket whaleman or a "black Jack," as black seaman were known.[47]

Mary Ellen worked as a clerk in Grandma Hussey's dry goods store. Although antebellum women were discouraged from participating in commercial affairs, women clerks and proprietors were common on Nantucket Island because whalers' wives and female relatives ran family businesses while the men were at sea. In the antebellum period, in fact, Center Street in Nantucket Town had so many women-operated shops it was called Petticoat Row, and Nantucket's women were notorious for their independence and entrepreneurial skills.[48] This exceptional gender freedom certainly was not lost on Mary Ellen. Nonetheless, due to her status as an indentured servant, Mary Ellen was not sent to school on the island, a fact that she recalled later with bitterness.[49] Nonetheless, the informal education Mary Ellen received, the practical business knowledge she acquired, and the social networks she developed proved extremely valuable to her later.

Traffic between Nantucket and Boston was heavy during the first half of the nineteenth century, so Boston was a logical destination for an emancipated bondwoman with abolitionist friends and business contacts. The details of Mary Ellen's life in Boston again fade into folklore, but it is generally agreed that she met and married an affluent Bostonian, James W. Smith, reputedly of Cuban or European descent and a carpenter, contractor, and owner of a tobacco plantation in Charles Town, Virginia, near Harper's Ferry.[50] Smith was also believed to be heavily involved in abolitionist activity, most likely sheltering and transporting fugitives via the Underground Railroad. When Smith died in the 1840s, Mary Ellen inherited his wealth, which has been estimated at approximately thirty thousand to fifty thousand dollars—the equivalent of one million dollars today.[51] Mary Ellen also inherited her husband's reputation for assisting fugitives as an Underground Railroad conductor. The evidence for Mary Ellen's Underground Railroad involvement is contextual but credible. As with Bowser and Tubman, however, secrecy was crucial to the success of Underground Railroad operations; therefore, Mary Ellen's actual Underground Railroad conducting in Boston has yet to be verified.

At the close of the 1840s, many blacks left New England for Canada and California. Some were Underground Railroad passengers, and some were Underground Railroad agents. Many were leaving to evade arrest or capture under the harsh terms of the new 1850 Fugitive Slave Law. The latter years of the 1840s also ushered in a mass migration of whites to California to join the Gold Rush, many of them from Nantucket, which had suffered an economic decline and a devastating fire in 1846; in 1849, at least twenty-five members of the Hussey-Gardner family migrated from New England to California.[52] Although Mary Ellen's activities during this time are again the subject of folklore, we do know she remarried after Smith's death, becoming Mary Ellen Pleasant, and moved to San Francisco around 1852.

Mary Ellen settled in the free state of California and claimed the status of a free woman of color. John Pleasant, her second husband, subsequently relocated to San Francisco; however, John's occupation as a cook on oceangoing vessels did not permit him and his wife to live together. Their long separations eventually led to lurid innuendo about Mary Ellen's immorality, which stained Mary Ellen's image and may have diminished later scholarly interest in her.

After Mary Ellen arrived in San Francisco, she found many of her former associates from New England. She had come to San Francisco with a considerable sum of money—"$15,000 in gold coin," she claimed.[53] Remembering, perhaps, the words and ways of Grandma Hussey, Pleasant did not advertise her wealth but camouflaged it by getting a job as a cook and housekeeper, one of the few avenues of employment open to a poorly educated black woman. Pleasant diversified her wealth by buying liveries, laundries, and boardinghouses, and she recruited her former associates from New England to invest her money in burgeoning enterprises such as Wells Fargo Bank and the Bank of California.[54]

Pleasant's friends from New England and New Orleans had touted her culinary skills to prominent bachelors in San Francisco, and Pleasant cashed in on the stereotype of the kitchen-ready mammy—fresh from New Orleans—to her advantage. Indeed, as Pleasant's reputation as a consummate housekeeper grew, so did her fortune. Her first housekeeping position was with the wealthy commission merchants, Case and Heiser. According to her biographer, Lynn M. Hudson, by the 1850s, "Pleasant had established herself as a charming housekeeper for some of the most elite families and bachelors in San Francisco."[55] From her daily diners and frequent boardinghouse guests, who regarded her as a charming servant, Pleasant received the demeaning title "Mammy,"[56] but her houseguests also dropped investment ideas and real estate tips that Pleasant parlayed into increased financial assets with the assistance of front men, including her old New England associates and a new associate, Thomas Bell. Completely unaware of Mary Ellen's wealth, San Franciscans referred to her as "Mammy Pleasant." In a 1953 popular biography of Pleasant, Helen O'Donnell Holdredge explained that Pleasant came to realize that "social expectations required her to wear her apron and collar" everywhere she went and "when she stepped outside of her role of housekeeper, she was regarded as arrogant and met disapproval."[57] Consequently, Pleasant was never recognized by her contemporaries as the wealthy woman she was, nor was she credited for the shrewd deals she brokered that made her a nineteenth-century multimillionaire. Pleasant was forced into the role of silent partner, obliged to put her financial assets in her (white) partner's name; no banker or broker would allow transactions involving large sums of money to be made by a domestic servant called "Mammy." Although the "Mammy" stereotype was incompatible with her millionaire status, "Mammy" was the role the public demanded of her. While Pleasant had little choice except to wear the "Mammy" mask, she also exploited it by using it as a decoy to divert attention from her entrepreneurial and political deal making.

In addition to her entrepreneurial transactions, Pleasant also engaged in abolitionist insurgency. According to biographers, she received fugitives from Underground Railroad agents back East who were part of her network of abolitionist friends in New England, although Holdredge attributed sinister motives to this operation. Holdredge claimed that as a result of Pleasant's help in gaining their freedom and finding jobs, these fugitives from slavery were indebted to her and that Pleasant placed the fugitives as spies in the homes of San Francisco's wealthy elite for the purpose of blackmail.[58] Despite acknowledging Pleasant's connections with prominent abolitionist friends and wealthy associates, Holdredge and others who perceived Pleasant through the stereotype of "Mammy" were apparently unwilling to grant her the personal power and social capital that such a wide network of associates could have given her.

Nevertheless, Mary Ellen's abolitionist efforts went well beyond the dubious schemes Holdredge attributed to her. An earlier biographer, Charlotte Dennis, the daughter of one of Pleasant's friends, reported that Pleasant had helped William West, a friend from New England, establish a boardinghouse that was, in reality, a secret safe house for fugitives.[59] Pleasant also assisted in the liberation of George Mitchell and Archy Lee, two enslaved men brought to California by their owners. Pleasant assisted Mitchell by hiding him from his owner and authorities until California's Fugitive Slave Law expired,[60] and when Lee's case was prosecuted in the California courts, Pleasant provided money for his defense.[61]

It is curious that, to date, Pleasant's Underground Railroad conducting in New England and in San Francisco has not been corroborated in surviving documents left by any of the prominent abolitionists she knew. It is also interesting that Hudson's 2002 biography is the first and only book-length scholarly study of Pleasant ever published. Pleasant's Underground Railroad exploits alone merit careful historical research, but they do not constitute the most spectacular abolitionist insurgency she claimed.

In 1858, when John Brown convened a constitutional convention in Chatham, Canada, to lay out his plan to instigate an insurrection at Harper's Ferry, Mary Ellen and John Pleasant were also in Chatham. Chatham resident Mary Ann Shadd Cary, editor and owner of the *Provincial Freeman*, listed Mary Ellen and John Pleasant as members of the Chatham Vigilance Committee, and Chatham records show that the Pleasants purchased four lots of Chatham property that year.[62] Although Pleasant's presence in Chatham during John Brown's visit is documented, her alliance with Brown and subsequent activities in support of the Harper's Ferry raid are still a matter of controversy.

In 1901, Pleasant granted an interview to her friend, Sam Davis, editor of the short-lived journal *Pandex of the Press*, in which Pleasant detailed the assistance she had given to John Brown. Pleasant said, "Before I pass away I wish to clear the identity of the party who furnished John Brown with most of the money to start the fight at Harper's Ferry and who signed the letter found on him when he was arrested."[63] Pleasant encouraged Davis to talk to Brown's children to corroborate her claims. Davis found Brown's son, Jason, who was living south of San Francisco in Santa Cruz and, according to Davis, Jason replied, "Yes, it is true. My father went to Chatham in '58 and met a colored woman who advanced him considerable money. I don't know her name."[64] Davis also found evidence that Pleasant withdrew a large sum of money in the spring of 1858 and had it converted to Canadian currency.

Scholars still dismiss the claim that Pleasant made to Davis about recruiting for Brown. Pleasant reported that she recruited supporters for Brown in slave cabins along the Roanoke River near Harper's Ferry and Charles Town, where, according to Susheel Bibbs, Pleasant's first husband's tobacco plantation had been located.[65] Pleasant told Davis that she had disguised herself as a man in the clothing of a jockey and, with an accomplice, visited cabins of the enslaved encouraging them to join the raid when it reached them.

One of Brown's raiders, African-Canadian Osborn Perry Anderson, managed to escape from Harper's Ferry and make it back to Canada, and he later wrote an eyewitness account of the raid that lends credibility to Pleasant's claim. According to Anderson, when the raid began, "many colored men gathered to the scene of the action," and Brown ordered him "to pass out pikes to the colored men who had come with us from the plantations, and *others* who had come forward *without having had communication with any of our party*."[66] The formal indictment against Brown also gives conclusive evidence that many enslaved men in the area took part in the raid, including four enslaved men named as co-conspirators owned by Lewis Washington and seven enslaved men owned by John Allstadt also named as co-conspirators. The indictment further states "each of the said slaves" had rebelled and made "insurrection against their said masters . . . against the authority of the Constitution and Laws of the . . . Commonwealth of Virginia."[67] However, Virginia officials later conspired to suppress the fact that enslaved men participated. Officials did not want to publicize the fact that slaves had supported Brown.[68]

Apparently, Pleasant's disguise worked perfectly, preventing her detection then and thereafter, although her daring ride through Charles Town is not the only evidence she offered of her co-conspiracy with Brown:

When Brown was captured they found among his papers a letter from me. . . . It contained these words, "The axe is laid at the foot of the tree.[69] When the first blow is struck there will be more money and help." The newspapers stated that such a letter was found and signed W.E.P. I read in the papers that the detectives were on the track of W.E.P. who wrote the letter and had quite a laugh when I saw that my poor handwriting had given them a false trail.[70]

Authorities used the letters found in Brown's carpetbag to subpoena many of Brown's co-conspirators, including Frederick Douglass; however, Pleasant was never subpoenaed or implicated.

According to her own account, Pleasant had evaded discovery as one of Brown's financiers and co-conspirators due to her illegible handwriting. Ironically, her early servitude, which resulted in a lack of formal schooling and, apparently, illegible penmanship, protected her from prosecution. Just as ironic, however, is the fact that Pleasant's gender has functioned into the twenty-first century to obscure her insurgency-in-masquerade in advance of the Harper's Ferry raid.[71] Pleasant's scouting in the area of Harper's Ferry dressed as a male jockey is still regarded as a sensational fabrication.[72] This is yet another example of gendered resistance and the reluctance of historians to credit black women for such gender-defying exploits.

*　*　*

Historians' reluctance to study Pleasant's life and the lives of other black women who engaged in abolitionist insurgency has much to do with an unwillingness to recognize nineteenth-century black women's exceptional ingenuity in subverting both racial and gender oppression. In all the cases discussed in this chapter, black women manipulated the stereotype of the hapless, deficient, enslaved black woman and used it as camouflage for their anti-slavery and anti-patriarchy insurgency. Either momentarily or permanently, Bowser, Garner, Tubman, and Pleasant became agents of their own or others' liberation. They exercised tactical ingenuity and rare insight into the illogic of both slavery and patriarchy. The success of these women's gendered resistance mystified antagonists, supporters, and scholars alike.

Although Harriet Tubman's sorties as an Underground Railroad conductor are well documented, her indigence, menial labor, brilliant escape strategies, and unwavering support for John Brown are not. Tubman's unorthodox gender behavior enabled her to use her gender to her advantage and to her pursuers' disadvantage, but it also deceived her supporters and later historians. Consequently, Tubman's tactical intelligence has been diminished and her womanly self-esteem erased from the historical record because her exploits were characterized as male behavior or as miracles.

Mary Elizabeth Bowser, Margaret Garner, and Mary Ellen Pleasant also transgressed race and gender conventions, even though historians largely neglected their strategic resistance for most of the twentieth century. The conspiratorial dissemblance of Tubman, Bowser, and Pleasant undermined their recognition in much scholarship that inscribed enslaved women as passive objects or manipulated victims. Although Margaret Garner's defiant misdeed lacks the deceptiveness inherent in the other women's insurgency, it, too, was a calculated and bold attack on both patriarchy and slavery. Margaret Garner momentarily stepped outside of an expected passive role and seized power granted only to elite white males: the power to destroy life. Ignoring the accusation of sexual victimization implicit in Garner's actions, the court, journalists, and nineteenth- and twentieth-century historians failed to see Garner's infanticide as anything more than defiance against slavery. However, Garner's misdeed at once expressed defiance against slavery and retaliation against rape.[73]

As we have seen, these nineteenth-century black women's resistance challenged the bizarre logic of both slavery and patriarchy by exploiting stereotypes of enslaved women and by transgressing gender propriety. If men had accomplished these women's courageous feats, there would likely be an industry of testaments and memorials to them. However, a full accounting of these and other black women's gendered resistance remains understudied, buried in obscurity, or reduced to folk legend. For too long, conventional assumptions that disregarded the gendered dimensions of enslaved women's attacks on slavery led scholars down "false trails" where the "secret weapons" brandished by many unprivileged, unlettered black women were missed or misunderstood.

NOTES

1. See, for instance, Darlene Clark Hine and Kate Wittenstein, "Female Slave Resistance: The Economics of Sex," in *The Black Woman Cross-Culturally*, ed. Filomina Chioma Steady (Cambridge, Mass.: Schenkman, 1981), 289.

2. Jean Fagan Yellin, "Introduction," in Harriet A. Jacobs, *Incidents in the Life of a Slave Girl: Written by Herself*, ed. Jean Fagan Yellin (Cambridge: Harvard University Press, 1987), xxvi.

3. Ibid.

4. Houston Baker, *Blues, Ideology, and Afro-American Literature: A Vernacular Theory* (Chicago: University of Chicago Press, 1984), 52–53.

5. Hine and Wittenstein, "Female Slave Resistance," 289–99; Adrienne Davis, "'Don't Let Nobody Bother Yo' Principle': The Sexual Economy of Slavery," in *Sister Circle: Black Women and Work*, ed. Sharon Harley and the Black Women and Work Collective (New Brunswick, N.J.: Rutgers University Press, 2002).

6. Davis, "'Don't Let Nobody Bother Yo' Principle,'" 117.

7. Harriette Petersen, "Mary Elizabeth Bowser," in *Notable Black American Women*, ed. Jessie Carney Smith (Detroit: Gale, 1992), 100–101.

8. Darlene Clark Hine and Kathleen Thompson, *A Shining Thread of Hope: The History of Black Women in America* (New York: Broadway, 1998), 133.

9. David D. Ryan, *A Yankee Spy in Richmond: The Civil War Diary of "Crazy Bet" Van Lew* (Mechanicsburg, Penn.: Stackpole, 2001), 11–12.

10. Catherine Clinton, *Harriet Tubman: The Road to Freedom* (New York: Little, Brown, 2004), 172.

11. What has been recovered of Elizabeth Van Lew's diary is missing many pages and sections. In the surviving pages of the diary, Bowser is not mentioned. A diary written by Mary Elizabeth Bowser herself was unwittingly discarded by her great-grand-daughter-in-law in 1952. Ryan, *A Yankee Spy*, introduction and 136.

12. In 1995, Mary Elizabeth Bowser was inducted into the U.S. Army Intelligence's Hall of Fame. Ryan, *A Yankee Spy*, 136.

13. Ella Forbes identified several additional African American women who spied for the Union behind Confederate lines. Lucy Carter, like Harriet Tubman, was given a special pass that allowed her to pass through the lines of the 16th New York Cavalry. Mary Louveste, owned by an engineer working on the captured USS Merrimac, stole some of the engineering plans and delivered them to Gideon Welles, Secretary of the Union Navy. Ella Forbes, *African American Women during the Civil War* (New York: Garland, 1998), 41.

14. Steven Weisenburger, *Modern Medea: A Family Story of Slavery and Child-Murder from the Old South* (New York: Hill and Wang, 1998), 77–78.

15. Weisenburger, *Modern Medea*, 10.

16. Davis, "'Don't Let Nobody Bother Yo' Principle,'" 103–27.

17. Jean M. Humez, *Harriet Tubman: The Life and the Life Stories* (Madison: University of Wisconsin Press, 2004); Kate Clifford Larson, *Harriet Tubman: Portrait of an American Hero* (New York: Ballantine, 2004); Catherine Clinton, *The Road to Freedom* (Boston: Little, Brown, 2004). For a comprehensive analysis of the historical Harriet Tubman, see Milton C. Sernett, *Harriet Tubman: Myth, Memory, and History* (Durham, N.C.: Duke University Press, 2007).

18. Clinton, *Harriet Tubman*, 86.

19. Sarah H. Bradford, *Harriet Tubman: The Moses of Her People* (Bedford, Mass.: Applewood, [1886] 1993), 95, 113.

20. Bradford, *Harriet Tubman*, 96; Clinton, *Road to Freedom*, 129.

21. Clinton, *Road to Freedom*, 129.

22. Ibid., 130.

23. Bradford, *Harriet Tubman*, 94.

24. Ibid., 94.

25. Ibid., 78.

26. Angela Davis contends that "one of the supreme ironies of slavery" was that "the black woman had to be released from the myth of 'femininity' in order to extract the greatest possible surplus from [her] labor." Angela Davis, "Reflections on the Black Woman's Role in the Community of Slaves," *Massachusetts Review* 13, no. 1/2 (1972): 87.

27. Shirley Yee, *Black Women Abolitionists: A Study in Activism, 1828–1860* (Knoxville: University of Tennessee Press, 1992), 79.

28. Clinton, *Road to Freedom*, 86.

29. Catherine Clinton, "Slavery Is War," in *Passages to Freedom: The Underground Railroad in History and Memory*, ed. David W. Blight (Washington D.C.: Smithsonian Books in association with the National Underground Railroad Freedom Center, 2004), 198.

30. In "Slavery Is War," Clinton states that Tubman "has not received her scholarly due" (199). Fergus Bordewich's *Bound for Canaan* titles the chapter on Tubman "General Tubman" and reinforces nineteenth-century notions that Tubman was "endowed with virtually superhuman personal qualities" (347). Fergus M. Bordewich, *Bound for Canaan: The Underground Railroad and the War for the Soul of America* (New York: Amistad, 2005).

31. Larson, *Bound for the Promised Land* (New York: One World/Ballentine, 2004), 137, 187.

32. Frances Smith Foster, *Written by Herself: Literary Production by African American Women, 1746–1892* (Bloomington: Indiana University Press, 1993), 70–71.

33. Larson, *Bound for the Promised Land*, 101.

34. Bordewich, *Bound for Canaan*, 352. Bordewich also discusses a moment on Tubman's third mission when Tubman carried a new suit of men's clothing for her husband, John, from whom she had been separated since her escape one year earlier. After learning that John had remarried, Tubman collected a group from the neighborhood who wanted to escape, gave one of the fugitives John's new clothes, and proceeded with the rescue in her own *women's* clothing (350–51).

35. Clinton, *Road to Freedom*, 168.

36. Ibid., 91.

37. Ibid., 91–2.

38. Ibid., 92.

39. Clinton, *Harriet Tubman*, ix–xiii; Larson, *Bound for the Promised Land*, xiv–xxi; Humez, *Harriet Tubman*, 3–8; Sernett, *Harriet Tubman*, chapter 10, "Historians Have Their Say," 293–319; Beverly Lowry, *Harriet Tubman: Imagining a Life* (New York: Doubleday, 2007), 3–9.

40. William Still, *The Underground Railroad: A Record of the Authentic Narratives, Letters, &c. Narrating the Hardships, Hairbreadth Escapes and Death Struggles of the Slaves in Their Efforts for Freedom,* (1872, rpt. New Jersey: Plexus, 2005), 458.

41. Clinton, *Road to Freedom*, 89.

42. Ibid.

43. Tubman began her missions as "Moses" while still in her twenties and was only forty in 1860 when Lincoln was elected (Ibid., 89).

44. Lynn M. Hudson, *The Making of "Mammy Pleasant": A Black Entrepreneur in Nineteenth-Century San Francisco* (Urbana: University of Illinois Press, 2003), 43.

45. Hudson, *Making of "Mammy Pleasant,"* 18.

46. Fredrick McKissack and Patricia C. McKissack, *Black Hands, White Sails: The Story of African-American Whalers* (New York: Scholastic, 1999), 27.

47. Ibid., 23.

48. Hudson, *Making of "Mammy Pleasant,"* 22.

49. Ibid., 23.

50. Lynn M. Hudson, "Mining a Mythic Past: The History of Mary Ellen Pleasant," in *African American Women Confront the West 1600–2000*, ed. Quintard Taylor and Shirley Ann Wilson Moore (Norman: University of Oklahoma Press, 2003,) 58; Helen O'Donnell Holdredge, *Mammy Pleasant* (New York: Putnam, 1953), 19.

51. Hudson, *Making of "Mammy Pleasant,"* 26.

52. Ibid., 29.

53. Ibid., 26.

54. Quintard Taylor, "Mary Ellen Pleasant," in *African American Women Confront the West*, 121–22.

55. Hudson, *Making of "Mammy Pleasant,"* 34.

56. In her pioneering critical work, *Black Women Novelists: The Development of a Tradition 1862–1972* (London: Greenwood, 1980), Barbara Christian elaborated the origins of the "Mammy" stereotype, its pejorative meaning in antebellum culture, and its use as a literary construct.

57. Holdredge, 171–73, 175.

58. Ibid., 39–40.

59. Hudson, *Making of "Mammy Pleasant,"* 35; Taylor, "Mary Ellen Pleasant," 122.

60. Taylor, "Mary Ellen Pleasant," 122.

61. *Ibid.*

62. Hudson, *Making of "Mammy Pleasant,"* 39.

63. *Ibid.*, 40.

64. *Ibid.*, 41.

65. Personal communication with Susheel Bibbs, December 2007 and January 2008. Susheel Bibbs, *Mary Ellen Pleasant: Mother of Human Rights in California* (San Francisco: MEP, 1996). Susheel Bibbs is an Emmy-award-winning TV and film producer, University of California lecturer, a leading historian on the life of Mary Ellen Pleasant and director of the Mary Ellen Pleasant Living Heritage Foundation. Bibbs's Emmy-winning documentary film, "Meet Mary Pleasant," aired in film festivals and on PBS in 2007–08.

66. Osborn Perry Anderson, *A Voice from Harper's Ferry: A Narrative of Events at Harper's Ferry* (Boston: 1861), available at http://www.libraries.wvu.edu/theses/Attfield/HTML/voice.html (accessed May 22, 2009).

67. Jean Libby, et al., *John Brown Mysteries* (Missoula, Mont.: Pictorial Histories, 1995), 16.

68. Herbert Aptheker, *American Negro Slave Revolts.* (New York: International, 1993), 352–53; Libby, et al., *John Brown Mysteries*, 25.

69. Pleasant's message is an abridged version of the scripture, "And now also the axe is laid unto the root of the trees: therefore every tree which brings not forth good fruit is hewn down, and cast into fire" (Matthew 3:10).

70. Hudson, *Making of "Mammy Pleasant,"* 41.

71. Personal communication in December 2007 and January 2008 with Susheel Bibbs confirmed that circumstantial evidence she has gathered in the form of letters from Pleasant's contemporaries corroborate that Pleasant did perform the scouting she described in the interview with Davis.

72. Taylor, "Mary Ellen Pleasant," 122.

73. Officials ignored Lucy Stone's courtroom indictment of Archibald Gaines as the father of the murdered two-year-old daughter as well as the infant that Garner intended to murder. Stone's and Garner's indictments left telltale traces in the historical record. After examining the record and reviewing the pattern of Garner's and Archibald Gaines's wife's pregnancies, Weisenburger concluded that "cultural logic" and "carefully coded insinuations" at the trial were compelling evidence "that Archibald Gaines must be the slave children's father." Weisenburger, *Modern Medea*, 44–48, 173.

# CHAPTER 4

# Enslaved Women's Resistance and Survival Strategies in Frances Ellen Watkins Harper's "The Slave Mother: A Tale of the Ohio" and Toni Morrison's *Beloved* and *Margaret Garner*

*Kristine Yohe*

Throughout the history of the United States, African American women have frequently been abused sexually, a circumstance particularly pervasive during slavery. Enslaved women's resistance to subjugation has taken many forms, from escape to suicide to murder. These women's responses to abuse have always been gendered: their resistance often had direct connections to their status as women, including their roles as cooks and house servants, as well as their status as mothers and objects of sexual predation. While the domestic sphere of many enslaved women provided ready access to their sometimes-covert resistance, it also meant that they were often victimized by sexual abuse. All of these circumstances were relevant to the enslavement, resistance, and survival strategies of Margaret Garner.

The historical Margaret Garner defied slavery not only through choosing to escape physically but also by deciding to end her daughter's life rather than allowing her to be re-enslaved. Garner's bold acts of resistance have inspired both print and visual artists to contemplate her motivations. Through examining three of these works—Frances Ellen Watkins Harper's 1857 poem "The Slave Mother: A Tale of the Ohio," Toni Morrison's 1987 novel *Beloved*, and especially Morrison's 2004 libretto, *Margaret Garner*, the most historically accurate and developed of the three—we can better understand Garner's brave actions and thereby fathom something of how it felt to be an enslaved woman with extremely limited options for autonomy. By contemplating the example of this one courageous woman, we can recognize how Garner's actions reveal the extremes that an enslaved woman would go to in order to resist tyranny, to assert her right to determine the fates of herself and her family, and to survive on her own terms.

Figure. 4.1. *Mother and Child*, sculpture by Carolyn Manto, 2012. Black Brigade Monument, Smale Riverfront Park, Cincinnati, Ohio. Photograph by Diane Schneiderman.

Heroic African American women in history have fought back in unique and compelling ways. For example, while Margaret Garner resisted through infanticide when she saw no other choice, Harriet Jacobs used her sexuality as a weapon of resistance and survival. As she details in her 1861 narrative, *Incidents in the Life of a Slave Girl*, Jacobs evades the enslaver's sexual harassment in part through becoming pregnant by another white man. Jacobs's experience exemplifies the sexual degradation and victimization of so many enslaved women, though she argues that most others were far worse off than she. Furthermore, Jacobs's resistance continued following the births of her children, for she thereafter hid for seven years in her grandmother's attic. Jacobs made clear that withstanding this extreme privation was preferable to undergoing the enslaver's abuse, sexual and otherwise. Eventually, she was able to escape to the North, and she was later reunited with her children.

While most enslaved African American women were not able to escape, some succeeded in doing so. Rather than using their sexuality as a weapon, some women used other means, including disguising their gender and/or race. In one notable example, Ellen Craft was able to escape enslavement with the innovative method of passing not only as white but also as a man. Craft thereby escaped openly, traveling with her husband, William, who represented himself as her enslaved property, from Georgia to Pennsylvania in 1848. Yet it is a poignant truth that most refugees from slavery, men and women, were unsuccessful in their escape attempts, if they even had the opportunity to try.

Margaret Garner's bid for freedom for herself and her children motivated nineteenth-century works of art as well as more recent ones. Notably, in 1857, just a year after the Garners' failed escape, African American writer Frances Ellen Watkins Harper published a poem, "The Slave Mother: A Tale of the Ohio," inspired by Margaret Garner's bold act of defiant love. Here, Harper notes that the heroic mother's actions in pursuit of freedom are made necessary by the absence of sanctuary in the northern United States. This historical and literary mother seizes her right to decide the fate of her children. More than one hundred years later, in 1987, Toni Morrison published her Pulitzer Prize–winning novel, *Beloved*, which takes as its genesis this same agonizing part of American history, reinterpreting Garner's infanticide into Sethe's relinquishing of her own young daughter. Most recently, 2005 saw the premiere of Toni Morrison and Richard Danielpour's opera, *Margaret Garner*, whose libretto had been published in 2004.

Through examining the various interpretations of Garner's history in the poem, novel, and opera, it becomes clear that her rebellious act resulted in metaphorical cultural survival even though her daughter did not literally survive. In other words, through the sacrifice of her child, Garner transcended her bondage, exerting her claim for maternal power over the tomb of institutional subjugation. Through asserting her right to decide what happened to her children, Garner defied slavery by surrendering the physical flesh in order to allow the metaphysical spirit to survive. Through these different genres, Harper and Morrison reconfigure the circumstances of Garner's decision, with powerful effect. The compression of the poem, the depth of the novel, the drama of the opera: all forms lend themselves well to this amazing story. For Garner's compelling refusal to allow her daughter to be returned to slavery challenged her contemporaries, as well as modern-day

Americans, to consider her act as one of maternal love. As an enslaved African, Garner rebelled; as a mother, she decided; as a woman, she resisted.

## Poetic Survival: Frances Ellen Watkins Harper's "The Slave Mother: A Tale of the Ohio"

When introducing Toni Morrison's *Beloved* to students, many teachers begin with Margaret Garner's history. Frances Ellen Watkins Harper's poem "The Slave Mother: A Tale of the Ohio" is quite effective at capturing the essence of Garner's story, especially the emotional anguish of this enslaved mother. The poem's title signals the contradiction that while enslaved women frequently were forced to become pregnant and to give birth, often they were not allowed to mother their children fully or freely; they usually were not able to determine their families' fates.[1]

In the poem, this enslaved mother, unnamed but clearly Margaret Garner, initially embraces the strategy of escape. She reaches the Ohio River, crosses it with her family, and seeks out a place of refuge, an oasis of safety. Joining the tradition of the Underground Railroad, these family members risk their lives for freedom. Although scholars now know that most of those trying to escape slavery failed, clearly the Garner family considered it a chance worth taking. In fact, many scholars—including Steven Weisenburger and Delores Walters—interpret Margaret and Robert Garner's ordeal as a family story, where the dynamics of their relationships added to the risks of their escape.[2] Furthermore, it is clear that it was unusual for an entire family to flee as a group. Escaping separately would probably have allowed for a greater chance for success, but this apparently loving family chose to stay together.

Harper shows in the first few stanzas of her poem that Garner's tenderness for the "treasures of [her] soul" is profound. She cherishes her children and feels terror at the thought of "the darkness of their future lot," their "doom."[3] Clearly, the consciousness that Harper creates for Garner is one of a devoted mother, one who dotes on her children and deeply values their familial connections. She will do anything for them, and she willingly sacrifices her own safety on their behalf.[4] Her dedication does not stop there, however, as she makes it clear that she will do whatever it takes to assert her belief in her right to protect her children.

The atmosphere of the poem, while literal, also metaphorically figures the frigid and barren environment of slavery, though glimmers of hope also exist. At several places in the poem, specific lines convey this backdrop of winter's chill, where the frozen river enables the crossing, although (unmentioned in the poem) traveling in the snow inevitably leaves tracks. Garner's crossing is accompanied by fleeting hopes for a better life, as Harper shows in stating that the mother has "Bright visions of deliverance . . . / Like dreams of plenty to the poor." But we immediately see that the dreams of this "heroic mother" are but futile and "vain," as "the pursuer" and "the hunter" overtake the fugitives.[5]

At this point in her poem, Harper pauses to make a political and social comment about the reprehensible situation of the post-1850 United States. While historically such other sites of slavery as Judea and Rome had possibilities of sanctuary for the enslaved, after the Fugitive Slave Law, Ohio does not. Neither the church nor the state provides for such desperate refugees; there is little to no possibility of a higher law superseding that which the government dictates, as this law, passed in 1850, just a few years before the Garner escape, provided for the harsh legal prosecution of anyone offering asylum to those fleeing slavery. Of course, some people of conscience (blacks more often than whites) did risk such punishment, including the Levi Coffin family who tried to help the Garners escape. But within the context of the poem, there is no one who can aid them.

This stark circumstance prompts the enslaved mother to her decisive and definitive act. Harper presents Garner as having no other choice but to "do a deed for freedom" by "find[ing] each child a grave."[6] Here, Harper challenges her readers to follow her logic that, if life consists of hell and slavery, then death is peace and freedom. In other words, this mother decides to protect her children by killing them:

> I will save my precious children
> From their darkly threatened doom,
> I will hew their path to freedom
> Through the portals of the tomb.[7]

Because Harper's Margaret regards the life that she knows as "doom," the only route to safety and "freedom" is death.[8] It is especially noteworthy that here this enslaved woman asserts her right to determine what happens to her children; she takes the initiative, she decides. Harper's Margaret—when faced with certain capture and what she perceives as a fate worse than death—chooses the preferable, even peaceful, outcome: death. The poem's last stanzas challenge Harper's readers in 1857 to act. If they are swayed by her poignant work of literature, her contemporaries must be, as she says in the last line, on "the side of freedom." If readers are inspired by Garner's "deed of fearful daring," if they are moved by the "icy hands of slavery," there is no other option than to fight against it.[9] In short, they must join the growing abolitionist uprising and end slavery now.

So while within history and literature Margaret Garner's initial survival strategy is to escape, circumstances force her to shift her focus to another courageous approach. She who gave her children life will also be the one to give them death. Harper deftly explores these motives and renders the emotions of this "Slave Mother," this woman who will stop at nothing to resist subjugation, to protect her children, to defy slavery. In Harper's 1857 interpretation, Margaret Garner is a heroic woman who dares to act, who dares to determine the fates of her children. One hundred and thirty years later, Toni Morrison gives us a woman who does that and more, for Morrison's fictional Sethe also resists the enslavers, decides to be a mother, and has the courage to protect her child through murder.

## Literary Transcendence/Literal Resistance: Maternal Love in Toni Morrison's *Beloved*

In Toni Morrison's 1987 novel *Beloved*, we encounter a woman, Sethe, who, like the historical Margaret Garner, commits what for many people would be an unforgivable act: she kills her daughter. If readers are to judge her without analysis or compassion, to just take her behavior at face value, they might be inclined to condemn her. When we consider Sethe's bold actions within slavery's dehumanizing brutality, however, recognizing that she kills the toddler to prevent her further mistreatment by the enslavers, we understand that Morrison encourages us instead to see this violent deed as a mercy killing. We realize that her reaction to slavery, her resistance as a mother, is—like Margaret Garner's—boldly defiant, brave, and protective. Therefore, Sethe, though a killer, becomes an admirable and sympathetic character.

Yet even the other characters in the novel struggle with how to judge Sethe's resistance. Both Stamp Paid and Baby Suggs, the rescuer and mother-in-law of Sethe, the main character, at various times become paralyzed with the situation, stuck and (as Baby Suggs realizes) unable to "approve or condemn Sethe's rough choice."[10] They understand what has driven her to such a desperate feat, but they cannot comfortably endorse it, so both characters remain unreconciled to this harsh reality. However, after his similar original response, Paul D, Sethe's current romantic partner and long-ago platonic friend from Sweet Home, the farm where they both were enslaved, eventually is able to understand, although he at first sees Sethe's killing of the baby simply as "wrong," insisting, "There could have been a way. Some other way."[11] Though Sethe contends that taking her daughter's life stops schoolteacher,[12] the last enslaver at Sweet Home, from having absolute control over her and therefore transports the girl to a place of safety, Paul D initially regards this "safety with a handsaw" and her claim to make such a determination as frightening and overwhelming. But by the end of the novel, he reconsiders, returning to take care of an ailing Sethe and hoping "to put his story next to hers."[13] Through depicting Paul D's gradual realization and by revealing the stirrings of Sethe's soul—including her deepest motivations of protection and attempts to embrace her role as a mother—Morrison asserts that one *can* kill out of love.

Not only does Morrison reveal Sethe's loving motivations though her other characters' reactions, she also does so through Sethe's own struggle with her decision. Because Sethe is literally and figuratively haunted by the spirit of her deceased child, it is apparent that she has not simply left her actions behind. Rather, she feels responsibility for them, further reinforcing her readers' interpretation of her as a devoted mother. She also refuses to relocate from the house, 124, believing that to withstand the haunting is her virtual penance for the killing. After Beloved returns and Sethe realizes that this is her reincarnated daughter, Sethe's attempts to make amends also contribute to an awareness that she regrets the necessity of the killing but sees it as having still been an act of authentic affection and protection.

Morrison shows that, like Sethe, other women in bondage resisted enslavement in a remarkable range of ways. Because the system of slavery dictated that African Americans were demeaned and considered by most whites to be worthless, Baby Suggs defies slavery's tyranny of hate and instead preaches to the newly free the power and the glory of self-love. Of their bodies, their flesh, she says, "Love it. Love it hard"; of their hands, in particular, she implores, "*You* got to love it, *you*!" Referring to racist whites, she continues, "And no, they ain't in love with your mouth. Yonder, out there, they will see it broken and break it again. What you say out of it they will not heed. What you scream from it they do not hear. What you put into it to nourish your body they will snatch away and give you leavins instead. No, they don't love your mouth. *You* got to love it." This radical response to slavery endears Baby Suggs to the community members, providing the first steps of much-needed healing and also anticipating the end of the novel, where Paul D urges Sethe to love herself, to see herself as her "best thing." In both cases, Morrison's intent runs counter to the prevailing dehumanization of slavery, bringing about the potential for healing through defiant and constructive resistance.[14]

In part because this novel was inspired, Morrison says, by Margaret Garner's resolute act, it forces its readers to consider this question deeply: What does it mean for a mother to kill her child out of love? This concept is a challenging one, and it can be hard for some readers to accept. But Morrison—via Sethe and, by extension, Margaret Garner—insists that her readers take this question seriously. As rendered by Morrison, the enslaved woman's choice of infanticide is powerful and redemptive, even while troubling and tough; it is a loving murder. In an interview with Alan Benson shortly before the novel was published in 1987, Morrison explains her response to learning about Garner's action years earlier: "For me, it was the ultimate gesture of the loving mother. It was also the outrageous claim of a slave. The last thing a slave woman owns is her children."[15]

Furthermore, in the foreword to an edition of Beloved published in 2004, Morrison discusses her motivations in writing the novel and in engaging the philosophy of, if not the exact biography of, Margaret Garner. This foreword seems to encapsulate what Morrison perceives as Garner's strategies to endure an exceedingly hostile culture, a perspective Morrison directly embodies in her novel via Sethe and her surviving daughter, Denver. She explains that when she left her editing job in 1983 to teach and write full-time, this shift created new life circumstances. This change in focus directly and indirectly led to heightened awareness in this novel, she reported, in part because she was newly conscious of her own freedom, causing her to consider her own life within the historical context of other African American women's freedoms: "I think now it was the shock of liberation that drew my thoughts to what 'free' could possibly mean to women. . . . Inevitably these thoughts led me to the different history of black women in this country—a history in which marriage was discouraged, impossible, or illegal; in which birthing children was required, but 'having' them, being responsible for them—being, in other words, their parent—was as out of the question as freedom. Assertions of parenthood under conditions peculiar to the logic of institutional enslavement were criminal."[16] Morrison continues by describing how she discovered a newspaper clipping about Margaret Garner in the early 1970s when editing *The Black Book*, a remarkably rich compendium of African American culture, and explains, in part, what attracted her to this story: "She had the intellect, the ferocity, and the willingness to risk everything for what was to her the necessity of freedom." The clipping that first attracted Morrison's attention, originally published in *The American Baptist* in 1856, just two weeks after the killing, was written by P. S. Bassett of Fairmount Theological Seminary in Cincinnati, Ohio, who visited with the Garners while they were imprisoned. The portion of Bassett's interview that appears in *The Black Book* includes his observations that Garner was *not* "excited almost to madness" but was "cool" when she killed her child and that her discussion of the event demonstrated "all the passionate tenderness of a mother's love." Bassett also characterizes Garner's intention to kill her children as a form of protection, whereby she "would much rather kill them at once, and thus end their sufferings, than have them taken back to slavery and be murdered by piece-meal."[17] Garner's courage, resistance, and perspective were singular, and that Morrison was inspired by her motivations seems entirely appropriate.

But as Morrison says in this foreword and elsewhere, she did not wish to be confined to Garner's life story when writing *Beloved*, as what she wanted to write was fiction. She therefore purposely limited her research about Garner and instead dug deeply into a sort of collective consciousness about slavery while also studying in more detail the tools of torture, so that she was able to explore intensely the motivations of an enslaved mother while paying respect to the realities of enslavement. Having known her own grandfather and great-grandmother who had been born into bondage helped Morrison access and understand "their very ordinary, unheralded lives. It's extraordinary what they did just to get through sixty years of existence."[18] The deep attention to slavery that Morrison embarked upon played a central part in her work's becoming a tribute to the experience of enslaved people, including but not limited to Margaret Garner. While Garner's story was formative in Morrison's work, it was not definitive: "The historical Margaret Garner is fascinating, but, to a novelist, confining. Too little imaginative space there for my purposes. So I would invent her thoughts, plumb them for a subtext that was historically true in essence, but not strictly factual in order to relate her history to contemporary issues about freedom, responsibility and women's 'place.' The heroine would represent the unapologetic acceptance of shame and terror; assume the consequences of choosing infanticide; claim her own freedom."[19] In other words, while Garner's story of rebellion provided Morrison's initial motivation for writing *Beloved*, it was only a starting point, allowing her to interrogate history while using Garner as a representative example. And, as Morrison has said in several venues, here she wanted to avoid the wide, epic sweep of many other works about slavery and instead take a very "narrow and deep" approach, seeking to explore what it felt like to be enslaved.[20]

While Harper seems to attempt to represent the thoughts of the historical Margaret Garner through her poem, Morrison willingly deviates from the historical record in her novel, instead exploring Sethe's decision to assert her rights as a mother. Focusing primarily on the experiences of Sethe, both within the grip of slavery and beyond, *Beloved* reveals some of the impossible demands on trying to be a mother, and indeed a human being, under such totalizing oppression, as well as what it means to defy this subjugation. In this novel, Morrison analyzes the motivations of an enslaved woman, seeking to reveal the forces that make up Sethe's psyche.[21] As Weisenburger writes in his book about Margaret Garner, *Beloved* presents an enslaved mother who refuses to be the passive object of others, instead claiming to be "far more significantly herself a feeling and thinking subject."[22] By sympathizing with Sethe as a "feeling and thinking subject," Morrison's readers begin to understand how this fictional mother in bondage could perform an act that transforms from unthinkable into heroic. Of course, these same ideas can also manifest in other genres. Therefore, fifteen years after successfully rendering these motivations in her novel *Beloved*, Morrison revisited Garner's story in her libretto, this time with the range of emotional and sensory impact made possible through the spectacle of opera.

## Operatic Redemption: Sacrifice, Resistance, and Survival in Toni Morrison's *Margaret Garner*

While the story of Margaret Garner's life provided the external motivation for *Beloved*, it also provided the internal spark for Morrison's libretto for the opera titled *Margaret Garner* (2004), with music composed by Richard Danielpour. Morrison's

Figure 4.2. *Margaret Garner*, world premiere, a co-production of the Michigan Opera Theatre, Cincinnati Opera, and Opera Company of Philadelphia on May 7, 2005, at the Detroit Opera House. Left to right, Gregg Baker as Robert Gardner, Denyce Graves as Margaret Garner, male chorus member (back row) and Angela Brown as Cilla. Photograph by John Grigaitis.

comment above, that history affords inadequate room for creativity when writing a novel, also applies in many ways to the opera. Yet the very name of the opera reinforces its historical specificity and creates unique pressures, particularly in the environment where the history took place, Northern Kentucky and Greater Cincinnati, Ohio. Having been influenced in her novel by Margaret Garner's story, in the libretto, Morrison examines the universality of this figure, rendering her historical salience into the realm of American myth. Morrison's returning to Garner's life through the orality of opera evokes the gathered women in *Beloved* who seek to exorcise the evil spirit: "In the beginning there were no words. In the beginning was the sound."[23] The merging of sound and words in the libretto exalt this story to a new level, resulting in a text with almost sacred echoes.

Although like *Beloved*, the *Margaret Garner* opera is not verbatim history, it much more closely follows the historical records of Garner's life. In an interview conducted in May 2005 with Janelle Gelfand of the *Cincinnati Enquirer*, Morrison explains her position: "We're not doing a documentary. We're trying to wrestle with some of the larger questions of those incidents that took place at that time, in that place," adding, "Is she human or is she property? The question of, is she a murderer, or has she stolen something, is the crux of the whole thing."[24] Yet the opera libretto includes some sharp distinctions between history and art, such as the treatment of Margaret Garner's husband, Robert. In reality, Robert Garner was a triumphant figure, surviving slavery and raising the two sons of Margaret, one of whom he probably did not father. In the opera, however, he meets an early demise devoid of his real-life heroism: he is lynched.[25] In the libretto, the circumstances of Margaret's death are also changed from what we know about her history, as in real life she died of typhoid, while in the opera she hangs herself.

In revisiting the Garner story in later years to write the libretto for *Margaret Garner*, Morrison has said that initially she wasn't keen on returning to this difficult terrain. But eventually, she recalled, part of what drew her back was the challenge to explore the material in another genre and that opera was ideal. As she explains in the program for the premiere of *Margaret Garner* by Michigan Opera Theatre, Morrison eventually was ready to go back to this story that had inspired *Beloved*: "Some ten years later, free of the exhaustion following the publication of *Beloved*, I realized that there were genres other than novels that could expand and deepen the story. The topic, the people, the narrative theme, passion and universality made it more than worthy of opera; it begged for it."[26]

Morrison's emphasis in these comments on the assertiveness and agency assumed by her operatic Margaret Garner also pervades her libretto. This text opens with a powerful selection in which the refrain is "No, no more!" Here, the enslaved people lament that they are to be auctioned off and separated, that they are to be further brutalized by slavery, and therefore implore God to stop such treatment while also asserting their refusal to accept this development.[27] In her interview with Gelfand, Morrison comments that she did so to emphasize the "resistance" of the enslaved people, whereby they claim power and authority, and that "they have something to say about their condition." Morrison also discusses the dilemmas facing enslaved women in particular, wherein issues of freedom and motherhood create impossible circumstances but where some, such as Margaret Garner, could proclaim their divine right to determine their children's fates. Noting that most slave narratives focus on the escapes of enslaved men, Morrison was especially taken with Garner's story: "That black slave woman was a revolutionary who clung to freedom, and said, 'I am in charge of my children.'"[28]

Garner's revolutionary status also appears in other ways in the libretto, such as when she considers the meaning of love. In one part of the opera, the enslaver's daughter, Caroline Gaines, reveals her incipient abolitionist leanings during her wedding reception, where she asks Margaret what she thinks of love, following a philosophical discussion with her father, Edward Gaines, new husband, George Hancock, and several of the wedding guests. This inquiry, which takes place in the piece "The Language of Love" in act I, scene 3, offends her father and the stuffy white wedding guests, all of whom regard asking an enslaved person her opinion on love to be not only bad manners and ridiculous but potentially threatening to the social order. After first trying to evade Caroline's question, Margaret does answer briefly, and later, when she thinks she is alone, she contemplates the meaning more deeply, as revealed in the poignant aria, "A Quality Love":

> No pretty words can ease or cure
> What heavy hands can do.
> When sorrow is deep,
> The secret soul keeps its quality love.
> When sorrow is deep,
> The secret soul keeps
> Its weapon of choice: the love of all loves![29]

Although the dominant attitude of the day was that the enslaved were incapable of such depth, Margaret makes it clear that she understands such ideas more profoundly than those who enslave her. Morrison underscores this distinction by immediately following the aria with Margaret's being raped by Edward Gaines just after Margaret exhorts the inviolability of her "secret soul." Echoing the necessity of developing self-love in *Beloved*, this scene reveals another level of psychological resistance for an enslaved woman, here one who is about to be sexually assaulted, so that self-protection involves maintaining a sense of oneself separate from the abuse and the abuser.

Defying and resisting slavery through escape, the libretto's Margaret and Robert Garner make it to Ohio with their two children, though in the process of leaving Kentucky, Robert is forced to kill Casey, the white overseer. After three weeks, they are caught by slave catchers, including Edward Gaines, who verbally abuses Margaret. While Robert is seized, Morrison's libretto does not provide any details beyond the fact that he is "bound and ready" and that a fire is to be lit. In the Detroit and Cincinnati performances in 2005, he was quickly mobbed and lynched by a gang of men with torches; in Philadelphia in 2006, this scene was slowed, but with the same outcome. Morrison writes in her libretto that before the children can be taken away, Margaret acts, exclaiming "Never to be born again into slavery!" as she kills both children. Immediately thereafter, Morrison's stage directions emphasize the bold resistance this mother's actions embody: "(*With defiant grandeur, Margaret embraces her life's circumstances*)."[30] In the performance in New York in 2007, these two actions were combined, with the quick lynching of Robert occurring simultaneously with the killing of the children.

In the libretto, Margaret's resistance continues in the courtroom in scene 3, where Edward asserts that he had been the "owner" of the deceased children. Margaret is silent and expressionless as a debate about slavery rages among Caroline, her husband, George, and her father, made all the more vigorous by the fact that Morrison has changed the year of the escape from its historical 1856 to 1861, on the eve of the Civil War. Edward claims his alleged supremacy:

> They didn't belong to her.
> She has no right to them,
> Living or dead
> Living or dead.
> It is clear in our system
> She owns nothing
> Least of all my slaves.[31]

Though Caroline tries to argue that the children had belonged to Margaret, the judges dismiss her argument as insignificant. Just as she is sentenced to be executed, Margaret speaks. In response to the townspeople's declaration that "She is not like you or me!" Margaret agrees "(*emphatically*)" with them: "I am not like you. / I am me." Though she is silenced, she refuses to be seated and denies the judges' right to control her:

> *You* have no authority.
> I am not like you.
> (*defiantly*) I am me!
> I am me!
> I am![32]

This existential claim also echoes a scene in *Beloved*, where Sethe's final words are "Me? Me?" said in response to Paul D's assertion that she is her "best thing."[33] In both cases, the enslaved mother takes a huge, and necessary, step: she resists slavery's doctrines in part by declaring her own self-worth, an essential part of the healing of self-actualization.

The opera libretto ends with Margaret Garner on the scaffold, where she has just been granted a reprieve from an imminent hanging, which was to have been punishment for killing her children, thereby destroying her owner's "property." Again, Morrison chooses to emphasize a strong woman who claims agency and asserts strategic defiance to the oppressive culture of slavery. For Margaret's final act is to hang herself. Asserting an eternal life with Christian overtones, her last words are "I live. / Oh yes, I live!"[34] Margaret becomes a sort of martyr, which Morrison confirms, saying of this final scene, "But it was almost like an offering. Look at this suffering. Judge her if you can."[35] Choosing the terms under which she lives, or dies, Morrison claims, is essential for Margaret. Though Edward Gaines's final words reinforce his continuing guilt as the brutal enslaver—"Unhealed, there is no peace"—the final blending of the choruses, that of the enslaved and that of the townspeople, into one is compelling. This mixed chorus, singing together for the first time in the opera, asks for forgiveness: "Have mercy. Have mercy on us. / Help us break through the night."[36] Though the country is on the brink of the Civil War, the healing perhaps can now begin. Here, Morrison asserts the importance of resisting the brutal status quo, of learning to work together, of making it through the quintessential dark night of enslavement to the dawn of a new era of freedom.

Resonating with the infanticides of the historic Margaret Garner, the protagonist of Harper's poem, and of Sethe in *Beloved*, this enslaved woman's survival at the end of the opera is not physical but spiritual. Her resistance is multi-layered, in which the oppressed people challenge slavery in every possible way. Particularly for the women, the mothers, this defiance allows them to claim themselves, to love their children, to begin to heal. All of these literary women embody the historical truth that the real Margaret Garner demonstrated: surviving and resisting slavery's hell required making unspeakable choices. In multiple genres, Morrison and Harper demonstrate that, for enslaved women like Margaret Garner, despite their excruciating sacrifices, redemption is possible.

## Notes

1. Frances Ellen Watkins Harper, "The Slave Mother: A Tale of the Ohio" (1857), in *Toni Morrison's Beloved: A Casebook*, ed. William L. Andrews and Nellie Y. McKay (New York: Oxford University Press, 1999), 21–3, hereafter cited as Harper. Here, Harper's repeated use of the evocative phrase "slave mother" creates a paradox of ironic contradictions. Note also that Harper has a separate, earlier poem with a similar name—"The Slave Mother" (1854)—but with a very different emphasis. The earlier poem depicts an anguished mother and child on an auction block as they are about to be separated forever. A refrain in the earlier poem, "He is not hers," prefigures the fact that, unlike the Garner character in the later poem, this mother has no strategies for survival and resistance. She is utterly powerless and, therefore, bereft and despairing. In both poems, the enslaved women are forced to produce children but not sanctioned to protect them, hence the irony of the titles.

2. I learned of these perspectives from Delores Walters when she shared with me a November 2004 letter she sent to Toni Morrison, and when I read a 2005 essay she wrote, "Margaret Garner in History, Fiction, and Opera," which was published in the conference program for *Toni Morrison & Sites of Memory: Fourth Biennial Conference of the Toni Morrison Society*, a July 2005 conference held in Greater Cincinnati and at Northern Kentucky University, for which I served as conference director. Steven Weisenburger makes a related case not only in the title but throughout *Modern Medea: A Family Story of Slavery and Child-Murder from the Old South* (New York: Hill and Wang, 1998).

3. Harper, 1, 12, 15.

4. It is interesting to compare Harper's depiction of Margaret Garner to nineteenth-century definitions of proper female behavior. While the Cult of True Womanhood—as explained by Jean Fagan Yellin, the preeminent Harriet Jacobs scholar, in a public address

I attended in 1991—dictated how white women should behave, with the home and hearth their only real sphere, African American women were denied the security of such possibilities. We know by reading Harriet Jacobs's text, for example, that these moral lessons also were quite apparent and compelling for women of color. Jacobs writes that she wishes she could follow a strictly virtuous path, but that slavery prevented it.

5. Harper, 27–8, 29, 31, 32.

6. Ibid., 43, 44.

7. Harper, 45–8.

8. Ibid., 46, 47.

9. Harper, 64, 57, 59.

10. Toni Morrison, *Beloved* (New York: Knopf, 1987), 180.

11. Ibid., 165.

12. Note that Morrison does not capitalize the name of this hateful character in the novel; it is lowercase throughout, seemingly an intentional sign of disrespect.

13. Morrison, *Beloved*, 164, 273. It is compelling to contrast this fictional depiction with the limited facts available from history. As we know that Robert Garner cared for his and Margaret's surviving sons (one of whom he most likely did not father) after her death, and as it was reported in 1870 in the *Cincinnati Daily Chronicle* that he was with her at the time of her death, it seems that Robert—unlike Paul D initially with Sethe—was able to reconcile himself to Margaret's killing of her child.

14. Morrison, *Beloved*, 88, 273.

15. Alan Benson, Interview with Toni Morrison, *Profile of a Writer: Toni Morrison*, VHS, dir. Alan Benson (London: RM Arts, 1987).

16. Toni Morrison, foreword to *Beloved* (New York: Vintage, 2004), xvi–xvii.

17. Morrison, foreword, xvii. P. S. Bassett, "A Visit to the Slave Mother Who Killed her Child," February 12, 1856, in *The Black Book*, ed. Middleton A. Harris (New York: Random House, 1974), 10.

18. Benson interview.

19. Morrison, foreword, xvii.

20. Benson interview.

21. It can be rewarding to consider this novel from a psychoanalytic perspective. In the course of describing Sethe's motivations, Morrison shows the influence of psychoanalysis, as first described by Sigmund Freud and later articulated by Jacques Lacan and others. For more on this angle of interpretation, see Evelyn Jaffe Schreiber, *Subversive Voices: Eroticizing the Other in William Faulkner and Toni Morrison* (Knoxville: University of Tennessee Press, 2001); and J. Brooks Bouson, *Quiet as It's Kept: Shame, Trauma, and Race in the Novels of Toni Morrison* (Albany: State University of New York Press, 2000).

22. Weisenburger, *Modern Medea*, 10.

23. Morrison, *Beloved*, 259.

24. Janelle Gelfand, "Author Brings Focus to Boone Slave's Life: Nobel, Pulitzer Prize Winner Reflects on Opera's Premiere," *Cincinnati Enquirer*, July 11, 2005.

25. I am indebted to my friend and colleague Delores Walters, one of the editors of this volume, for clarifying for me how important this change was. Instead of sharing with the

public a story of a devoted family with a strong black male figure, Morrison and Richard Danielpour, the opera's composer, have stated that they pursued a wider historical truth in the opera, rather than confining themselves to one family's literal history. Of course, it is certainly true historically that many African American men caught escaping from slavery were indeed murdered.

26. Toni Morrison, "A Note on *Margaret Garner* from Toni Morrison," in program for *Margaret Garner* (Detroit: Michigan Opera Theatre, 2005), 8.

27. Toni Morrison, libretto, *Margaret Garner*, with music by Richard Danielpour (New York: Schirmer, 2004). For my purposes of emphasizing the resistance and defiance of enslaved women, it is interesting to note that Morrison writes in the stage directions that the "Slave Chorus" should sing the refrain of this piece—"No, no! No more!"—"(*confidently, with a sense of defiance*)" (Morrison, *Margaret Garner*, 9).

28. Gelfand, "Author Brings Focus to Boone Slave's Life."

29. Morrison, *Margaret Garner*, 25.

30. Ibid., 33.

31. Ibid., 34. This passage, about "ownership" of enslaved children, resonates with Harper's 1854 poem, "The Slave Mother." See note 1 above.

32. Ibid., 36.

33. Morrison, *Beloved*, 273.

34. Morrison, *Margaret Garner*, 38.

35. Gelfand, "Author Brings Focus to Boone Slave's Life."

36. Morrison, *Margaret Garner*, 38.

# CHAPTER 5

# CAN QUADROON BALLS REPRESENT ACQUIESCENCE OR RESISTANCE?

*Diana Williams*

Because of its reputed role in facilitating quasi-marital contracts across the color line between white men and free women of color, the quadroon ball offers an interesting perspective on American conceptions of consent. For more than two centuries, countless pieces of Americana have represented female "quadroons"— women possessing one fourth black and three fourths white "blood," including folk and minstrel songs, poetry, short stories, popular novels, ex-slave narratives, collectible dolls, and even science fiction stories. A typical description of such balls appeared in the *Providence Gazette* on August 7, 1820:

> Every Saturday night is ushered in with splendid quadroon balls . . . none but quadroon ladies (that is, women of mixed blood) and white gentlemen are allowed to attend. . . . Those ladies are prohibited . . . to marry a white man, and they are too proud and high minded to marry one of their own colour, consequently in this land of sensuality they become openly, without any degradation, kept mistresses, and will, it is said while engaged, if it be for a week, month or year be true to their employers. It is also said to be the common practice of the mothers of such daughters to educate them for the purpose of pleasure, and barter them away during their minority to the best bidder.

Although the balls quadroons supposedly attended in New Orleans so as to attract the attentions and financial support of would-be white male sexual partners appear more often in print media than in American visual culture, in recent decades they have been enjoying a kind of renaissance in film, including a 2001 film adaptation of best-selling author Anne Rice's second novel, *The Feast of All Saints* (1979).

Rice's novel belongs to a genre of pulp fiction objectifying interracial sex and slavery as subjects for titillation and entertainment—what we might call historical blaxploitation, or what historian Catherine Clinton has called sexploitation.[1] Perhaps the most famous work in this genre—identified as "plantation porn" on goodreads.com—was *Mandingo* (1957), the debut novel of Kyle Onstott's wildly

Figure 5.1. Box Office, *Quadroon*, July 12, 1971. Presidio Production. Image courtesy of Boxoffice Media, LCC.

popular Falconhurst series. Significantly, Rice authored *Feast* after the film adaptation of *Mandingo* appeared in 1975.[2] Most of these texts focused on slavery, but some purported to represent the lifestyles of New Orleans's free women of color. In 1971, for example, a Texas-based film studio released what may have been the first motion picture representation of a quadroon ball in the B-movie *Quadroon* (1971). Promotional materials for the film had advertised it as revealing "the shocking truth about the passion slaves of 1835 New Orleans," informing prospective viewers that it "rips the veil of secrecy from History's strangest chapter!"[3]

Three decades after the appearance of *Quadroon*, two new historical films emerged: *The Feast of All Saints*, a Showtime miniseries adaptation of Rice's 1979 novel, and *The Courage to Love*, a drama based on the life of Henriette Delille, a New Orleans free women of color who founded the city's first order of black nuns. With the heyday of *Mandingo* long over, evidently neither of these films was received as exploitative. Yet a comparison of promotional images for *Quadroon* and *Courage*—both of which featured very-light-skinned black women in bust-enhancing profile, gazing fetchingly at the viewer—suggests that the newer films retained the prurience of the older ones. *Courage* ostensibly celebrated Delille's decision to become a nun and reject "her family's wishes" that she submit to a presumed destiny in interracial concubinage, or what the DVD packaging euphemistically referred to as "the traditions of an arranged marriage." Yet the images released to promote the film featured Vanessa Williams not in prayer but rather in full bosom-exposing quadroon ball regalia, with the white male romantic love interest gazing longingly at her in the background.

Lavishly produced, *The Feast of All Saints* is visually reminiscent of a Merchant Ivory production, except that it features an all-star black cast, including James Earl Jones, Eartha Kitt, Forest Whitaker, Ossie Davis, Pam Grier, Jasmin Guy, and Jennifer Beals. The response of many of the Amazon reviewers is revealing, including one who praised *Feast* and who expressed frustration with "the usual slavery movies. . . . [whose] plot is always the same white america oppressing blacks!" In contrast, the reviewer argued, the film "actually taught me something about my history, that there were free people of color who were aristocrats."[4] The film develops a sharp contrast between the material conditions of free women of color and those who were enslaved: it precedes the quadroon ball scene with an auction-block tableau in which a mother shrieks as her young children are sold and then dragged away screaming. This family's agony and horror provides a striking counterpart to the smiling countenances of the women in the next scene, resplendent in jewels and white gowns, pirouetting in the arms of their white suitors under a glittering chandelier as their mothers gaze on approvingly. The response of viewers such as the one just cited is undoubtedly due at least in part to the film's presenting the enslaved woman on the auction block, much like representations of Margaret Garner and her family, as helpless victims of the market. Her free counterparts in the ball, on the other hand, appear to have full control of the means by which they market themselves as mistresses to white men, as one white male character explains:

> "It's all quite formal, they're chaperoned by older women, mothers, aunts, grandmothers. They size you up, decide if you have the means to keep them in style."
> "Matchmakers?"

"Very capable *businesswomen*. They guard their assets like the crown jewels."

"Extraordinary!"

"It's called *plaçage*. Promises, rituals, and long-term means. You won't see one of these beauties alone until you set them up!"

*    *    *

"If you'll excuse me . . . I see a vision that requires closer inspection." *(laughter)*

"Careful, they're here to inspect *you*."

The screenwriters might have lifted this exchange from any of several published travel accounts from the antebellum period purporting to document these scenes and the relationships they facilitated, not only in newspaper accounts such as the one quoted earlier but in book-length travel accounts published by such authors as Alexis de Tocqueville and Frederick Law Olmsted, neither of whom spent much time in the city.[5] With rare exceptions, accounts of the balls appear almost exclusively within this largely self-plagiarizing genre, geared to would-be tourists and readers outside of New Orleans.[6]

This chapter seeks to reconcile the persistent myth of the self-directed quadroon finding love and quasi-marriage at a glamorous and respectable quadroon ball with the known history of the sexual exploitation of black women, both slave and free.[7] It approaches the ball setting and the supposed security and elevated social status of the quadroons who attended with skepticism. White men frequently engaged in sexual relationships with women of color, including free women of color, in pre–Civil War Louisiana, yet fictionalized representations of the balls distort and obscure important realities about race, sex, and power in the nineteenth century.

In Southern cities, women of color, both free and enslaved, were especially vulnerable to the types of sexual abuses that white working-class women in developing urban centers elsewhere experienced; moreover, they had even fewer legal protections.[8] White men exercised sexual access to women of color in a variety of blurred and overlapping forms, including slavery, domestic servitude, prostitution, and other relationships, all of which could be placed under the rubric of what Louisiana law termed concubinage. Some of these relationships involved women of color who were free, leading some historians to term them "consensual." Shifting legal definitions and lack of first-person evidence make it difficult to distinguish among these different status categories. In antebellum Louisiana, a woman of color could not become a white man's legal wife, nor could she obtain justice for the crime of rape, which the state explicitly defined as a crime against white women in 1855 and 1857. This racial construction of criminal assault had much older roots, as an 1818 statute defined assault as a crime only when committed against "any free white person."[9] Indeed, the 1806 Black Code stipulated that "free people of color ought never to insult or strike white people . . . but on the contrary that they ought to yield to them in every occasion, and never speak or answer to them but with respect under the penalty of imprisonment."[10] In other words, state lawmakers construed sex with a woman of color as consensual by definition. As a result, the voluminous literature on litigation involving women of color in antebellum Louisiana contains virtually no mention of any bringing a rape suit. Either free women of color never experienced rape, which is highly unlikely given what we know of the endemic sexual assaults on young women in northern cities, or they lacked legal protection against it. Both the statutes and their interpreters presupposed an eagerness among black women to become the "concubines" of white men. Indeed, in 1851, the Louisiana Supreme Court declared in a suit involving an enslaved woman the legally convenient premise that "it is rare in the case of concubinage that the seduction and temptation are not mutual."[11] That this claim constituted a notable exception to the legal presumption that the slave was the extension of her master not only goes unremarked but raises important questions about constructions of consent in a society constituted through the notion of a social contract among its citizens.[12]

Although travel accounts and judicial pronouncements present colorful narratives of consensual interracial concubinage or informal marriages between white men and women of color in Louisiana, they fail to address the fantasy of consent underpinning the post-Enlightenment sentimental ideal of a love match between a breadwinning husband and a nurturing wife firmly ensconced in the private sphere.[13] This fantasy paralleled the rise in popularity of nineteenth-century transracial love stories—such as those documented extensively by Werner Sollors—that according to Mary Louise Pratt "neutralize concrete dimensions of slavery."[14] In an age in which arranged marriages based on the economic interests of extended families were supposedly passé among white middle class readers, the possibility of interracial relationships as a form of social mobility for women of color was doubly disruptive and taboo. Thus antebellum popular representations to romanticize informal marriage across the color line, even for white writers with widely ranging perspectives on slavery and abolition, almost inevitably became cautionary tales about the reality of social inequality and the corrupting possibility of mercenary "interest."[15]

The diary of Ann Maria Davison offers a far less sanguine perspective on the agency of free black women in sexual relationships with white men. Davison was a white Northern abolitionist forced by widowhood to take residence in the South with her daughter and affluent son-in law. She had soon offended her new neighbors by trying to teach about twenty children of color, some enslaved, how to read in a short-lived Sunday school; her anti-slavery sentiments became so well known that one of her fellow Presbyterian church members gossiped, she recalled, that "it was seriously contemplated to tar and feather me." Isolated from the companionship of like-minded white people, Davison bore witness through her diary to examples of racialized female dependency, vulnerability, and subordination.[16]

In one such example in 1857, Davison recorded gossip about one of her neighbors passed on to her by the local black midwife. Davison's description of the unfortunate women of color who ended up in the clutches of her neighbor, Thomas Harper, calls attention to how fragile the distinction between freedom and enslavement could be for women of color[17] and how unsavory living as the colored "wife" of a white man could be:

> This woman Theresa is the slave of Mr. Harper. He lives with her as his wife. She has six children. Four are his, two are black; he whipped her for having the black children. She is very much dissatisfied in being compelled to be her master's concubine: but he makes her submit. She tells the black women that she wishes to be with her own color. Harper took this girl when a child. Her mother Sarah did not like it. He whipped Sarah, for saying something against it, and to get clear of her, he sold her off.
> [ . . . ]
> This Thomas Harper . . . is one of the strongest kind of defenders of the system of slavery. Ever ready, and most energetic, in taking up runaways. Before he had this Theresa for a wife, he had . . . got hold of a free woman, somehow, and after keeping her three or four years, and managing to destroy all proof that she was able to make, to retain her freedom, he sold her for a slave for life.[18]

Like the travel accounts on which the *Feast of All Saints* quadroon ball scene is based, Davison's diary entry calls attention to the fact that white men openly exercised access to the bodies of women of color (a category in which she included Indians) in a variety of ways, both in urban New Orleans and in Louisiana's rural parishes.[19] Yet her account differed considerably from those of the white and mostly male professional writers who published accounts of their travels. Not only as an abolitionist but also as a woman who chafed at her dependency in a white man's Louisiana household, Davison had a less positive view of the "freedom" of those women of color who were not legally slaves. She presented both the slave Theresa and the unnamed free woman who lived with Thomas Harper as victims of a malevolent patriarch—neither compliant nor passive, but victims nonetheless.

Until they began to heed the objections of black feminists, many historians in the 1960s and 1970s continued to describe black women who engaged in sex with white men as "agents" who were somehow complicit with slavery and racism.[20] Subsequent generations of historians have become only slightly more cautious about describing enslaved women as consenting to sex with their masters.[21] Yet few have taken on the task of interrogating and not simply reproducing nineteenth-century accounts suggesting that New Orleans's free women of color insisted that their daughters eschew marriage in favor of illicit yet profitable relationships across the color line. Moreover, some insist on framing these ill-documented relationships within a resistance paradigm. "Instead of falling victim to the system," one historian suggested in 1991, free women of color "fashioned identities and lives outside of the dominant model" of (white) womanhood; in other words, they constructed a different moral code for themselves.[22] A more recent account—based largely on secondary sources—also attempts to portray New Orleans's free women of color as heroines and icons of resistance.[23] Yet the author's argument that these women should be valorized for cultivating moral standards on their own terms is predicated on the assumption that the choice to be the legitimate wife of a man of color was unavailable, redeploying a demographic argument employed more frequently to explain the motivations of white men who lived openly with colored concubines in colonial Louisiana.[24] Surprisingly, none of the extant scholarship on Louisiana's free women of color has broached the subject of rape,[25] even though Darlene Clark Hine has argued "as long as they occupied an enforced subordinate position within American society," women of color who sold sex ought to be seen as victims of rape. Calling for historians to problematize commonly held assumptions about the volition of free women of color, Hines's point that black women cultivated a "culture of dissemblance" around the painful subject helps account for why many remained silent on the issue.[26]

Because the dominant portrait of women of color has been as seductive temptresses, I hesitate to present quadroon balls as examples of their agency. Indeed, historian Walter Johnson has called for a critical reexamination of the "agency" paradigm itself, arguing that the term—often used in slavery studies as synonymous with humanity, resistance, and independent will—is "saturated with the categories of nineteenth-century liberalism, a set of terms which were themselves worked out in self-conscious philosophical opposition to slavery." Much scholarship purporting to "give the slaves back their agency," he claims, invokes "a notion of the universality of a liberal notion of selfhood" where it is least appropriate and forestalls both "a consideration of human-ness lived outside of the conventions of liberal agency" and a serious effort to reconsider what truly constitutes "resistance."[27] Feminist political theorist Carole Pateman points to another possible reason for the creation of the fantasy of quadroon consent, arguing that "if universal freedom is to be represented as the principle of civil society, all individuals, including women, must enter into contracts; no one can be left out. In civil society, individual freedom is exhibited through contract," and the only contract available to women at the time was the marriage contract.[28] As Deborah Gray White has argued regarding enslaved women, the difficulty black women faced in embracing their freedom in this regard was that when they "offered themselves," even if only in order to trade on their sexuality to attain freedom for themselves or a child, they "breathed life into the image of Jezebel" used to justify their subordination.[29]

Any historian seeking to disentangle the quadroon myth from the lived reality of free women of color in antebellum New Orleans would do well to interrogate the myth's internal logic and the reasons for its remarkable durability. It means questioning why a woman of color would bother to negotiate a written but legally nonbinding contract of financial support with her daughter's white suitor. It means asking why "the mothers always regulate the terms and make the bargain,"[30] and why white fathers would shower largesse on their daughters, investing resources in a genteel upbringing, then fail to participate in helping to broker their relationships. Finally, why would they resort to the special ball venue in a city where white men enjoyed access to women of color wherever they went? The more such questions one asks, the less plausible the travel accounts seem.

Furthermore, the women at the balls made famous by travel writers who sojourned in New Orleans may not have been free at all. Women can earn more money at prostitution than they can at most other jobs open to them in what Pateman calls "patriarchal capitalism,"[31] and urban slaveholders seeking to profit from their investments could not have failed to observe this. Indeed, some suits that came before the Louisiana Supreme Court suggest that some masters sold or leased out the women they enslaved for the express purpose of concubinage and/or prostitution, despite the state's official prohibition of such transactions as contrary to good morals.[32] As early as the 1790s, New Orleans slave owners had loudly objected to attempts to prohibit slaves from attending dances frequented by whites and free people of color, suggesting that these owners may have been more interested in the profits to be made from prostituting their slaves than in ensuring their access to recreation.[33]

But what if free rather than enslaved women of color populated the quadroon balls? A scholar seeking to frame their presence in terms of agency could follow the example of Christine Stansell, who recognized this problem in her study of white working-class women who occasionally turned to prostitution to supplement their meager incomes in antebellum New York City. In "a society in which many men still saw coerced sex as their prerogative," Stansell writes, "the prostitute's price was not a surrender to male sexual exploitation but a way of turning a unilateral relationship into a reciprocal one."[34] Pateman, however, problematizes the fictitious nature of reciprocity in such a context, arguing that despite liberal contract theory's construction of those who sell their labor as having contracted "property in their person," because this "property" cannot be alienated from the body of its "owner," what is being exchanged might be more accurately identified as obedience, and thus such contracts "inevitably create subordination."[35]

Scholars must take a much closer look at available documentary sources concerning New Orleans's balls before speculating about the status, motives, and agency of the women who attended them. Before the Louisiana Purchase, as Henry Kmen has observed, "neither color nor condition of servitude barred anyone" from public balls for people of color.[36] Although the myth required the complete exclusion of free men of color from the balls, they are known to have attended those that occurred before 1800; indeed, a group petitioned to object when the Spanish authorities suspended the dances that year.[37] The government responded by briefly attempting to reduce the "disorder" allegedly caused by the dances by preventing all white people from attending, even as spectators.[38] The "disorder" with which the authorities were concerned may have been the indiscriminate mingling of races and castes, but there were other problems as well. For instance, the colored soldiers who petitioned them requested that guards be appointed to prevent "maliciousness" that occurred at the dances when they were away on expedition and unable to provide such protection themselves. They complained that "some people came to the dances . . . determined to disrupt the peaceful diversions—some by provoking fights . . . others by putting chewed tobacco on the seats so that the women would stain their garments."[39] In short, it appears that the so-called "tricolor" balls of Spanish Louisiana offered people of color the opportunity to take part in leisure activities from which they were normally excluded, and in so doing elicited hostility from white residents, calling to mind the 1823 observation of William Brown, a free black theater owner in New York whose business was destroyed by rioting whites: "White people do not know how to behave at entertainments designed for ladies and gentlemen of colour."[40] This problem evidently persisted well into the nineteenth century, forcing the city council to pass an ordinance in 1828 forbidding white men from attending "dressed or masked balls composed of men and women of color."[41]

Only following the Louisiana Purchase in 1805 did an enterprising businessman hit upon the idea of excluding men of color from these balls and turning them into what some historians have described as "fields of operation for prostitutes," reportedly providing "rented rooms right on the premises" for the convenience of his patrons.[42] Rather than a vestige of a more racially fluid, seignorial Latin culture, these quadroon balls were a capitalist innovation in a newly constituted and rapidly "Americanizing" society of citizens. The idea quickly caught on among other entrepreneurs—the owner of the St. Philip Street Theater found "quadroon balls" more profitable than staging plays. A number of competing venues held such gatherings over the course of the antebellum period, and judging by antebellum travel accounts, they quickly became a must-see attraction for male out-of-town visitors. These balls offered not only the opportunity to drink and dance with women of color but also, in the case of the Globe Ballroom, a gambling room in which one could play craps.[43] One 1847 account noted that people leaving the theater were quickly accosted by "eager cabmen proposing to convey them to the Quarteroon Ball."[44] Many travel writers who claimed to have attended these balls took pains to inform their readers about the specific dollar amount necessary to "possess" these women, or, perhaps less expensively, to lease their "favors . . . for stipulated periods."[45] The reported cost of "possession" was comparable to the going rate for a young female "fancy" slave. One traveler professed to have been overwhelmed by the dancing skill of the quadroons, who evidently danced for, not with, the men who had paid a cover charge (as he had) and checked their weapons at the door: "I wonder some of the opera lessees in Europe do not import some for their corps de ballet [but for] the expense. . . . A handsome quadroon could not be bought for less than one thousand or fifteen hundred dollars! though the market is well supplied at that price."[46]

Together, these accounts again raise the question of whether the balls served chiefly as another form of the slave market rather than a courtly display of the city's colored female elite. Visiting in 1832, Alexis de Tocqueville described the "ball of the quadroons" that he attended as "a sort of bazaar."[47] Another tourist commented a decade later that "few strangers . . . ever visit New Orleans without attending, at least for once, these nocturnal haunts of libertinism."[48] Like so much else in New Orleans, the balls quickly became tourist traps and inauspicious places for a genteel free woman of color to seek a stable, long-term relationship. Indeed, just one year before Frederick Law Olmsted referred to the Globe Ballroom as the special haunt of Paris-educated "Quadroons," a New Orleans policeman closed it, arresting more than sixty people of color, "both male and female, bond and free," for violating city ordinances prohibiting the unlawful assemblage of "white and colored people."[49] One historian has observed the "curious irony" of the spatial proximity of the Orleans Ballroom, another space associated with the quadroon balls, to the auction block in Jackson Square—less than one city block separates them.[50] Some travel writers, like Olmsted, described the quadroons at these balls as having been free(d), and while he may have been correct on this point, it seems unlikely that they were expecting to meet what he describes as "suitors" who intended to support them in "a style suitable to the habits she has been bred to."[51]

The evidence suggests that the balls may have appeared genteel, but they were strictly about business, and business was evidently so good that white female prostitutes sought to participate, as the mayor observed in 1835 when he referred to the balls as "the sink of the most dissolute class of women." When the city councilmen debated his proposal to ban white women from these balls, one argued that it was necessary "to tolerate the order of things established for debauched women," (in other words, interracial balls) because it would keep this "abominable caste" of

white women from soliciting at whites-only balls given for "respectable families."
White prostitutes should be permitted to attend quadroon balls, he argued; if any
legal action should be taken, it should be to fine and imprison those seeking entry
into respectable whites-only balls. His colleague responded that he would support
this motion, but only if informed as to how to differentiate between vicious white
women and respectable ones. Because women of the former class did not display
a brand of shame on their faces, he argued, it would be very difficult to apply this
rule fairly.[52]

The problem of keeping "viciousness" and "respectability" fixed along segregated
boundaries of color was precisely the issue facing the city council. Dissolute white
women were supposed to remain invisible in order to maintain the appeal that
light-skinned colored women held for white visitors. The specific feminine allure
of the quadroon balls lay in their exhibition of "slave-market whiteness," in which
female slaves advertised as delicate, genteel, and "well-bred" served to commodify
sex in a form that could fetch a very high price. It is little wonder that needy white
women sought to capitalize on it as well. Consumers only valued what Walter
Johnson has called "slave-market whiteness" when it was "legible as imitation" of
the real thing.[53] When "real" white women sought out these venues, it became a
matter of concern for city leaders because, unlike their colored counterparts—slave
or free—white women could theoretically sue for rape, or for damages for breach
of marriage promise, seduction, or abandonment. In Louisiana, if a white woman's
children could prove their paternity, they could legally claim some financial support from their father. Sex with a woman of color posed none of these risks. We are
far from knowing precisely who was at the balls and what kinds of social relations
the balls fostered. But their name and the discussions they prompted suggest that
the free or enslaved status of the women in attendance was less important, both
to visitors and white authorities, than their racial status.

Barbara Fields has argued that prohibitions on racial intermarriage show "society in the act of inventing race."[54] Framed by this prohibition and its disparate
consequences for black and white women, the stories of quadroon balls fostered
a legally established status distinction that pertained to white men, irrespective of
their class standing. Sexual possession of a woman was considered an important
accoutrement of male mastery and power throughout the nation.[55] In the theater
of the slave auction, white men publicly bid against one another, creating dramatic scenarios in which only the wealthiest or most credit-worthy could emerge
victorious. Accounts of the quadroon balls offered a different kind of theater, one
that attenuated class differences among white men by staging transactions more
privately. The balls may even have served to democratize access to "fancy" women:
now available as rentals, they required a smaller financial commitment than those
at the auctions and could be possessed by less affluent men.[56] Even the labor of

free women of color in the nineteenth century was sufficiently undervalued to place it within the reach of working-class white men. Antebellum stories of the quadroon balls did important cultural work in articulating the terms of American citizenship in a republic based on white male privilege.

Postbellum accounts of the quadroon balls by such writers as George Washington Cable and Charles Gayarré are retrospective, framing the balls as artifacts of the pre–Civil War era. Such reports have led historians to conclude that such lavish displays vanished after the war.[57] Tellingly, quadroon balls apparently lost their appeal precisely at the moment when slavery was abolished and interracial marriage became legal. This timing raises the question of why general emancipation would disrupt a tradition among free quadroons of pursuing extralegal sexual relations with white men. Indeed, during and shortly after the war, white Northern visitors continued to perceive women of color as having no higher ambition than to become white men's sexual partners. One Massachusetts soldier stationed in Louisiana in 1864 noted in his memoirs that "the women [of color] seem proud of their almost white children, holding the fruit of their adultery as evidence of their charms."[58] The same year, when Union General Benjamin Butler testified about his experiences with "contrabands" entering his soldiers' camps, he declared that he was "obliged to make some stringent regulations" regarding the women, "because they are brought up to think that no honor can come to them equal to that of connection with a white man," and white men's willingness to take advantage of this posed problems for military discipline.[59] Under such circumstances, why should the balls have ceased? Descriptions of the antebellum balls conjured an elaborate choreography of physical intimacy and social distance—not unlike the situation under slavery. After the war, as people of color clamored for new rights and refused to passively accept exploitative aspects of the "free labor" regime, the sense of social distance between whites and people of color seemed less secure, transforming the balls' implications.

*    *    *

Quadroon balls, it is argued, were sites for black female agency; a close rereading of the documentary evidence such as travel accounts and newspaper reports points to this fact. By historicizing these accounts and placing them in relation to scholarship and other kinds of documentary evidence focused on women of color, one can conclude that the balls are inauspicious sites for locating the kinds of agency we might seek to celebrate. Yet this is by no means to conclude that such women's voices, or the dynamics of their intimate relationships, are lost to history. While first-person sources such as diaries and the kind of personal papers most archives tend to preserve are admittedly scarce,[60] other types of sources, including civil and criminal court records, as well as Civil War widows' pension applications, contain vast troves of information that historians have scarcely begun to explore.[61] The women who pervade these accounts defy easy conventionalization, and their perspectives were rarely the kinds of things travel writers observed or appellate judges sought to publicize. They may not make compelling subjects for a Showtime miniseries, but their stories contain much food for thought for those interested in gendered resistance.

NOTES

1. Catherine Clinton, *The Plantation Mistress: Woman's World in the Old South* (New York: Pantheon, 1982), 225.

2. Earl F. Bargainnier, "The Falconhurst Series: A New Popular Image of the Old South," *Journal of Popular Culture* 10, no. 2 (1976): 298–314; on the film *Mandingo*, see Clinton, *Plantation Mistress*, 223–31.

3. Press book for *The Quadroon*, 1971, in author's possession.

4. Results of DVD search on "The Feast of All Saints" in Amazon.com database. http://www.amazon.com, Quotes and Trivia (accessed October 1, 2005).

5. See, for example, Alexis de Tocqueville, *Journey to America* (New Haven, Conn.: Yale University Press, 1960), 164, and Frederick Law Olmsted, *A Journey in the Seaboard Slave States* (New York: Dix & Edwards, 1856), 594–96.

6. Virtually every traveler who passed through New Orleans and published an account wrote something about sexual relations between white men and women of color there. While many of the male travelers claimed to have attended the balls, none mentioned having danced with anyone there. For useful reference bibliographies of travel accounts of the antebellum South, see Thomas Dionysius Clark, *Travels in the Old South: A Bibliography* (Norman: University of Oklahoma Press, 1956). Monique Guillory offers the suggestive comment that "the balls are most often recollected in travelers' logs rather than reports from native New Orleanians." Monique Guillory, "Under One Roof: The Sins and Sanctity of the New Orleans Quadroon Balls," in *Race Consciousness: African American Studies for the New Century*, ed. Judith Jackson Fossett and Jeffrey A. Tucker (New York: New York University Press, 1997), 81.

7. The arrangements to which the balls supposedly gave rise are shockingly ill-documented. Focusing on New Orleans in the late eighteenth and early nineteenth centuries, the supposed heyday of institutionalized interracial concubinage, historian Thomas Ingersoll concluded in 1999 that "neither the word [plaçage] nor evidence of its being common is to be found in the archives." In 2008, historian Justin Nystrom cited testimony from an 1874 Louisiana Supreme Court case concerning a sexual relationship between a free woman of color and a white man; one of the witnesses said that the woman "was placée with" the man. Tantalizing as this example is, it cannot alone confirm the travel accounts' depiction of formalized interracial concubinage as a "tradition," especially a tradition that court records suggest would seem to have been more honored in the breach than in the observance. See Thomas Ingersoll, *Mammon and Manon in Early New Orleans: The First Slave Society in the Deep South, 1718–1819* (Knoxville: University of Tennessee Press, 1999),

220; Justin Nystrom, "In My Father's House: Relationships and Identity in an Interracial New Orleans Creole Family, 1845–1875," *Louisiana History* 49, no. 3 (2008): 289n4.

8. The literature on working-class women emphasizes their lack of protection because of their dislocation from the traditional farm family. Obviously such family dislocations were even more prevalent among free and enslaved women of color. See Christine Stansell, *City of Women: Sex and Class in New York, 1790–1860* (New York: Knopf, 1986); Ellen Ross and Rayna Rapp, "Sex and Society: A Research Note from Social History and Anthropology," *Comparative Studies in Society and History* 23, no. 1 (1981): 68–72; Lisa Forman Cody, "The Politics of Illegitimacy in an Age of Reform: Women, Reproduction, and Political Economy in England's New Poor Law of 1834," *Journal of Women's History* 11, no. 4 (2000): 131–56.

9. U. B. Phillips, ed., *The Statutes of the State of Louisiana* (New Orleans: Emile La Sere, 1855), 161. On rape, see Judith K. Schafer, *Slavery, the Civil Law, and the Supreme Court of Louisiana* (Baton Rouge: Louisiana State University Press, 1994), 85–86; on assault, see H. E. Sterkx, *The Free Negro in Ante-Bellum Louisiana* (Rutherford, N. J.: Fairleigh Dickinson University Press, 1972), 241.

10. *Louisiana Acts 1806*, p. 188–90.

11. *Vail v. Bird*, 6 La. Ann 223 (1851), quoted in Schafer, *Slavery*, 187.

12. This chapter is indebted to Amy Dru Stanley's work on the connections between labor and marriage contracts in the nineteenth-century United States. See Amy Dru Stanley, *From Bondage to Contract: Wage Labor, Marriage, and the Market in the Age of Slave Emancipation* (New York: Cambridge University Press, 1998).

13. See Stephanie Coontz, *Marriage, a History: From Obedience to Intimacy; or, How Love Conquered Marriage* (New York: Viking, 2005).

14. See Werner Sollors, *Neither Black nor White yet Both: Thematic Explorations of Interracial Literature* (New York: Oxford University Press, 1997); Mary Louise Pratt, *Imperial Eyes: Travel Writing and Transculturation* (New York: Routledge, 1992), 100.

15. See, for example, J. H. Ingraham, "The Quadroon of Orleans: A Tale," in *The American Lounger; or, Tales, Sketches, and Legends, Gathered in Sundry Journeyings* (Philadelphia: Lea & Blanchard, 1839), 255–73; Lydia Maria Child, "The Quadroons," *The Liberty Bell* (1842): 115–41.

16. Ann Maria Davison Diary, September 10, 1848; January 25, 1858; January 2, 1860. Original manuscript in Schlesinger library, Radcliffe Institute, Harvard University.

17. See also Judith K. Schafer, *Becoming Free, Remaining Free: Manumission and Enslavement in New Orleans, 1846–1862* (Baton Rouge: Louisiana State University Press, 2003), especially chapter 6, "The Struggle to Stay Free," and chapter 7, "Kidnapping Free People of Color."

18. Davison Diary, November 26, 1857.

19. See Carl A. Brasseaux, Keith P. Fontenot, and Claude F. Oubre, eds., *Creoles of Color in the Bayou Country* (Jackson: University Press of Mississippi, 1994), 8–13.

20. For an example of this, see John Blassingame, *Black New Orleans, 1860–1880* (Chicago: University of Chicago Press, 1973); for feminist criticisms, see Hazel V. Carby, *Reconstructing Womanhood: The Emergence of the Afro-American Woman Novelist* (New York:

Oxford University Press, 1987), 39; Angela Davis, "Reflections on the Black Woman's Role in the Community of Slaves," *Black Scholar* 3, no. 4 (1971): 3–15. In a similar vein, Diane Miller Somerville has criticized Eugene Genovese's influential 1970s work for romanticizing "miscegenation" in the antebellum South as consensual, arguing that this "euphemization of the sex act between master and slave serves a useful ideological purpose" in making his argument for paternalism in master-slave relationships. Diane Miller Sommerville, "Moonlight, Magnolias, and Brigadoon; or, Almost Like Being in Love: Mastery and Sexual Exploitation in Eugene D. Genovese's Plantation South," *Radical History Review* 88 (January 2004): 68–82.

21. See, for example, Mia Bay's criticism of post-DNA scholarship on Sally Hemings that assigns her "an extraordinary degree of agency in negotiating the terms of her relationship with Jefferson." Mia Bay, "In Search of Sally Hemings in the Post-DNA Era," *Reviews in American History* 34 (2006): 407–26.

22. Virginia Meacham Gould, "In Full Enjoyment of Their Liberty: The Free Women of Color of the Gulf Ports of New Orleans, Mobile, and Pensacola 1769–1860" (PhD diss., Emory University, 1991), 232.

23. See, for instance, Joan M. Martin, "Plaçage and the Louisiana Gens de Couleur Libre," in *Creole: The History and Legacy of Louisiana's Free People of Color*, ed. Sybil Kein (Baton Rouge: Louisiana State University Press, 2000), 57–70.

24. For a critique of the uses of demography in this literature, see Jennifer Spear, *Race, Sex, and Social Order in Early New Orleans* (Baltimore, Md.: Johns Hopkins University Press, 2009), 216–17.

25. This gap in the regional literature also exists in more nationally oriented studies. Free black women are hardly mentioned in Diane Miller Somerville, *Rape and Race in the Nineteenth Century South* (Chapel Hill: University of North Carolina Press, 2004).

26. Darlene Clark Hine, "Rape and the Inner Lives of Black Women in the Middle West: Preliminary Thoughts on the Culture of Dissemblance," *Signs* 14, no. 4 (1989): 919.

27. Walter Johnson, "On Agency," *Journal of Social History* 37, no. 1 (2003): 113–24.

28. Carole Pateman, *The Sexual Contract* (Stanford, Calif.: Stanford University Press, 1988), 110–12.

29. Deborah Gray White, *Ar'n't I a Woman? Female Slaves in the Plantation South* (New York: Norton, 1999), 34.

30. Thomas Ashe, *Travels in America* (London: Blunt, 1808), 345.

31. Pateman, *Sexual Contract*, 194.

32. For examples, see *John H. Hanna v. Theron A. Bartlette*, 10 Rob. 438 (1845); *Trudeau's Executor v. Robinette*, 4 Mart La. 577 (1817); and the manuscript record in the Supreme Court of Louisiana Collection, University of New Orleans, Docket #2506, *Carmelite, a Negress, Slave, v. Jean Lacaze*, 7 La. Ann. 629 (1852).

33. Ronald R. Morazan, "'Quadroon' Balls in the Spanish Period," *Louisiana History: The Journal of the Louisiana Historical Association* 14, no. 3 (1973): 310.

34. Christine Stansell, *City of Women: Sex and Class in New York, 1789–1860* (Urbana: University of Illinois Press, 1987), 185.

35. Pateman, *Sexual Contract*, 113.

36. Henry A. Kmen, "The Quadroon Balls," in *Music in New Orleans: The Formative Years, 1791–1841* (Baton Rouge: Louisiana State University Press, 1966), 46.

37. See, generally, Morazan, "'Quadroon' Balls in the Spanish Period."

38. Kmen, "Quadroon Balls," 46.

39. Morazan, "'Quadroon' Balls in the Spanish Period." 314.

40. Marvin Edward McAllister, *White People Do Not Know How to Behave at Entertainments Designed for Ladies & Gentlemen of Colour: William Brown's African & American Theater* (Chapel Hill: University of North Carolina Press, 2003).

41. John Calhoun, comp., *A Digest of the Ordinances and Resolutions of the Second Municipality of New Orleans, in Force May 1, 1840* (New Orleans, 1840), cited in Roger Fischer, *The Segregation Struggle in Louisiana, 1862–1877* (Chicago: University of Illinois Press, 1974), 17–18.

42. Kmen, "Quadroon Balls," 47, 49.

43. Quadroon balls are mentioned in Amos Stoddard, *Sketches, Historical and Descriptive, of Louisiana* (Philadelphia: Mathew Carey, 1812), 321; Isidor Lowenstern, *Les Etats-Unis Et La Havane; Souvenirs D'un Voyageur* (Paris: Bertrand, 1842), 302–3. On the Globe Ballroom, see the *New Orleans Daily True Delta*, February 9, 1853.

44. Albert James Pickett, *Eight Days in New-Orleans in February, 1847* (Montgomery, Ala.: Author, 1847), 38.

45. Stoddard, *Sketches*, 321.

46. Edward Robert Sullivan, *Rambles and Scrambles in North and South America* (London: Richard Bentley, 1852), 223.

47. Tocqueville, *Journey to America*, 164.

48. Louis F. Tasistro, *Random Shots and Southern Breezes, Containing Critical Remarks on the Southern States and Southern Institutions, with Semi-Serious Observations on Men and Manners* (New York: Harper and Brothers, 1842), 20.

49. *New Orleans Picayune*, December 25,1855.

50. Monique Guillory, "Under One Roof: The Sins and Sanctity of the New Orleans Quadroon Balls," in *Race Consciousness: African American Studies for the New Century*, ed. Judith Jackson Fossett and Jeffrey A. Tucker (New York: New York University Press, 1997), 70.

51. Frederick Law Olmsted, *A Journey in the Seaboard Slave States* (New York: Dix & Edwards; London: Sampson Low, 1856), 594–96. Postbellum fictional accounts of quadroon balls follow Olmsted's example in labeling them as "aristocratic," and it is this image that dominated two films that attempted to portray the balls. See, for example, George Washington Cable, "Madame Delphine," in *Old Creole Days* (New York: New American Library, 1961), 18–19.

52. *New Orleans Bee*, November 28, 1825, French edition, author's translation.

53. Walter Johnson, *Soul by Soul: Life inside the Antebellum Slave Market* (Cambridge: Harvard University Press, 1999), 150–56.

54. Barbara Jeanne Fields, "Slavery, Race, and Ideology in the United States of America," *New Left Review* 181 (1990): 107.

55. Anne McClintock, "Family Feuds: Gender, Nationalism and the Family," *Feminist Review* 44 (1993): 61–80; Stephanie McCurry, *Masters of Small Worlds: Yeoman Households,*

*Gender Relations, and the Political Culture of the Antebellum South Carolina Low Country* (New York: Oxford University Press, 1995); Edward E. Baptist, "'Cuffy,' 'Fancy Maids,' and 'One-Eyed Men': Rape, Commodification, and the Domestic Slave Trade in the United States," *American Historical Review* 106, no. 5 (2001): 1619–50.

56. Monique Guillory argues that "through this strategic commodification of the quadroon body . . . women of color seized an opportunity beyond the confines of slavery to set the price for their own bodies." I have little use for this argument, which I view as an untenable effort to fit "quadroons" into an "agency" paradigm. The market set the price for these bodies, and if the travel accounts Guillory relies on are to be believed, there was a rather large supply of "quadroons" available for the "taking," keeping the price quite low. Monique Guillory, "Under One Roof: The Sins and Sanctity of the New Orleans Quadroon Balls," in Fossett and Tucker, *Race Consciousness*, 83.

57. Alecia Long's work on prostitution in New Orleans emphasizes that "long term affairs between white men and free women of color" were "institutionalized" and brokered "by the mothers of women of color." Her argument that such "economic agreements . . . all but disappeared" after the Civil War contains the implicit suggestion of their stability before it occurred. Alecia Long, *The Great Southern Babylon: Sex, Race, and Respectability in New Orleans 1865–1920* (Baton Rouge: Louisiana State University Press, 2004), 7, 11, 59.

58. Henry T. Johns, *Life with the Forty-Ninth Massachusetts Volunteers* (Washington, D.C.: Ramsey & Bisbee, 1890), 138.

59. Ira Berlin et al., eds., *Freedom: A Documentary History of Emancipation, 1861–1867,* vol. 3, series 1, *The Wartime Genesis of Free Labor: The Lower South* (Cambridge: Cambridge University Press, 1990), 445.

60. For an exception, see Virginia Meacham Gould, *Chained to the Rock of Adversity: To Be Free, Black, & Female in the Old South* (Athens: University of Georgia Press, 1998).

61. In addition to Judith Schafer's two books cited above, which focus on Louisiana's court records, promising work with Civil War pensions includes Elizabeth Ann Regosin, *Freedom's Promise: Ex-slave Families and Citizenship in the Age of Emancipation* (Charlottesville: University Press of Virginia, 2002).

PART II

# Global Slavery, Healing, and New Visions in the Twenty-First Century

# CHAPTER 6

# "Freedom Just Might be Possible"

## Suraj Kali's Moment of Decision

*Jolene Smith*

Suraj Kali woke every morning at six o'clock to begin her workday in slavery, pounding gravel into sand with a hammer. Her family had been held in slavery in Uttar Pradesh, India, for generations, children inheriting from their parents a bogus, illegal debt that could never be paid off. "My parents, my in-laws, they all died as slaves," she explained. For many years, Suraj assumed that she and her husband and children would have the same fate. A life of slavery was all they had ever known. They were each born into it, since Suraj's parents and grandparents had all been enslaved to the same family. The fact that the Kali family members literally were possessions of another family was unquestioned. It was

Figure 6.1. Suraj Kali, 2001, photograph courtesy of Peggy Callahan, Free the Slaves.

also unquestioned that every day the Kalis were forced to work all day in their slaveholder's stone quarry and were paid nothing.[1]

Sadly, her story of enslavement is not uncommon. Regularly, Free the Slaves, the organization I work for, hears about horrific cases such as this from nearly every country in the world. Nowhere is exempt. Yet what was uncommon about Suraj Kali's experience gives great hope for eradicating slavery: she also has a story of liberation, and one in which she was the key protagonist. Unlike in the past, there are now social movements of sufficient strength in at least some parts of the world that are making more and more liberation stories possible, encouraging more and more leaders of resistance like Suraj Kali to demand freedom for themselves and others, despite great risk. And they are living to tell about it.

The fact that slavery still exists in the twenty-first century is nothing less than appalling, and it points to a great failing of human societies. Yet progress is being made, as evidenced by juxtaposing the resistance experience of Suraj Kali and that of Margaret Garner, another courageous woman who defied her slaveholders in a bid for freedom. Like Suraj Kali, Margaret Garner also relied on a social movement—abolitionism—which in Garner's case ultimately failed her. Of the hundreds of slavery survivors whom we at Free the Slaves have had the honor of interviewing, it is Suraj Kali's story that to me most closely reflects the struggle of Margaret Garner—willing to make unthinkable sacrifices to achieve freedom for herself and those she loved. Suraj Kali's story also best illustrates, in stark contrast with Margaret Garner's, how similar acts of personal struggle can have strikingly different consequences, depending on whether they happen within the context of a wider movement that is demanding change and whether that movement is successful at a given time. This contrast illuminates additional reasons to stand in awe of the risks and sacrifices made by individuals who preceded or built the foundation for movements that followed them. These risk takers remind us that when individuals link arms to demand change together, progress can be made.

## Twenty-Seven Million Enslaved

There are twenty-seven million slaves in the world today—twice the number of people taken from Africa during the transatlantic slave trade.[2] For these women, men, and children, slavery means

- being controlled by violence or its threat,
- working without payment,
- being economically exploited, and
- being unable to walk away.

This same definition of slavery has held true throughout human history. The institution of slavery has adapted to flourish in new socioeconomic contexts, but at its core it remains its ugly self. It was true for Margaret Garner, who was forced to work on a farm in Kentucky in the mid-nineteenth century, and it was true for Suraj Kali in the quarries of India in the first decade of the twenty-first century. Like Suraj Kali, Margaret Garner feared that she and her family would die in slavery. The daily brutalities meted upon them and the courageous ways in which each woman confronted this injustice, centuries apart, were strikingly similar. When each woman made her own daring bid for freedom for herself and her family, however, the outcomes were starkly and heartbreakingly different. This difference provides an additional lens through which we can see the horrific circumstances of people in slavery in the nineteenth century and underscores the value of social justice people's movements in the struggle against slavery, which in turn gives us hope that slavery can be eradicated.

This hope is juxtaposed with the fact that there are more people in slavery today than at any other time in human history. In the twenty-first century, purchasing a human being for the purpose of enslavement is inexpensive. Margaret Garner was born into slavery in Kentucky in 1833 a time when adult enslaved people were being sold for around $1,000. Adjusted for inflation, that is equivalent to $40,000 in current U.S. currency. Today, a slave typically costs around ninety dollars. This low price is a function of the vast number of people who are vulnerable to enslavement and the relative ease and low risk that characterize the act of enslaving another person in the twenty-first century. The population explosion since World War II, especially in areas of the world with fewer economic opportunities, paired with the fact that many people do not have the benefit of a social safety net, has resulted in millions of people being vulnerable to slavery. Slavery is now illegal in every country in the world, unlike in Margaret Garner's era, yet slavery persists wherever a criminal can evade detection or pay off law enforcement to turn a blind eye to tricking or otherwise coercing a vulnerable person into slavery.[3]

In economic terms, the "market" is flooded, and an oversupply of enslaved people has pushed down the price of purchasing another human being. There has been such a dramatic fall in this price that the basic economy of slavery has changed. Because of the inexpensive purchase price and minimal costs associated with keeping people enslaved alive and working for the benefit of the slaveholder, today slavery is more profitable than ever. Margaret Garner, who was enslaved on a farm, likely earned John and Archibald Gaines a 5 percent return on the cost of buying, feeding, housing, and clothing her. Individuals like Suraj Kali enslaved in mining or agriculture in modern India typically generate a profit of more than 50 percent. In brothels in Thailand, where people in slavery are held for much shorter periods, the return can be as high as 800 percent.[4] This unprecedented profitability and the ubiquity of people vulnerable to slavery have proven enticing to the world's human traffickers and slaveholders who feed their greed through the theft of human lives. In 2005, the International Labour

Organization found that each year an estimated $31.7 billion in illicit profits is made from forced labor.[5]

Slaveholders and human traffickers are taking advantage of these high profit margins by enslaving people in virtually every country in the world. The highest concentration of slavery occurs in Asia and Pacific Rim countries, followed by Latin America and the Caribbean, then sub-Saharan Africa, but Global North countries are not exempt.[6] In 2004, the U.S. government estimated that from 14,500 to 17,500 people are trafficked into the United States each year and forced into industries such as prostitution, domestic service, and agricultural labor.[7] This number is widely believed to be far higher, especially when taking into account the number of children in forced prostitution.

In addition to the slavery that exists within the borders of nearly every country, slavery-tainted goods cross borders every day and end up in shopping malls and grocery stores around the world. Most of the products made by enslaved people are fed into local economies in the Global South, like the stones and sand mined by Suraj Kali and her neighbors, but there is also a wide range of products tainted by slavery that flows into the global economy. The United States Department of Labor counts 122 goods produced by forced or child labor in fifty-eight countries.[8] Some of these slavery-tainted items—rugs, jewelry, and cigarettes, for example— enter the global economy as finished goods. Many other products—such as sugar or cotton clothing—can involve slavery somewhere in their manufacturing or processing. These goods are regularly imported into the United States and a host of other countries to feed consumer demand.

On the other hand, some slavery-tainted goods are entirely home grown. Agricultural slavery is the third most common form of slavery in the United States, after forced prostitution and domestic servitude.[9] Traffickers frequently prey on the dreams of Mexican and Central American men and women by first offering to bring them to the United States to work and then trapping them with false and illegal debts. Individuals are often trafficked to fruit farms in Florida and California, where they are beaten and threatened and forced to work off their "debt" in abominable conditions. The produce from these farms is routinely shipped to supermarkets across the country.

Consumers are literally buying into slavery through their purchases, the last link in a long chain of oppression that connects consumers with people enslaved in farm fields and mines around the world. In most slavery-tainted products, slavery is connected to the harvesting or extraction of raw materials that occurs at the very bottom of complex supply chains. To date there have been few attempts to monitor the production of raw materials according to international labor standards. In general, businesses have not invested time, personnel, or capital in examining their supply chains at the level of raw materials or demanded that their secondary and tertiary suppliers do so either. Nor have consumers demanded it. There is a collective ignorance on the part of both consumers and businesses that renders both powerless to end their support of the modern-day slave trade.

This ignorance begins with the fact that a large number of people in the United States believe that slavery ended in 1865, and although awareness is growing through media coverage and education efforts by nongovernmental organizations, public understanding of the issue is partial at best. Many law enforcement officials have yet to receive adequate training on how to identify slavery and human trafficking. Only a handful of grant-making foundations in the United States list slavery or human trafficking as a program focus; these groups are rare trendsetters in the field of philanthropy. No global problem on the scale of modern slavery receives so little attention. Recognition of the issue is growing but has not yet reached the point of public outcry whereby the existence of slavery anywhere in the world is deemed simply unacceptable.

## Believing that Freedom Is Possible

Neither Margaret Garner nor Suraj Kali depended upon such public outcry. Margaret Garner's story, eloquently documented in other submissions in this volume, is unknown in Suraj Kali's village. Yet, a fundamental attitude toward freedom ties Kali and Garner to a strong legacy of resistance. Suraj Kali was determined that her children—three sons and two daughters—would not die in slavery. In the remote village of Detipur in the Shankargargh region of northern India, she, like Margaret Garner before her, began to believe that freedom just might be possible. That they were able to imagine an existence different from the one they or anyone they knew had experienced is astonishing.

Believing that freedom is possible is the first step, but not the last. Suraj Kali made the decision that even the remote possibility of achieving freedom for her, her family, and her fellow villagers was worth risking her life, even when the risk included the real possibility of leaving her children without a mother, her husband without a wife. What that moment of decision must have been like for individuals in Kali's or Garner's position is difficult if not impossible to imagine for a person born into freedom. Weighing all of the cruelties, the indignities, the terrors of the unknown, they nevertheless made their bids for freedom. Not only did they risk their own lives in their quest to be free, but both women also understood that they were risking the lives of their children as well.

This speaks to the horrific nature of being enslaved: going to bed each night shaking from exhaustion from the day's work, hungry, weak from untreated illnesses, eviscerated from seeing loved ones treated in unspeakable ways, worried for their safety or even survival, despairing that things might never change. In the case of Suraj Kali's village, it meant waking up every morning knowing that a hammer was waiting for each member of the family, no matter how young or old. The men chiseled out large pieces of stone from the parched, dusty quarry. The women used a sledge-hammer-like device to break those down into smaller rocks. The children pounded the smaller rocks into sand. Every day of their lives.

Treatment of women and girls in slavery often has additional brutal twists, as throughout history. As Delores Walters has argued, at least some of Margaret Garner's children were fathered by her slaveholder through repeated acts of rape.[10] In the early twenty-first century, it is still commonplace for enslaved girls and women to be raped by their slaveholders. This is true even for those who are not forced into prostitution. Boys and men are sometimes exploited in this way as well, but it is the general rule for women and girls, not the exception. Slaveholders commonly rape enslaved people as yet another means of control. Forced abortions and forced breeding still happen in 2011. In addition to the sheer brutality of this exploitation, it also brings additional health risks for women and girls in slavery. Pregnancy in already malnourished and maltreated women and girls bears significant health risks for mothers and infants, unsafe abortions can result in serious injury, and the risk of contracting sexually transmitted diseases increases.

In cases where women and girls manage to break free from slavery, especially in situations where they have been trafficked away from their home to another region then manage to return home, survivors often face difficulties reintegrating into their communities. In communities from which many girls and women are trafficked, it is widely understood that most females are raped while they are in slavery, which some cultures interpret to mean that female survivors of slavery are "tainted" because they are no longer virgins or have somehow acted impurely. This can cause women and girls to be deemed "unmarriageable" and unworthy of a respected place within their society. This is particularly problematic in countries where women do not have access to legal status or the right to own land except through a husband or other male family member. Their options for supporting themselves become severely limited, and they become vulnerable to the false job offers of human traffickers. Without sufficient economic opportunities, slavery survivors can fall back into slavery.

In light of the hell of the experience of slavery, it becomes easier to fathom how, when presented with even a narrow possibility to escape, millions of people throughout history and into the present have risked their lives and died while attempting to free themselves. Most of us will never know about the enslaved people who today are attempting escape but are caught by their slaveholders first and killed, or who die a slow death because of their brave attempts to resist or escape from enslavement.

## The Possibility of Death

Suraj Kali understood this very real possibility of death, and like Margaret Garner and many before her around the world, she risked death in search of freedom for herself and her family. However, Kali and Garner's journeys toward freedom were quite different. The only way for Margaret Garner and her family to make a bid for freedom in the nineteenth century was to physically escape their slaveholder's grasp and attempt to cross the geographical boundary to a place where slavery was illegal. Suraj Kali's journey, in contrast, was not so much a geographical one as a journey of knowledge, will, and fortitude. Yes, she could have tried to steal away with her family when the slaveholders and their thugs were not looking and made a run for it like the Garner family with the aim of getting far enough away from their slaveholder that he would not likely succeed in hunting them down. But because social justice people's movements had succeeded in making slavery illegal in India and in every country in the world by Suraj Kali's time, she had access to such a movement in her region. Therefore, Suraj Kali had another option: demanding her freedom without leaving her place of enslavement.

Inspired by grassroots anti-slavery activists who visited her village and who secretly discussed with her the possibility of breaking free, Suraj Kali began to talk to her fellow villagers about how they could change their lives. She explained what she had learned from the activists—that being held in servitude against their will was against the law; that everyone in the village should be able to live in freedom; and even that every child should be able to go to school—unthinkable notions in this village. With the help of local activists, Suraj Kali started a women's group that met regularly. The women gave each other as much moral and material support as they could and all began to plan their break for freedom. Over time, Suraj Kali and the members of the women's group inspired the entire village to understand that everyone deserved freedom.

One day, when the village decided it was ready, Suraj and her neighbors banded together to confront the slaveholder and demand that he set them free. They literally joined arms and refused to move until the slaveholder relented—and he did relent, but not before sending his thugs to beat them up. The villagers did not waver, despite the violence, hunger, and exhaustion. Finally, the slaveholders simply gave up, because it was clear that the people they had enslaved would no longer comply. With the help of local activists, the villagers also demanded the rights to a part of the stone quarry where they had been forced to work so they could sell stones and sand to support themselves. Suraj Kali told the slaveholder, "If you cannot give us land like that, then shoot us dead." Shortly after her village gained freedom, she explained, "Now we are not tied to anyone. We are buying and selling stones of our own. We are not tied to anyone. We are able to teach our children." Within the course of a few days, the people of Detipur village went from having their every move controlled and their humanity denied for generations to being able to direct their own lives and to actually control and run their own small-scale business.[11]

It was not an easy path. As in the nineteenth century, gaining freedom was not a guarantee of sustainable freedom or even the wherewithal to physically survive. The conditions of being free can include less food and even worse shelter than in conditions of slavery, especially during the first days and months in freedom. While someone in slavery only has access to the bare minimum for subsistence, the lack of economic opportunities upon becoming free can mean having access to even less. But when people like the villagers of Detipur make a collective, conscious decision to claim their right to freedom, they tend to find ways of working to support themselves and each other, even if that work is backbreaking and tedious. Achieving basic economic sustainability and maintaining this strong commitment to other community members means that they are much more likely to sustain their freedom and much less likely to ever fall under the control of a slaveholder again.[12] Eventually, as occurred in the village of Detipur, there is also a strong likelihood that the formerly enslaved will find the means to build a school in their village and to educate their children.

The knowledge that slavery was against the law and that freedom was their right was enough to inspire Suraj Kali and her neighbors to confront their slaveholder and withstand the violence that preceded their liberation. At the time, very few slaveholders in their remote region of Northern India had ever been brought to justice. Nor did this particular liberation strategy involve direct law enforcement. The first step in Suraj Kali's journey to freedom was learning about her rights and realizing that involuntary servitude was illegal. She then shared this knowledge with her neighbors. Her understanding that every person has a right to be free was crucial, as was her willingness to risk her life and possibly the lives of her family members. The final essential piece to her success was her realization that if she, her family, and her neighbors all stood together, they might have a better chance at freedom and a better chance at remaining free.

## The Contemporary Anti-slavery Movement

We will never know how many resistance leaders in India were inspired by Suraj Kali and her neighbors to take their first bold and dangerous steps into freedom, bringing their communities with them. We do know that Suraj Kali's story has motivated thousands of people around the world, as Margaret Garner's has moved others throughout the generations. While Garner's story was a lightning rod for a polemical national debate, Kali shared her story through contributing to Free the Slaves's video interview library of testimonies from those closest to slavery. This footage helps educate people about twenty-first-century slavery and to spread the word that that slavery, in fact, can be beaten.[13] Communities like Suraj Kali's are proving this to us all.

Free the Slaves finds effective, ongoing, community-based anti-slavery work in areas with a high incidence of slavery and then works with these local groups to free people and dismantle the systems that allow slavery to exist. In 2011, Free the Slaves is working in six countries—Brazil, Democratic Republic of Congo, Ghana, Haiti, India, and Nepal—in addition to the United States. The organization's headquarters is in Washington, D.C., a natural base for ongoing work to persuade governments and businesses to use their power to eradicate slavery. Free the Slaves presents Freedom Awards each year to shine a spotlight on heroes within the anti-slavery movement. All of Free the Slaves's work is buttressed by social-science-based research on the nature of slavery and the most effective ways to combat it. As noted, Free the Slaves's drumbeat for eradication is communicated primarily through its video library of interviews, the world's largest on modern slavery, where survivors share in their own words why slavery can and must end.

When we started Free the Slaves in 2000, there were only a few U.S. organizations, elected officials, and business leaders who were actively addressing modern slavery. Thankfully, in 2011 there are many more, and their ranks are growing. The Alliance to End Slavery and Trafficking (ATEST) is a powerful coalition of organizations focusing on strengthening the U.S. government's response to modern slavery. Polaris Project runs a national hotline for people to report cases of slavery. Synagogues, churches, and temples have incorporated anti-slavery activities into their regular services and celebrations. This, the fourth and one hopes the final great abolitionist movement, is strengthening.

Narratives of slavery past and present come together at Cincinnati's National Underground Railroad Museum, which has gripping exhibits about slavery and liberation spanning centuries. Visiting there, it is impossible to ignore the grand sight of the Ohio River where so many individuals like Margaret Garner dared to demand their basic human right to freedom, and where so many were tortured and killed. Slavery happened right there, in the middle of the United States heartland and not all that long ago. Blatantly, right under the noses of many people who considered themselves morally upright, slavery continued. Individuals personally witnessed this atrocity every day and did nothing to stop it. They were onlookers, not change agents.

In October 2010, the museum was joined by the world's first museum-quality, permanent exhibition on modern-day slavery and human trafficking at the National Underground Railroad Freedom Center. A powerful exhibit, "Invisible: Slavery Today," brings past and present together. Freedom Center visitors, many of them students, come face to face with the reality that slavery did not end in the nineteenth century. The exhibit draws on the work of Free the Slaves and six other activist organizations to extend the twenty-first-century work of abolishing slavery across the globe by sharing the stories of individuals trapped by slavery today and analyzing the causes of slavery, the economic forces that have allowed it to grow, and the responses of governments, the justice system, nonprofit organizations, and the public. Visitors are introduced to antislavery activities underway around the world and are invited to take action by supporting state and national anti-slavery legislation, purchasing fair-trade products, volunteering, fundraising, and raising awareness about the warning signs of slavery and what each of us can do about it.[14]

My colleagues and I have had the opportunity to bear witness to the horror of slavery—and the first moments of freedom—in countries around the world. But it is on the banks of the Ohio River, where slavery was allowed to flourish right in the middle of my country, that I most vividly feel the responsibility and the opportunity to be part of the solution, not just an onlooker. I imagine that every person who read about the Underground Railroad in history class as a child wondered at some point, as I did, if I would have been one of those helping people to freedom, despite the risks, or would I have been a coward who did nothing and turned the other way. Tragically, with more people in slavery today than at any other time in human history, none of us has to wonder. This question is being asked of each of us right now.

## Sustainable Freedom, Continued Resistance

Years after Suraj Kali achieved her own freedom, my colleague Supriya Awasthi remains in touch with her and the activists who worked with her and reports that Suraj Kali continues to be an inspirational leader in her community. In 2008, Kali told her, "I have come out of slavery. Now I will never go back into it, neither will I let anybody from my village be a slave."[15] She is constantly looking for ways to help the entire village move forward. For example, when healthcare workers travel near Detipur, she arranges for the whole village to receive care. She is also coordinating a women's group—much like she did when freedom was only a concept—of fourteen members who support each other in moving past the abject poverty that many of them are still confronting. They have made progress: all the members now have houses, all receive the "social security" benefits that the government often fails to provide unless the people organize to demand their payments, and all have a modicum of decent work to support themselves economically. Together they have reached many of their own goals since the days when they were fearful to even voice their desire to make their own choices and stand up for their rights.

Suraj Kali has reached many of her personal goals as well, especially her primary one—making sure her children do not die in slavery. All five of them are living a free life. Each of them is married and earning his or her own living. Suraj Kali's husband died soon after reaching freedom, but he did live to see the day that his children could go to school. Suraj Kali worked her way out of the stone quarry and found a job as a caretaker at a guesthouse (a small hotel) near her village, where she is earning many times what she did during her first days in freedom. The expectation in Suraj Kali's community is that women like her—a widow with children who are earning enough to support her in her older age—will simply move in with one of her daughters or sons. But as she has done repeatedly in her life, Suraj Kali is breaking with society's expectations of her and chooses to live by herself.

## NOTES

1. Thanks to my Free the Slaves colleagues Peggy Callahan, co-founder and executive producer, and Supriya Awasthi, South Asia director, who interviewed Suraj Kali on September 11, 2001, near Ghond village, Uttar Pradesh, India. The video of this interview is housed at the Free the Slaves library in Torrance, California.

2. Kevin Bales, *Disposable People: New Slavery in the Global Economy* (Berkeley: University of California Press, 1999; rev. ed., 2004), 8–9.

3. See Mark Reinhardt, *Who Speaks for Margaret Garner? The True Story That Inspired Toni Morrison's* Beloved (Minneapolis: University of Minnesota Press, 2000), 11. Bales, *Disposable People*, 16; Siddharth Kara, *Sex Trafficking: Inside the Business of Modern Slavery* (New York: Columbia University Press, 2009), 78–79, 205.

4. Bales, *Disposable People*, 16–18.

5. International Labour Office, "A Global Alliance against Forced Labour: Global Report under the Follow-up to the ILO Declaration on Fundamental Principles and Rights at Work," Report 1B, ILC, 93rd Session, Geneva, 2005. This report estimates that there are 12.3 million people in the world trapped in forced labor. The ILO's estimate corresponds closely with those of Kevin Bales and Free the Slaves, except in the case of India, where Free the Slaves's estimates differ from the ILO's.

6. International Labour Office, "A Global Alliance against Forced Labour."

7. U.S. Department of Justice, *Assessment of U.S. Government Efforts to Combat Trafficking in Persons* (Washington, D.C.: Department of Labor, June 2004), 5.

8. U.S. Department of Labor, Office of Child Labor, Forced Labor, and Human Trafficking, *List of Goods Produced by Child Labor or Forced Labor* (Washington, D.C.: Department of Labor, 2009), iii.

9. Kevin Bales and Ron Soodalter, *The Slave Next Door: Human Trafficking and Slavery in America Today* (Berkeley: University of California Press, 2009), 51.

10. Delores Walters, "Re(dis)covering and Recreating the Cultural Milieu of Margaret Garner," introductory chapter in this volume.

11. Callahan and Awasthi interview with Suraj Kali.

12. Free the Slaves Associate Director for Partnerships Ginny Baumann first observed this, together with Supriya Awasthi and Free the Slaves' partner organizations.

13. The short documentary *Silent Revolution* tells the story of villagers in Suraj Kali's state of Uttar Pradesh, India, who achieved freedom using a similar methodology to that of Kali and her neighbors. See http://freetheslaves.madebysurvivors.com.

14. See http://www.freedomcenter.org/slavery-today. Freedom Center partners for "Invisible: Slavery Today" include Free the Slaves; International Justice Mission; Polaris Project; Child Voice International; GoodWeave; TransFair USA; and the Department of Homeland Security Blue Campaign.

15. Report from Supriya Awasthi, Free the Slaves South Asia director, December 28, 2008.

# CHAPTER 7

# MARGINALITY AND ALLEGORIES OF GENDERED RESISTANCE

## Experiences from Southern Yemen

*Huda Seif*

Forces of spirit possession cut across time and space.[1] The compelling presence of the devil and malevolent spirits called *jinn* in the Delta region of southern Yemen in the 1990s echo accounts of spirits, tricksters, or *aye* in West African and New World cultures. Margaret Garner's life history as interpreted by Toni Morrison in *Beloved* connects us with a spiritual world of memory and possession that mirrors the experience of women spiritual healers and their patients in Yemen's *al-Wadi* Delta. Internal and external struggles for control dominate Morrison's narrative of enslaved American women and the lives of women agricultural work- ers in southern Yemen. Complex forms of gendered resistance shape the lives of women in both cultures. In the following pages, I will argue that the deployment and circulation of narratives of (dis)possession by the devil, particularly among women, represent a gendered form of understanding marginality and of confront- ing exploitation, domination, and material adversity.

## The Valley of the Spirits

A few hours after arriving in a small town in the Delta region of southern Yemen in the early summer of 1996, six years after the unification of previously socialist South Yemen with tribalist/conservative North Yemen, I sought refuge from the scorching midday sun under the shade of an old lime tree in the middle of a large commercial estate. I was to embark on a yearlong research project leading to a doctoral dissertation. Dazed and disoriented, I sat next to my two suitcases, one filled with books on the history of agriculture in the region that I had collected from street vendors in the capital city of Sana'a, the other containing the entirety of my personal effects. In front of me was an army of agricultural laborers, men and women, queued in front of a one-room mud structure with a low, thatched

Figure 7.1. Women laborers from the Delta region of Abyan, southern Yemen, 2007. Photograph by Huda Seif.

roof that stood in the middle of the estate. The laborers wore stained, torn clothing and were equipped with rusty sickles and machetes. One by one, they entered the mudroom and re-emerged a few minutes later with a green plastic bag. Before disappearing into the lush green banana leaves, they stopped under the lime tree and inspected the contents of their bags: monthly wages of less than fifty U.S. dollars.

There was only one other dwelling in sight—a mobile home of two rooms with full amenities that belonged to my host, the owner of the estate and the man who gave me permission to carry out my research. The owner lived in his family home in a nearby town but kept the mobile home for his frequent supervisory trips to the estate. His armed bodyguards simply settled themselves in the surrounding bushes, where they could easily monitor, around the clock, the safety of their boss and all activities in the surrounding field. Local morality would not permit that I share the two-room home with him. On becoming fully cognizant of my housing crisis, I began to contemplate on how to settle into a simple makeshift hut in the nearest labor settlement that had been unknown to me only a few days before. Although established more than fifty years ago, the settlement did not have a name, and its residents simply referred to it as *al-Wadi*, or the Valley. The laborers who queued that day were among the residents of the settlement. They were the people whose everyday lives and struggles I had come to study.

I collected my courage and decided to approach one of the women from the queue as she passed by the lime tree where I sat. She hardly noticed my presence, for she was fully engaged in counting, with her dusty and calloused hands, stacks of almost pulverized Yemeni banknotes, tied in thick bundles with a rubber band.[2] "What did you do to earn this money? And what are the stains on your clothes?" I asked. The woman seemed in her late forties, with worn plastic sandals that seemed two sizes too small, exposing the deep cuts on her calloused feet. The dripping sweat from her forehead formed clear lines on the thick film of white dust covering her dark face. She slowly shifted her attention from the old banknotes and stared at me as if registering my presence for the first time. She took some time to look at my cropped and uncovered hair—uncommon in that place and time—then again slowly moved her gaze down to my leather boots, specially purchased for fear of the scorpions and snakes of the region. It seemed a long moment before the woman replied to my questions with a clarity that sounded condescending and made me feel like a mental patient and she my doctor. *"Ahlan, ahlan bil ukht al'azizah"* (Hello, and welcome my dear sister). How can I break this news to you without scaring you away with your fancy boots?" Looking at the field across from us, she added with a secure sense of dignity, "You see, we are soldiers of the landlord, and we are hired to banish the *jinn* (evil spirits) that infest this field." Pushing a handful of the rotten banknotes close to my face, she continued, "This money is for the number of *jinn* we kill per day or per month. The bloodstains that you have recognized on my clothes are those of the bleeding *jinn*."

The woman's response prompted laughter from some of her colleagues in the queue who had been watching us with amusement. Encouraged by the audience, she continued with her story, this time carefully pointing her index finger at a woman who was leaning against the mud wall where the foreman was distributing the money.

"Do you see that poor woman sitting there? Do you also want to know why she is not standing in the queue with the others and why her clothing is not stained?" Without waiting for my response, she added, "Because she cannot kill *jinn*. Instead they shattered her. You will be too, if you do not watch out for yourself. One must acquire the skills to fight the *jinn* or they will dispossess you just like the many people who inhabit the Valley." The woman at whom my interlocutor pointed had a protruding belly that suggested advanced pregnancy, but she showed no reaction to the comments about her weakness.

Like the other women in the long queue, my interlocutor wore torn, loose, see-through garb called *dira'* atop a colorless, long-sleeved men's shirt. She also wore cotton slacks underneath to offset the transparency of the long garb and covered her hair with a colorful but faded scarf. Months later I understood that the cotton slacks also served as protection during menstruation. None of the women in sight was veiled or stood apart from male co-workers in the queue with the machete and sickles. Indeed, the practices of veiling and gender/sex segregation that are often written about in the ethnographies on the Middle East did not apply here.[3] This first encounter was a crucial moment in guiding the nature of my research. Subsequently, I learned that my interlocutor's name was Rahmah. She was one of a group of six women who had chopped enough bananas and papayas to fill a big truck that same day while their male counterparts loaded the fruits in stacks. Rahmah was also a professional healer of those afflicted with spirit possession and a well-respected spirit medium who chased possessing spirits from the bodies of her female co-workers. The squatting and allegedly *jinn*-shattered woman was named Sa'idah and was one of Rahmah's patients. She also seemed to be in her forties and her protruding belly of the last four years was said to be an "arrested pregnancy" caused by an evil eye. But despite the mocking statements about the *jinn* massacres and bloodstains from the field, both Sa'idah and Rahmah, like most women in the Delta, knew a great deal about the devil and devil possession and evil eyes.

Far from being just a gesture for sarcasm, narratives on the devil and his capacities to dispossess and alienate impoverished individuals from their bodies informed all aspects of everyday life. These stories are part and parcel of larger allegorical narratives that shed critical light on a long history of oppression, marginality, and resistance. In particular, these narratives creatively deploy a form of gendered resistance that was quite extensive in the Delta area of southern Yemen at the time of my research.

During the months that followed, I found myself privy to the social relations of power that harshly conditioned the everyday lives of the Delta people who queued once a week or once a month for their less than a dollar-a-day wage for eight to ten hours of work each day, six days a week. It was an existence that depended on the labor of the entire family, including children who took care of their younger siblings while parents were out laboring in the fields. Although the workers were unified under the overall banner of landless agricultural laborers in the post-socialist era of which I write, in reality they were an amalgam of different social groups, each with different histories.

The devil figure played a crucial role in mediating a plethora of contradictions and tensions in power relations that tied destitute and landless laborers with potent and exploitative landlords. More critically, the devil figure articulated a variety of dissenting responses to everyday experiences of marginality resulting from intertwined sexual, gender, race, and class relations in southern Yemen. As for the bloodstains on the workers' shirts, they were marks left by substances that ooze from freshly cut papaya branches.

In the allegorical narratives and performances of dispossession and healing that I will discuss, the devil is redeemed in marginal spaces as a potent social agent by marginal subjects who seek to articulate their dissenting views against material dispossession, social marginality, and political domination. By "allegory" I mean modes of narratives in which the characters and events are deployed to symbolize deeper or underlying meanings.[4]

By invoking the devil figure, marginal groups are able to simultaneously question centuries-old perceptions of social difference and contemporary realities of socioeconomic class relations and to critique dominant discourses of moralities that author such perceptions by legitimizing these class realities as based on divine truth and unquestionable ordainment. This chapter will reveal just one instance in which the critical deployment of the devil and narratives of possession and healing serve as a sociocultural mode of remembering and resisting domination in marginal social spaces. How was this done in this community? The potency of the devil figure, or *al-shaytan*, as it is locally known, in these narratives is very much related to its validation in the Holy Qur'an.[5] However, in Yemen as elsewhere, authority, religious or otherwise, may be contested.[6] Accordingly, disease-causing spirits and the rituals required for their amelioration are called *zār*, but the legitimacy of this phenomenon is disputed among practicing Muslims in Yemen, as will be explained. Yemenis and neighboring East Africans use the term *jinn* to refer to evil-dealing spirits, which exist as part of the zār pantheon.

Healers like Rahmah protect their co-workers in southern Yemen by engaging in healing performances that narrate resentment and resistance.[7] A comparable expression of mediated or questioned authority among the dispossessed was displayed by African women enslaved in the Americas. Teresa N. Washington refers to this as the concept of *aye*, a Yoruba word that describes a spiritual force thought to be inherent in Africana women such as Margaret Garner. According to Washington, it is the *aye* of Margaret Garner that is re-membered and re-embodied by Sethe, the Margaret Garner figure of Toni Morrison's imagination in *Beloved*.[8] Sethe's mother-in-law, Baby Suggs, the powerful, loving matriarch and preacher whom Washington calls "the quintessential *aye*," works to heal the community of the newly freed, calling them to the Clearing to "mend their spirits." This process reveals individual and collective powers hitherto unrecognized.[9] Sethe therefore is healed, forgiven, and sustained by the beloved community of believers who gather in the Clearing, a metaphorical, sacred space not unlike the one Rahmah creates for the patients she protects.

As enslaved Africans in America struggled for survival against "the financially motivated, sexually depraved, and morally bankrupt whims of their oppressors," according to Washington, *aye* mothers "returned the creations of their wombs to the tomb-like 'wicked bag' that holds destruction, creation, and re-creation." Margaret Garner teaches us that these tormented *aye* "are not destroying their progeny," but are, as Sethe remembers, putting them "where they'd be safe."[10]

## An Empire's Legacy: Contemporary Global Realities

The Delta of which I write is located about forty miles east of the historic port town of Aden in southern Yemen. It is a fertile valley that stretches across the two governorates of Abyan and Lahj and has contained the nation's leading fields for cotton and banana production since the 1950s. As is the case elsewhere in the lowland area in Yemen, annual rainfall is not reliable and fields are watered through tube-well irrigation and torrent floods that occur two or three times a year. After achieving independence from the British in 1968, South Yemen formed a socialist republic (The People's Democratic Republic of Yemen, or PDRY), which administered a succession of land reforms and nationalized the economy. Large, feudal-like estates were seized from local sultans by the socialist government and subsequently converted into state-run farms or cooperatives managed by previously landless peasants.[11]

The dams and canals that were left by the British were tremendously improved and new ones built by the region's new allies, the Soviet Union and China, during the Cold War era. Following the end of the Cold War and the fall of the Soviet Union, PDRY became politically and economically unified with the Yemen Arab Republic to form the Republic of Yemen. Four years later, a civil war between the North and South crushed Yemen's Socialist Party and asserted the dominance of North Yemen's conservative, tribalist regime.

A new land-based, capitalist class emerged in southern Yemen, composed of the old feudal lords of the pre-socialist era who have recently returned and been reinstated as the beneficiaries of International Monetary Fund economic reform policies consisting of liberalization, privatization, and structural adjustment measures that the country has adopted. Ironically, the socialist visions that built the dams and improved the colonial canals for historically dispossessed classes of peasants are currently benefiting the new capitalist Shaykhs and religious landlords of the post-socialist era.

Today, the Delta accommodates thousands of *feddans* of labor-intensive, privately owned commercial estates.[12] A mass of dispossessed and exploitable women, men, and their children work with minimum technology under harsh conditions[13] and reform policies that disadvantage them within the market economy.[14] Precarious working conditions include unprosecuted homicides carried out by paramilitary troops belonging to landlords to ensure the containment of any form of rebellion. Because men tend to leave, seeking better employment elsewhere, women, including those alluded to earlier, do the majority of the labor-intensive field work.

Except for the sporadic noise from the distant highways encircling the Delta villages and the scattered labor settlements around them, the green fields and the sound of the steady din of water pumps conjure up the façade of a languorous rural ambiance of serenity and simplicity. For decades, travel agents have capitalized on these images to lure European tourists to stop by for a dose of Arabian rural life on their way to the exotic eastern regions of the Hadramawt and the wondrous mud skyscrapers of Shibam. But a close look beneath this façade will quickly reveal intricate and all-too-familiar realities of material, social, and sexual exploitation based on class, race, and gender inequalities.

## Modernity and the Legacies of Slavery and a Culture of Inequality

The globally recognizable relations of marginality and exploitation in the Delta region of southern Yemen are hardly entirely the side effects of uncontrolled capitalist economic transformations that are currently sweeping the region. Nor can the realities of widespread and extreme marginality, intimidation, and economic hardships be explained simply on the basis of Third World colonial underdevelopment or contemporary North-South global inequalities or even lack of advanced technologies in the so-called Least Developed Countries (LDC), of which Yemen is a leading figure.[15]

Rather, the abysmal social realities of the Delta's mainly black, marginalized Yemeni people bespeak particular social histories and conditions of marginality that are shaped by local histories and realities of socioeconomic practices of slavery that were only "legally" outlawed in the 1960s but not socially eradicated, and identity politics that thrive as ancient caste-like practices of social categorization and find legitimacy within the otherwise overarching and purportedly egalitarian Islamic paradigm of social equality.[16] These centuries-old historical and social factors are translated within increasingly global capitalist production relations, the results of which may rationally appear to the uncritical observer as being class based.

Given the sociocultural complexity throughout their history, the majority of landless agricultural workforce in the Delta are identified as "non-Arab" people of African origin within an otherwise amalgam of larger and dominant clusters of social groups who collectively identify themselves as Arabs, signifying tribalists, *Saada* (those who trace their genealogies from Prophet Mohammed), and *Qudha* (a lineage whose males have historically specialized in Islamic jurisprudence, or *Fiqh*, and mostly serve as judges in the traditional court system based on customary laws, known as *'urf* ).[17] Within the Arab category, there is also a handful of occupational groups such as smiths and barbers, who endure low social status but nevertheless enjoy economic independence. Those identified as "non-Arabs" have darker complexions and generally identify themselves with regions such as Zabeed or Hajar.

All social groups in Yemen tend to be heterogeneous, including those identified as non-Arabs; those previously enslaved (or *'Abeed*);[18] *Al-Akhdam* (servants who are itinerant outcasts who inhabit society's most marginal end); and a much larger grouping, *Al-Hajour* (people from Wadi Hajar of the further southern region of the Hadhramout Valley). A common denominator of all those identified as non-Arabs is their inability to claim or guarantee access to land. Their landlessness puts them in a perpetually precarious situation of dependency within a politico-cultural economy that is largely agrarian and where control of land signifies both symbolic and material autonomy. Although landless, the Hajour generally work as seasonal or long-term sharecroppers for specific landlords.

The Delta's so-called non-Arab population started to increase exponentially during the 1950s, when cotton production was introduced by the British. Unlike earlier production of locally consumed grains that used locally available slave labor, large-scale cotton production demanded an intensive labor force beyond that available in the Delta. Additionally, fruit production, especially banana and papaya, was introduced by the colonial agricultural administration to feed not only the robust colonial representatives and administrators in the region but also the huge European expatriate business community based at the time in the coastal town of Aden. Despite the harshness of the work environment, the demand for wage-based, outside labor for both cotton and food production lured historically and culturally disfranchised groups from the highlands and lowlands of northern Yemen as well as the southern regions such as Wadi Hajar of the Hadhramout valley. The Delta provided the newcomers with a work opportunity, a haven from even harsher conditions elsewhere, and limited social mobility. The following astute observation, by one wise woman from the Hajour group, conjures up the sense of difference and liberation to which I am alluding: "As migrant Hujour, we were different from the slaves of the Delta region. Our fieldwork was harder and longer than that of the slaves because the slaves were close to the sultans (*mullak al-ardh*) and considered part of the household. But we were freer. We came and went as we pleased. At the end of harvesting seasons, sometimes we received part of the harvest, other times small wages barely enough to survive. For this reason, we were obliged to engage with more than one landlord at a time."

## Possession Narratives among Women as Allegories of Gendered Resistance

Among the residents of the Abyan valley, the devil, *al-shaytan*, and other entities, *jinn*, loom rampantly as tricksters. The impoverished laborers of the contemporary commercial estates circulate stories that say the fields hum with devil whisperers that loot human souls in a multitude of social encounters.

In these narratives, the devil can conquer deprived human bodies and broken spirits and manifest its authority through excruciating demands to which the victims must attend. If neglected, the devil may physically and mentally incapacitate the victims by causing severe depression (*ka'abah*), distress (*tafash* or *dhig al-nafas*), chronic fear and terror (*khowf wa ru'ub*), and a multitude of physical ailments such as muscle aches (*kasar*) and migraines (*waja'ra's*). In acute cases, partial paralyses diminish one's ability to get out of bed and go to work, leaving the victim unable to earn a living (*qut al-yowm*). A young, unmarried woman was said to have been so disabled by the devil that she could no longer work in the fields. Her loss of income further diminished her family's already meager income from the husband. Other times the devil may steal meager monthly food rations (*sibar*) from impoverished households at night. Fatima, a woman who had experienced possession, expressed her exasperation by pressing her palms in a quick, sliding gesture, which meant her hard-earned wages had lately been vanishing into thin air.

Beyond such damage to individuals, widely circulated narratives on the devil among the most marginalized of the Delta also relate a multitude of social injuries, thus making disintegration even more rampant. In all these cases, experiences of marginality and vestiges of poverty, including communal violence, antagonism, jealousy instigated by tensions over scarcity of resources, lack of privacy due to congestion, and physical exhaustion may all provide the context through which the devil may play a decisively negative role. Folks in these communities claim that the devil is directly linked to a host of crimes, creating mistrust among neighbors already broken by poverty and thus diminishing all possible developments of neighborly coalition and communal partnership. Others say that the devil causes friction between relatives, pushing already fragmented families into further disintegration. Another woman suspected that someone within her extended family circle had caused the misfortunes that afflicted her husband because he was earning more than his brother. "They consult the devil to cause you afflictions beyond repair," she explained. "The devil consumes them by filling their hearts with jealousy." In rare cases, possession victims have visions during which the devil can become a lewd figure exerting intolerable sexual demands, especially on its female victims. Through all these encounters, the devil can inflict upon its victims uncertainties and misfortunes that eventually lead to emaciation and diseases that annihilate not only the laboring body but also the social body.

What, then, are the individually and collectively sought remedies to offset this mighty and tyrannical evil force? Relief must be sought through various healing procedures, which may be inexpensive or costly but come with no guarantee of complete recovery. Women residing in the Delta may avail themselves of services to curb devil possession via healers who can summon and exorcise the demons. One easy but hardly effective form of recourse from devil intrusion is keeping handwritten verses from the Qur'an wrapped with transparent plastic and tying them with thin sewing threads kept close to visible parts of the victim's body, usually around one's neck or wrist. The plastic wrapping is to protect the verse from humidity. But this does not seem to succeed in protecting the poor against the malevolent forces of the devil. Burning resin gum incense just before dawn and dusk prayers at dwelling thresholds may also keep malevolent spirits at bay.

## Khadhra's Ordeal

In the house of Khadhra, a mother in her late thirties with four children, the activities of the devil had exceeded tolerable limits. Khadhra was timid and had very few friends. Her husband had deserted her a few years back. Until 1990, Khadhra and her husband had worked in a state-managed farm, and the family had lived comfortably. Things began to change when in the post-socialist era of privatization the state farm they worked for was reclaimed by its pre-revolutionary owner. Both lost their employment when the new owner downsized operations. Khadhra found work on another privatized farm, but her new employer took no responsibility for the family's health or other needs.[19] Her husband started to work as an independent porter in Zingubar market, but his income was not secure. Some days he came home with two hundred Riyals (about two dollars), but nothing for the next three days. To make ends meet, she started to sell bread that she baked with her fifteen-year-old daughter, who also took care of the household while Khadhra worked in the fields. With their incomes, the family was barely making ends meet. Things deteriorated further with the husband's departure and the news of her divorce.

Khadhra's biggest ordeal began just months after her husband's departure. She began to experience vivid night visions in which a Shaykh (a powerful or religious man) appeared. He demanded that Khadhra sprinkle herself with perfume every night before going to bed, at a time when her income was barely enough to feed her family of five. "I had hardly time to put my head on the pillow before the first cock woke us up again," she told me, "but this Shaykh was asking me to clean myself and put on incense."

She became increasingly troubled by her inability to comply with the unreasonable demands of the Shaykh-ly specter. Why, she asked herself, was he so insensitive to the realities of her hardship? Could he not see that she was already tormented by poverty and spousal abandonment? She did not have the money for the luxury that the Shaykh required. When she failed to meet his demands, the specter made her miserable by stealing food from her one-room mud house.[20] Some of her colleagues in the field suspected that the specter was a wandering spirit known as a zār and urged her to see a zār medium (*'alaqah*) who could help her control the Shaykh through a ritual called appeasement (*ridha'*). Among other activities, such mediums communicate with zār spirits and help those inflicted with zār to come to terms with their new status as "people inflicted with zār" (*nas ma'ahum zār*) by calming down the entity also through the appeasement process.[21]

Khadhra was too busy working several jobs to seek the advice of a zār medium. When the specter's demands became intolerable, however, and began to disrupt her daily activities, Khadhra decided to consult with Jum'ah, a female medium. Jum'ah had to determine not only the nature of the menacing spirit entity (whether zār, or non-zār) but also the particular category of zār spirit.

Khadhra's initial consultation with Jum'ah proved futile. After seeking to identify the Shaykh, the medium said the spirit was too powerful, that it transcended her authority as a medium. She said the Shaykh refused to talk to her because, like Khadhra, she was of slave descent.[22] Realizing that the belligerent Shaykh was not a zār spirit that she could control through a contractual appeasement, Jum'ah referred Khadhra to another authority, a devil exorcist.

Throughout her ordeal, Khadhra had suspected the Shaykh was a devil. Jum'ah's inability to control the belligerent Shaykh reaffirmed this suspicion. Khadhra then sought the help of a Sayyid, a religious Shaykh from the dominant social group (Saada). The man identified the specter as a devil trying to create doubts and uncertainties (*waswas*) so as to dissuade her from her duties as a Muslim woman. As a remedy, the healer prescribed a small piece of paper with verses from the Qur'an handwritten on it and sprinkled it with blessed water (*mai Zam Zam*).[23]

He recommended that she wear this close to her body before going to bed.[24] This calmed Khadhra, but only temporarily. Shortly thereafter, the specter reappeared, this time enraged that his victim desired to be freed from it. Upon his return, the spirit became even more demanding, this time making lewd, explicit demands. Khadhra then decided to seek a professional exorcist.

## Mabrouk the Exorcist

Mabrouk was a notorious exorcist who healed devil-possessed victims throughout the labor settlements. Like Khadhra, he was from a marginal social group and was equally impoverished. Neither versed nor knowledgeable about the Holy Qur'an and its widely contested interpretations, Mabrouk was a self-taught man who acquired his healing skills while undergoing torture in prison. Yet like many of the illiterate, marginal, middle-aged individuals with whom I became acquainted in southern Yemen, Mabrouk considered himself a devout Muslim. Typically, he explained the existence of the devil as a manifestation of a divine will that must be reckoned with. He also rationalized his exorcising power as a divine gift revealed to him as he had undergone severe physical torture that left one of his eyes constantly open, as if vigilant, enabling him to combat the maliciously potent conspiracy of the devil that others could not see.

Unlike the learned men who employ the Holy Text and the power of interpretation when healing sick bodies and broken spirits, Mabrouk utilizes the violence of interrogation and torture to extract confessions for wrongdoing. He literally beats the devil out of his patient's body. "I am in control only when the devil inhabits the human body. Outside this domain, he is the boss" (huwwa illi ya'mur), Mabrouk added. In other words, he has the authority to summon the devil only when the latter inhabits human bodies. This is a claim that clears him from the accusation that his skill is related to witchcraft and sorcery (sha'wada and sihir), which are said to involve entering freely into a pact with the devil to obtain personal benefits, a practice forbidden by Islam.

Mabrouk's method involves summoning the devil and engaging in a lengthy dialogue with him to get at the devil's reasons for conquering his victims' bodies with the ultimate purpose of freeing the victims of possession. Once summoned, the devil literally speaks through the tongue of his victim and details his reasons for possessing. Unlike the wandering spirits of the zār—which may represent a gamut of local social identities (for example, Shaykh, Sayyid, Khadim) and different nationalities (such as Arab, British [representing colonial officers], Ethiopian, Somali) who may speak in foreign tongues (yurtun)—the devil always speaks in Arabic and disguises himself as a powerful persona with authority. Apart from healing the (dis)possessed victim, the exorcist's job is to force the devil to reveal his "true" identity and confess his wrongdoing.

## On the Method of Summoning the Devil

A practical healer, Mabrouk does not claim to possess religious authority when healing. He employs little paraphernalia and observes short, preliminary procedures that do not involve the customarily ritualistic incense burning and recitations of verses from the Holy Qur'an that religious healers typically deploy. Nor does he use any assistants, family members or otherwise, as other famous healers do. On the contrary, his method crudely resembles police interrogations combined with pragmatic civil and criminal court procedures through which he subsequently reaches a verdict and prescribes punishment ('*iqab*) to the possessing devil and retribution (*jaza'*) to the possessed victim.[25]

Mabrouk's court-like theatricality involving confession and retribution can be appreciated once the context through which he acquired his power to heal devil possession is understood. When I inquired about how he obtained the power to heal without himself possessing *Baraka* (divinely ordained blessings that can heal and which is mainly associated either with individual Sayyids from a dominant social group or highly versed religious authorities), he explained in political terms: "Hunger generally allows one to see and know the truth" (*Al-maja'ah takhalli al-wahid yashuf wa ya'rif al-haqiiqah*). In this sense, Margaret Garner and the fictional Baby Suggs also assess ("see") the restrictions inherent in the system of slavery and resolve to free themselves, their children, and fellow enslaved from mental and physical bondage.[26]

In Mabrouk's case, his own exposure to torture while in police custody during which he confessed to stealing from his employer led to his transformation to a healer who appreciates the power of torture and confession. For this healer, torture—hence violence—delivered the earthly results that one with his power expects to hear and achieve. "Seeing injustice and the interrogation of the devil is not something one can teach," he explained to me one day after he had forced a possessing devil to confess his wrongdoing and subsequently chased him from the body of a young homosexual man: "[it is] something one acquires through experiences." The devil was pretending to be a "nasty Sultan," he expounded.

## Healing Khadhra

After Mabrouk took Khadhra's case, I was invited to sit in the summoning performance, which took place at Mabrouk's mud-house on a Friday afternoon after prayer. Fridays are religious days of specific prayers when the devil is extremely vulnerable. Those who die and are buried on Fridays are considered lucky ones. But Mabrouk's choice was based on his availability and that of his audience, whose testimony was crucial to the credibility, validation, and healing processes. When all of the participants arrived, the healer went straight to the process of summoning the devil culprit, acting simultaneously as chief police torturer, prosecutor, and judge who delivered the verdict. The possessed woman sat docilely in front of him on a lower seat. Next to him was a big stick, his only paraphernalia. He then commanded the unknown entity that possessed the woman to declare its presence through Khadhra's tongue. Initially, the woman remained silent. He repeated the process of commanding the possessing entity to reveal itself as follows:

"Confess to us: Who are you? Let yourself be known to us if you have the courage to face me and this audience." When he received no answer, he repeated his questions, this time raising his voice higher: "I ask you to come and face me. I know you are the devil."

When his questions yielded no answers, Khadhra's body began to tremble as she started to cry feebly as Mabrouk shouted in an even louder voice. After several vain attempts, he began to hit the woman with the stick steadily and with growing intensity. The process lasted a few minutes; the room filled with suspense punctuated by Mabrouk's screams, his beating on the woman's back with his stick, and Khadhra's whimper while the audience remained quiet. After several blows, the devil finally spoke (through Khadhra): "I am not a devil and stop calling me a devil because my name is Shaykh Muhsin. I am not from this place and I am not afraid of you."

Suddenly Khadhra's whimper ceased and she was no longer submissively stooped. Looking straight into the healer's eyes, she addressed him in a loud, clear voice that was uncharacteristic of her while her entire body stiffened, protruding with authority. She moved away from where she had been aloofly seated in front of the healer and into the center of the dirt floor of the mud room, this time facing the participants seated on pieces of old mats. Everyone in the room jerked back, aghast, as Khadhra moved through the room with her hands clasped behind her in an authoritative gesture that challenged everyone, smiling all the while with eyes wide open and lips tightly shut with transforming determination. She surveyed everyone in the room and suddenly pointed her finger at me, asking, "And who is this black one? Is she a man or woman?" Everyone giggled but me. It was not the first time that I had been singled out for mockery, especially with regard to my short hair. I had learned not to take such attacks personally but to accept these statements as expressions of uncertainties regarding my status as an outsider to the community. Here it was simply reaffirmed through the devil, albeit humorously.

Mabrouk, sensing that the summoned entity was stealing the scene, screamed a command: "Sit back where I asked you to sit. You are not called here to make jokes. You're here to answer my questions and to release this poor woman from your filthy demands. Tell us who you are! You are an immoral one (Inta 'adim al akhlaq')." Through Khadhra, the voice replied once again, this time standing closer to the seated healer and even more composed and challenging: "I have told you, I am a respectable Shaykh. Show some respect, you feces cleaner. Why are you calling me names? What do you want from me?" At this point Mabrouk, angry and heaping beatings on the woman, chased her, saying, "I want to know: what do you want from this poor woman? (*Eish tuba min hal miskinah?*). Why are you torturing her? Can't you see she has nothing to offer you? Can't you leave her alone? Can't you leave her home and body? Can't you let her earn her children's livelihood (rizq)?" This prompted the following exchange:

*Voice:* I have the power to control whomever I wish. I can make people do what I want them to do. This is my right as a mighty demon. It is a God-given power. I am a Shaykh and neither you nor anyone else can stop me.

*Mabrouk:* I am here not to obey your commands but to order you to reveal your real self and to ask you to leave this poor woman alone. If you are strong, as you claim, then what do you want with her? Why do you torment her? Why? Why? You devil (*Leysh ta'adhdhibha hal dhabhanah? Leysh? Leysh?*)," (hitting hit the woman with the stick every time he asked "Why?").

*Voice:* I don't care about your orders. My existence depends on controlling her and everyone. Stop calling me a devil. I am a respectable Shaykh. Respectable! Respectable! (*Muhtarim, Muhtarim*).

*Mabrouk:* You are wrong. I can stop you from harming this poor woman, and I demand you to leave her in peace. Leave her alone so she will be able to take care of her children. Leave her alone, and the food of her poor tiny children. Go away to where you came from. Confess you are wrong. Confess! Confess! (*I'tarif innak qaltan; I'tarif! I'tarif ya qaltan!*)

With this, Mabrouk hit the woman until she, or the devil, cried, "You are wrong. You are wrong. Shaykhs are not bad." To this, Mabrouk responded, "You are wrong. You are a liar. You are the devil. Confess. Confess." And finally the voice complied:

*Voice:* All right, all right, I confess. (*Khalas, Khalas, ba'taraf. Ma'ad ba'adhiha.*) I will not harm her again. I am wrong. I am wrong. I am bad. I am filthy. I won't hurt her again. I will leave her now. No More! No More! Never again! Forgiveness! Forgiveness! (*Tobah, Tobah, Al'afu! Al'afu!*).

With this last statement, the voice speaking through Khadhra began to weaken. In its place was, once again, her soft whimper. Within less than an hour, the woman had returned to her old, timid self and meek body. The lewd devil hiding behind the façade of a Shaykh was publicly exposed, lampooned, and chased away, promising he would leave the afflicted alone. But the devil is notorious for not keeping his promises. Indeed, as Mabrouk cautiously explained, breaking promises was one of the satanic attributes (*min sifat al-sheytan innoh la yufi bi wa'doh*). This may only be a temporary relief. There was no guarantee that the devil would not claim the poor woman's body again.

## Theorizing Possession and Possession Narratives

Mabrouk's seamless method of exorcising the devil, like that of many other marginal healers, may seem simple. His straightforward theatrical performance may even run the risk of seeming naïve and amateurish when compared to other forms of exorcism performances reported elsewhere. But surely it gives us pause. The creative deployment and subsequent lampooning of a religiously legitimated, mighty devil figure within a narrative of (dis)possession and healing performance cannot simply be taken as an instance of anthropologically observed cultural "enactment" of a shared belief system involving duping religious acceptance of supernatural powers. Rather, I suggest that these narratives and their deployment should be taken as an allegorical social text and performance that seeks to articulate a host of social issues and social relations and the tension resulting from a multitude of experiences of domination and marginality, including those pertaining to gender, sexuality, and class. In other words, possession narratives are allegorical social texts that do not just narrate social relations of power and experiences of domination and marginality, but, more important, they also present critical responses to such relations of domination and marginality. There are several layers of creative actions, both individual and collective, that work simultaneously here and need to be distinguished to appreciate them.

First, the devil as a religiously provided intermediary agent for social and moral wrongdoing can serve as a conduit of transgressions and absorb multiple meanings through which social relations of power (gender, sexual, class, religious, race) can be represented and subsequently condemned as immoral. The dominant discourse includes the authoritative constraints on faithful Muslims as expounded in the Qur'an and deploys the devil figure to construe the marginal as an immoral "Other."[27] For example, a very powerful and well-respected religious man who was also one of the most prominent landlords in the Delta once said to me, "Poverty neighbors blasphemy" (*Al-fuqru kufur*), suggesting that the propensity to commit immoral acts and to abandon one's faith are higher among the poor. Another said to me, "Poverty may be tantamount to the devil" (*kada al-fuqru an yakouna shaytan*), citing Omar ibn Al-Qattab, one of the Prophet Mohammed's closest disciples.

Within these narratives of possession, the religiously legitimated devil figure provides an equally legitimate opportunity for the poor to renounce social and economic inequality.[28] To this end, Khadhra could voice her dissent opinion against old and recent forms of poverty, exploitation, and marginality through the devil figure within possession narratives while still conforming to divine ordainment of accepting poverty. In such subversively creative action of blaming the devil to "speak," through her, she avoids the moral entrapments of the dominant discourses that condemn any dissent against poverty as immoral sentiments such as greed (*tama'*) and envy (*hasad*). In so doing, Khadra shifts away from her subjective self the social responsibility of breaching the religious moral codes against dissent. I will elaborate on this last point in later sections of this paper. By keeping their characters within the confines of a normatively bounded binary opposition of humans and nonhumans (and not social classes), such possession narratives and healing performances seem to operate within the normative boundaries set by dominant discourses, a conformity that renders these narratives and performances less radical responses to exploitation.

Class-consciousness aside, Khadhra's possession narrative provides an ethnographic window to appreciate yet another dimension of social relations of power pertaining to sexuality and gender. Yemen's dominant moral economy, based on perceptions of sexualities, race, caste-like descent, and genealogies, underlies a complex system of social identities. From the standpoint of this economy, Khadhra's biological sex as a female is irrelevant to her marginal social body, which is designated as "immoral." She is therefore exempt from adhering and/or aspiring to the moral codes of modesty (in this case veiling, segregation, and confinement) in a society where the rules of modesty are considered prerequisite to demanding and achieving honor and respectability as a male or female. Tautologically, Khadhra's ability to transgress segregation (her ability to work outside the house in a male space) is also the reason for her status of "immorality" within which she is forced to accept the reality of the sexual demands of her landlord Sheikh or other persons with authority over her. In this moral economy, acceptance of sexual demands by a woman marked as immoral does not lead to contradictions within the otherwise strict moral codes of modesty of the dominant morality, which forbids heterosexual practices outside marriage contracts. Implicit in Khadhra's narrative of possession by the lewd Shaykh, however, is not only a refusal to categorize her body as immoral but also a critique of power and domination (physical, social, and economic). To explain, her refusal of the Shaykh's lewd demands in her night visions bespeaks of the moral contradictions in her society and can be interpreted as not just a subjective consciousness of class but also a subjective refusal of gender and sexual domination.

In other words, possession narratives and performances, in addition to their qualities as critical social comments (against inequality and detrimental social difference), provide a psycho-social setting for catharsis and redemption. The performances are emotionally charged, dramatic, and comic spaces for voicing social grievances. They also allow for momentary relief from cumulative tensions from resented social inequalities and ensuing material hardships. The crying and laughter of the improvised public healing sessions are reminiscent of Baby Suggs's ministering to her congregation in the Clearing in *Beloved*, in that both improvisations result in critical, yet momentary relief.

Furthermore, the cathartic potency of this healing space occurs as a face-to-face—albeit enacted—reconciliation with forces of oppression that are otherwise unfeasible in everyday life. Hence for the healing performances to come to fruition, a confession of ill-doing must be obtained from the possessing entity and clemency granted by the afflicted. Fruition in this case does not necessarily mean getting rid of the menacing spirit but acceptance of peaceful cohabitation. Healing performances are open to the afflicted community of neighbors, friends, and relatives whose presence is essential for the healing to occur, and the presence of an audience validates the collective will to allegorically voice individual and collective resentments against inequality while metaphorically locating the perpetrator of their inflictions. It is allegorical because the contestation of worldly poverty suggests impious challenges to a divine will that ordains fate and destiny *(naseeb)*.

## A Will to Power

The complexity of these narratives of devil possession lies in their propensity to become social texts that can be appropriated by both dominant and marginal classes. Given the validation of the devil figure as an indubitable immoral force, a reading legitimized by the Holy Qur'an, the devil enjoys a central social position similar to that of a sponge absorbing a multitude of meanings. The devil succeeds over his victims when they have failed to show strong moral values: piety *(taqwa)* and full trust in God. Such authoritative validation of the devil as the ultimate "evildoer" allows the demon figure to become accessible to and appropriable not only by dominant moralities but also by marginal agencies. Dominant moralities appropriate this divine ordainment by declaring poverty, and hence marginality, as a fragile social condition that permits the devil to conquer the spirit of the impoverished human *(min madakhil al-shaytan)*. On the other hand, marginal agents consciously represent the devil as aspiring to be part of the dominant class that they critically lampoon as the devil.

Globally, women from marginal social groups seem to excel in this effort, whether in the context of contemporary expressions of Islam in Yemen or historical expressions of Christianity during the enslavement era in the United States. Recall Khadhra's ability to vacillate between her roles as the devil and the good Shaykh, giving Mabrouk the healer the chance to further lampoon the Shaykh by calling him names. Recall, too, Khadhra's insistence on refusing the lewd demands of the Shaykh that appears to her as a specter at night. In her visions, she can refuse him, but in reality, she is like many other marginal women, who may not be in a position to reject such demands and often fall victim to them.[29]

Thus, I suggest that these narratives of possession can be interpreted as "a will to power" recovered from the dominant group by those on the edge of society. In this endeavor, they seek to liberate marginal bodies from the grip of the dominant morality and its consequences of inequality and economic marginality. Like an iconoclastic philosophy with its own will, these narratives seek to contradict the truth claim of the dominant moral discourse and its authority.

Besides the obvious effects of cathartic relief, one may rightly argue that there is little effective political resistance in these narratives and performances of possession and healing. The entertaining spirit of the healing performance may be appealing to its audience as comic relief for interrupting the cumulative tension from pernicious relations of power. The dialogues between the possessed and the healer may be humorous amid a tragic situation. But outside the social circle of its audience, the comic scene can take a different life where, in Henri Bergson's words, it may "continue in successive rumblings, like thunder in a mountain."[30] At the same time, one cannot ignore the collective consciousness that is conjured up in the coming together of patient, healer, and audience (comprising an afflicted community) for the implied purpose of questioning collective experiences of poverty. The possessed may act at times as a comic or fool. But surely the meaning of this laughter and the sublime purpose of the possessed comic cannot be limited to what Bergson insightfully calls a "momentary anesthesia of the heart."[31] Like the intelligence that Bergson observes as the appeal of comic spirits, the possessed in devil performances also appeal to a certain intelligence, both within and outside of the close social circle in marginal social spaces.

In the Delta of southern Yemen, religious authorities and those who assign themselves the responsibility of moral policing have continuously decried the preponderance of devil possession and healing performances in marginal social spaces as a sign of moral decay, if not the absence of morality altogether. Within authoritative circles, possession performances are feared, despite their marginal location, as a treacherous liaison that subverts social cohesion. The everyday reality of the fierce reactions from religious authorities, state officials, medical experts, and Islamic extremist groups who condemn these narratives and performances through public media as un-Islamic (bida') and vestiges of ignorance suggest that the cacophonies of these staged activities are not lost on the intelligence of these authorities.

A final word of caution: What I have tacitly celebrated as creative resistance and a marginal will to power may actually have adverse effects that undermine the intents of its agencies. While the attempt to heal possession may offer a creative, momentary liberation of the marginal from the grips of domination and the religious validation of such domination, these efforts may also adversely validate the claims of the very moral authority that they seek to challenge. Thus, when pro-slavery forces interpreted Margaret Garner's act of infanticide as a manifestation of deranged barbarianism (rather than liberation), they thereby reinforced the slaveholders' moral views of the enslaved as nonhuman savages. The views of religious moral authorities in Southern Yemen are likewise reinforced by their condemnation of possession healing performances as un-Islamic practices of concordance with the devil.[32]

While these narratives and performances of possession successfully voice collective resentments toward domination and may succeed in destabilizing established moral authorities and codes, the preponderance of the devil figure in marginal spaces may only reinforce the claims of dominant discourses that attribute immorality to these marginal spaces. Like most acts of defiance, the critical and creatively cathartic narratives and performances run the risk of carrying adverse and often contradictory effects that will continue to provide a rationale for violent moral domination.

## NOTES

1. Spirit possession is a widely researched topic. As Janice Boddy has argued, "Possession cuts a broad swath through Asia, Africa, Afro-America, and Latin America, with some incidence in Oceania and historical and contemporary (chiefly Mediterranean) Europe." Janice Boddy, "Spirit Possession Revisited: Beyond Instrumentality," *Annual Review of Anthropology* 23 (1994): 409. However, the particularity of the political manifestation of this phenomenon in Yemen and linking it to a wider context of resistance to slavery and marginality from a global perspective is a more recent approach.

2. The Yemeni currency, the Riyal, had seen severe depreciation that year. One U.S. dollar was equivalent to 95 Yemeni Riyal in 1996.

3. In the context of a dominant ethnographic representation of Yemen that accepts the image and lifestyle of women from dominant classes as the culturally authentic image, this chapter and its portrayal of the experiences of women from marginal social classes will challenge such depictions as a reproduction of dominant moralities. For a longer discussion of this trend in ethnographic representation that undermines the experiences and realities of different social groups, especially of women's lifestyles in Yemen, see Huda Seif, "Moralities and Outcasts: Domination and Allegories of Resentment in South Yemen" (PhD diss., Columbia University, 2003).

4. In my effort to interpret the social meaning of circulating possession narratives as the nexus of resentment in marginal spaces, I have been inspired by (and borrowed heavily from) different theoretical sources: Paul de Man, *Allegories of Reading: Figural Language in Rousseau, Nietzsche, Rilke, and Proust* (New Haven, Conn.: Yale University Press, 1979); Paul de Man, "Dialogue and Dialogism," *Poetics Today* 4, no. 1 (1983): 99–107; Mikhail Bakhtin, "Discourse in the Novel," in *The Dialogic Imagination: Four Essays*, trans. Michael Holquist and Caryl Emerson (Austin: University of Texas Press, 1981); Augusto Boal, *Theatre of the Oppressed*, trans. Charles A. Mcbride and Maria-Odilia Leal McBride (London: Pluto, [1979] 1993); and Henri Bergson, *Laughter: An Essay on the Meaning of the Comic*, trans. Cloudesley Brereton and Fred Rothwell (New York: Macmillan, 1912) have all inspired me

to read allegorized narratives launched at marginal spaces as social texts and prompted me to dwell on both the political context within which they are deployed and the class-informed intentions of the narrators. In addition to Toni Morrison's transcendental work, equally inspiring have been the seminal works of Margaret Atwood (*Lady Oracle*, 1976), Doris Lessing (*Children of Violence*, 1952), and Virginia Woolf (*The Waves*, 1931). All these authors have utilized the dialogical process allowed by the novel or novella as a textual/narrative means for asserting the subjective voices of the otherwise marginal self.

5. Here, the category *shaytan* is often used interchangeably with *jinn*. Although the two are closely intertwined as well as distinguishable, it is useful to highlight the fact that both entities are invoked interchangeably and in contradistinction to the human category or *al-ins*. Within the Qur'anic literature, the *shaytan* category, especially *Iblis*, is depicted as a fallen angel that God has thrown out of heaven because he refused to worship Adam (the first man). The *jinn* category is a more ambivalent entity, often invisible, that God has created in opposition to the visible *ins*. The two entities are invoked when one wants to talk about supernatural figures, as opposed to human ones.

6. For a discussion of a selective appropriation of the enslavers' symbolic power by enslaved people who then created their own competing traditions, see Vincent Brown, "Spiritual Terror and Sacred Authority: The Power of the Supernatural in Jamaican Slave Society," in *New Studies in the History of American Slavery*, ed. Edward E. Baptist and Stephanie M. H. Camp (Athens: University of Georgia Press), 180.

7. These women also lead an everyday lifestyle that may or may not conform to certain previous ethnographic depictions with respect to veiling practices and sex segregation, for example. Despite their invisibility in the ethnographic record, women such as Rahmah who occupy the nether end of Yemen's social hierarchy have supported their families for generations.

8. These spiritually endowed beings are discussed in Teresa N. Washington, "The Mother-Daughter Àjé Relationship in Toni Morrison's *Beloved*," *African American Review* 39, no. 1/2 (2005): 171–88.

9. Ibid., 175.

10. Ibid., 174–75. Traditionally, the spiritual power of *aye* can be transmitted genetically from mother to daughter. In Jamaica Kincaid's *Autobiography of My Mother*, a perfect union envelopes mother and daughter, a spiritual and metaphysical merging so complete that the unnamed daughter reflects, "I could not see where she left off and I began, or where I left off and she began." The physicality of this fusion meant that "I fit perfectly in the crook of my mother's arm, on the curve of her back, in the hollow of her stomach." In this way, it can be understood, as Morrison underscores, that the act of women who rescued their children by killing them was akin to a mother killing herself.

11. For accounts on similar histories of political transformation and trajectories in northern Yemen, see Sheila Carapico, *Civil Society in Yemen: The Political Economy of Activism in Modern Arabia* (New York: Cambridge University Press, 1998) and "The Economic Dimensions of Yemeni Unity," *Middle East Report* 184:9–14 ; Helen Lackner, *P.D.R. Yemen: Outpost of Socialist Development in Arabia* (London: Ithaca, 1985); Brinkley Morris Messick, *The Calligraphic State: Textual Domination and History in a Muslim Society* (Berkeley: University of California

Press, 1993); R. B. Serjeant, "South Arabia" in *Commoners, Climbers and Notables: A Sampler of Studies on Social Ranking in the Middle East*, ed. C. A. O. Nieuwenhuijze (Leiden: Brill, 1977); Stephen Day, "Updating Yemeni National Unity: Could Lingering Regional Divisions Bring Down the Regime?" *Middle East Journal* 62, no. 3 (2008): 417; Ahmed Mohamed Shuja'a Al-Deen, Abdo Ali Othman, and Abdullah Ali Al-Ghuly, "Socio-Economic and Demographic Study of Marginal Groups and Social Strata in the Four Main Cities in Yemen," Ministry of Development, CSO (1997).

12. Since December 2010, massive prodemocracy movements, labeled the Arab Spring, have swept the political landscape in the Middle East Arab countries. In the Republic of Yemen, this has brought a sea change that ended the three-decade rule of the regime of President Ali Saleh. Despite these radical changes, however, the socioeconomic situation in the Delta remains unchanged. It is still too early to predict the ramifications of these political changes in relation to agricultural workers in general and minorities in particular. *Feddan* is a nonmetric unit of area commonly used in the Middle East measuring approximately 0.42 hectares or 1.038 acres.

13. Deadly forms of cerebral malaria and diarrhea, severe malnutrition, and a host of diseases have all maintained high rates of infant mortality and premature deaths.

14. The use of both minimum technology and intensive human labor are among the most common structural adjustment measures recommended for economic development in many Third World countries. The IMF's structural adjustment measures purposefully downplay technology to promote the capitalization of an abundant labor supply, which is kept unprotected to ensure that it remains cheap and exploitable.

15. For a similar argument, see Jeffrey Sachs, *The End of Poverty: Economic Possibilities for Our Time* (New York: Penguin, 2005).

16. This egalitarianism applies to ethnic and racial differences within Muslim communities. It does not extend to equality between men and women and between Muslims (believers) and non-Muslims or Dhimis (nonbelievers within or under the jurisdictions of an Islamic State).

17. The social identities of the last two groups are largely maintained via an endogamous marriage practice with varying degrees of severity. For example, the Saada strictly limit marriage to others within the same group, whereas intermarriages among those in other dominant Arab groups may occur.

18. Freed slaves are still labeled *'Abid*, or slave, in Yemen. In the Arabic lexicon, a black person is referred to as *zingi* (Negro), a term used synonymously with slave. I have observed that the synonymy is so normalized that it does not raise any concern in most parts of the modern Arab-speaking world where I have lived or visited, including Jordan, Kuwait, and Saudi Arabia.

19. Some of the benefits that the socialist era of the late seventies and eighties included were free comprehensive healthcare and education for all. Many Southerners reflect back on this era with extravagantly expressed nostalgia and regret that people never appreciated the system enough.

20. This story in which the Shaykh steals is in itself a contradiction to the social qualities that Shaykhs in the society actually claim, including honesty, kindness, virtuousness, and the like.

21. The term *zār*, with only slightly altered pronunciation of the letter *z*, is shared by many different languages, including Arabic, Amharic, and Somali. Janice Boddy argues that the term is thought to have a Persian or more "plausibly" Amharic derivation rather than Arabic. See Janice Boddy, *Wombs and Alien Spirits: Women, Men, and the Zār Cult in Northern Sudan* (Madison: University of Wisconsin Press, 1989), 131–32. With variations, belief in *zār* or possession is also found among practitioners of Christianity, Candomble, and Voodoo. See also Boddy, "Spirit Possession Revisited," 415. For a discussion of a more individualized, less communal, but also African-derived practice of Obeah, see Margarite Fernández Olmos and Lizabeth Paravisini-Gebert, eds., *Sacred Possessions: Vodou, Santería, Obeah, and the Caribbean* (New Brunswick, N.J.: Rutgers University Press, 1997), 6.

22. Here descent matters since it refers to a social interaction. But both the *zār* and devil possession inflict all. Religious authorities, however, do not recognize the *zār* spirit, whereas the Devil's existence and ability to cause trouble to humans is explicitly articulated in the Qur'an to which all classes of social categories of Muslims adhere.

23. Water that is brought back by pilgrims who visited the Prophet's tomb in Saudi Arabia.

24. A verse from the Holy Qur'an is commonly recited as a source of tranquility for those afflicted with nightmares.

25. The distinction between a positive law and a normative order here is arguable, since both are human and therefore socially constructed despite the fact that the latter is purportedly based on divine authoritative sources such as the Qur'an and *hadith* (Prophet's sayings). Although an argument of this sort is valuable, it falls beyond the scope of this discussion and my expertise. Mabrouk did not suggest any knowledge on the established distinctions made between a "normative" Shari'a law and a positive law (*qanun*). Suffice to say here that from my observations in southern Yemen, divine order or shari'a were deployed to legitimize causes such as protecting private ownership of prominent landlords, just as the *qanun* (positive law) was invoked to discredit religious authorities. For an anthropological understanding of issues pertaining to Yemen's legal history, see Messick, *Calligraphic State*, 133–200.

26. See Barbara Schapiro, "The Bonds of Love and the Boundaries of Self in Toni Morrison's *Beloved*," *Contemporary Literature* 32, no. 2 (Summer 1991): 200–201; David Lawrence, "Fleshly Ghosts and Ghostly Flesh: The Word and the Body in *Beloved*," *Studies in American Fiction* 19 (1991): 189–201; Deborah Horvitz, "Nameless Ghosts: Possession and Dispossession in *Beloved*," *Studies in American Fiction* 17, no. 2 (1989): 157–68.

27. For a more detailed understanding of this "othering" process, see Seif, "Moralities and Outcasts."

28. Continuing Bakhtin's metaphor of the underground, it can be argued that the devil metaphor within narratives of possession in healing spaces provides a social text through which both healers and patients can come together for the purpose of weaving an underground dialogical instance where the authoritative world can be creatively interrogated and condemned as demonic and immoral. In this context, the immoral devil figure within narratives of possession seeks to relocate a supposedly normative inequality and social difference by shifting them from an undisputable divine realm into a dialogical social realm where it can be contested as a class issue. Marginal healers, in short, together with their patients, successfully create a healing space that sanctions a dialectical tension reflecting

conflicts in society that rise through personal misfortunes, hardship, and temporary possession. In so doing, these healers and patients allow, albeit at the edge of society, inequality to be dialogically adjudicated.

29. In the settlement where I lived, there was a beautiful young woman named Asma. She was married to her cousin, who was a garbage collector in Aden. Asma had four children who ranged in age from one to six and was the only one not working in the fields like her parents and her three sisters. Everyone in the settlement believed that only the eldest of Asma's four children belonged to her husband. On the contrary, everybody knew that the other three were the spitting image of her employer's son, a big landlord and a descendant from one of the previous sultan families in the area. Although ashamed silently, Asma never admitted this and decided to benefit from the situation by being able to stay home and look after her children while all her sisters and friends labored long hours under the scorching sun in the field. To my surprise, her husband pretended nothing had happened and went about his life. He was simply not in a position to "protect" his family's honor. He also dealt with the situation by constantly being absent from the settlement under the pretense of work demands in Aden.

30. Bergson, *Laughter*, 5.

31. Ibid., 6.

32. See Delores M. Walters's introductory chapter in this volume. Under nineteenth-century Christianity, pro- and anti-slavery views co-existed—the latter condemning slavery as a brutal, evil system, the former condoning slavery as a civilizing influence.

# CHAPTER 8

# RESURRECTING CHICA DA SILVA

## Gender, Race, and Nation
in Brazilian Popular Culture

*Raquel L. de Souza*

On April 28, 2008, I spent the day translating for the prominent Black Brazilian film-maker, Joel Zito Araújo, who was finalizing his documentary *Cinderellas, Wolves, and Prince Charming*, detailing the intricate networks of the sexual tourism indus-try.[1] Araújo's film reveals a pattern in which white European men travel to Brazil in order to fulfill their sexual desires and fantasies, more often than not with women of African descent. The Afro-Brazilian women and male homosexuals Araújo in-terviews state that through their participation in sex tourism they are enabled by

Figure 8.1. Press photo from *Xica da Silva* (1981), starring Zeze Motta and Walmor Chagas, directed by Carlos Diegues. A Unifilm/Embrafilme release.

their foreign suitors to acquire material goods and enjoy leisure and entertainment activities that they would otherwise not be able to afford. The implication is that such activities are almost exclusively the domain of middle- and upper-class white Brazilians. Current-day racial hierarchies that are central to Araújo's documentary are rooted in the distant past. He depicts the inherent intricacies of sexual encounters and/or resistance to sexual violence occurring within disparate power relationships. Araújo's documentary highlights the complexity of discussing agency for Black women who are in subordinate positions to their male partners. Modern-day sexual and/or romantic relationships occurring between partners of highly unequal socioeconomic power is an especially relevant framework from which to view the resistance of Chica da Silva, the daughter of an enslaved Afro-Brazilian woman and a white Portuguese nobleman, who lived in eighteenth-century Minas Gerais.

## Resisting Bondage: Challenging Conventional Notions of Black Female Resistance

Since the beginning of colonization, women of African descent have developed and utilized a variety of strategies to resist white supremacy, sexism, homophobia, and other forms of oppression and exploitation. These strategies of resistance, despite their significance in shedding light on the lives of enslaved women, have yet to be adequately investigated. To speak of agency in the context of the forced migration of Africans and subsequent bondage within a system marked by highly unequal power relationships is indeed a challenge. Yet it is crucial to invest in developing alternative frameworks that expand the most common understandings of resistance to include recognition that men and women of African descent have not passively acquiesced to their enslavement and exploitation.[2] Rather than render Africans and their descendants, particularly Black women, into passive subjects who submit to their inferiorized positioning and are incapable of challenging those who exploit and deprive them of their humanity, I seek an alternative framework that transforms our marginalized and objectified status within mainstream narratives so that Black women become protagonists of their own history.

This chapter contextualizes an alternative to narratives of Black passivity and lack of agency through a critical analysis of mainstream media portrayals of the historical character of Chica da Silva. She was an enslaved woman born in eighteenth-century Brazil who obtained manumission and socioeconomic ascendance through her involvement with a very wealthy Portuguese man who was sent to the interior of the State of Minas Gerais to oversee the exploration of diamond mines. Chica guaranteed her survival and the well-being of her offspring through her association with the diamond contractor. Faced with few alternatives for economic stability, her association with a "benefactor" might still be interpreted as a choice to commodify her body. I believe, however, that Chica's resistance to subjugation warrants a more complex assessment.

I contend that mythologies surrounding racial slavery and race relations in Brazil, which were fomented by slaveholders and perpetuated by social scientists and intellectuals, have provided the framework that many Brazilian artists have employed in developing carnival themes and composing songs, theater plays, a major movie production, and a soap opera about the history of this eighteenth-century enslaved woman. These portrayals in Brazil simultaneously embody and are informed by continuing discourses about slavery, race, race relations, and sexuality that emanated during Chica da Silva's lifetime more than 250 years ago. Within a perspective that seeks to challenge mainstream narratives about Black female resistance, Chica's relationship with a nobleman who was a Portuguese government representative should be viewed as an act of resistance by an enslaved Black woman who took charge of her own destiny, her body, and her sexuality in order to survive. By using her body, a valuable commodity in colonial Brazil, she freed herself from bondage and was able to obtain power and prestige. Yet today her resistance is trivialized in mainstream media and popular culture.

My analysis of the historical character of Chica da Silva is intended to unveil and challenge stereotypical depictions of her in contemporary culture. To this end, I focus on her representation in the 1976 movie *Xica da Silva*,[3] directed by Cinema Novo director Carlos Diegues, providing a critique of Diegues's appropriation of her life history to fit a particular political and ideological agenda. Stuart Hall's analysis of the role played by the construction of stereotypes illuminates key elements of such intellectual projects: "Power, it seems, has to be understood . . . not only in terms of economic exploitation and physical coercion, but also in broader cultural or symbolic terms, including the power to represent someone or something in a certain way—within a certain 'regime of representation.' It includes the exercise of symbolic power through representational practices. Stereotyping is a key element in this exercise of symbolic violence."[4]

Like Margaret Garner, Chica da Silva is the subject of fictional works—in da Silva's case, an opera, a soap opera, and a film—that make statements about slavery and the lengths to which enslaved women went to resist bondage. Rather than accurately portraying historical facts, however, these works tell stories that are meant to be larger than the woman herself, as they are depicted to fit particular narratives and political agendas, often embodying the aspirations of competing interest groups. In both cases, while there is scant historical information that conveys the viewpoints of these two women, portrayals of Margaret Garner and Chica da Silva in ahistorical mainstream media adaptations, especially film, have an enormous impact on how they are interpreted as historical figures. As cultural critic and feminist theorist bell hooks observes, "Movies do not merely offer us the opportunity to re-imagine the culture we most intimately know on the screen, they make culture."[5] In both instances, the women's names are used for the titles of the fictional works and the protagonists' significance is remembered and partially restored. Chica da Silva's image, however, is intentionally distorted, as I shall demonstrate. This anthology brings together feminist/womanist narratives of women's resistance to oppression, but I must offer one cautionary note to the reader. Juxtaposing the narrative of Margaret Garner in relation to women in other colonized and enslaved realities who chose violence as a means of dialogue and resistance to violent and oppressive regimes with Chica's choice to associate herself with a representative of the Portuguese crown, seemingly becoming the subject/object of exotic/erotic consumption, presents a dilemma. This quandary has to do with whether Black women's resistance is defined narrowly as choosing death as the only dignified act of resistance or whether seeming acquiescence and passivity can be framed as a technique for survival and an opposition to subjugation. Oversimplified perceptions of resistance strategies reduce the radical interventions made by these women to a neat, hierarchical resolution, which ultimately is inadequate. Moreover, framing resistance within an easy dichotomy between respectable and admirable behavior versus hyper-sexualized trading of one's own body and surrendering to colonial objectification may distract the reader from understanding the nuances of deliberate and conscious processes of personal and social transformation that Chica da Silva, Margaret Garner, Sally Hemings, Elizabeth Clark Gaines, and others embarked upon in their liberatory struggles.[6]

Support for a complex perception of acts of resistance is found in the analysis of violence, home, and community by Nancy Jesser, who describes Toni Morrison's *Beloved* as "a meditation on transformations of the body and soul . . . [a] simultaneous working through of history and memory by describing bodies and social structures . . . dwellings and places the characters move through and escape to . . . making possible the gatherings and joinings necessary for emancipatory struggles."[7] Chica, like other women resisters analyzed in this collection, made strategic and tactical choices of multiple self-representations within the oppressive and exclusive colonial structures of the African Diaspora. She was determined to create the necessary places of survival while simultaneously negotiating the spaces of colonial self-indulgent preoccupation with the exotic. This anthology of gendered resistance to the regimes of colonization and its attendant institution of slavery invites the reader to witness personal and social transformations that are made visible through the analyses of the life histories and emancipatory struggles of women engaged in multiple forms of resistance as an expression of their fundamental right to self-determination and ultimately freedom.[8]

## Chica da Silva: The History of a Myth

Chica da Silva was born in Diamantina in the Brazilian state of Minas Gerais sometime between 1731 and 1735, though many questions about her life remain unanswered in early-eighteenth-century legal documents. In *Chica da Silva and the Diamond Contractor: The Other Side of the Myth*,[9] Brazilian historian Júnia Furtado uses a wide range of documentation gathered from archives in Brazil, Portugal, and the United States. Tracing back the presence of Chica da Silva in popular culture in Brazil, Furtado found that a lawyer from the former Arraial do Tejuco, a city now known as Diamantina, was the first to write about her life. Joaquim Felicio dos Santos was the assigned lawyer in charge of handling the papers regarding João Fernandes's inheritance in 1853. He had access to a vast amount of documents and registered oral testimonies pertaining to Chica. Santos later published a book, *Memórias do Distrito Diamantino* (*Memories of the Diamantino District*), in 1868, wherein he dedicated a chapter to the history of Diamantina to Chica and to those who were a part of her world.[10] This book by Santos gave visibility to Chica da Silva, who was then cited by other writers such as famous Brazilian poet Cecília Meireles.

Furtado examined court records, census data, museum collections, church records, traveler's reports, and other sources in order to contextualize the historical background in which the popular culture icon of Chica da Silva was created. Although Furtado's goal is to establish the historical context in which she reveals the discrepancies between the historical record and Chica's portrayal in mainstream media, she does not provide a theoretical framework that uncovers the interconnectedness of gender, race, class, and sexuality as intersecting categories that have framed Black women's experiences within various historical contexts. Such an intersectional approach is also crucial in an examination of the stereotypical representations of Black women and historical characters such as Chica da Silva. In other words, a Black feminist critique of such distortions is a perspective that may greatly enhance Furtado's analysis.

Furtado's research demonstrates that in 1753, João Fernandes de Oliveira, a member of a noble Portuguese family, arrived in Arraial do Tejuco, in the northeast of Minas Gerais. He had been sent by the Portuguese crown to Brazil to administer the mining of diamonds on lands that had recently been acquired by his father because early in the eighteenth century, Portuguese settlers encountered gold and later diamonds and other precious stones in Minas Gerais.[11] As a contractor, João Fernandes represented both his family's interests and those of the government in Portugal. In that same year, João Fernandes purchased the enslaved woman Chica from her previous enslaver, although there is no official documentation of his motivations for purchasing her. Furtado states that usually slaveholders in Minas Gerais did not grant manumission right after purchasing an individual; usually only the enslaved who were very close to their enslavers would be freed, and only through a will that would be effective only after the slaveholder's death. Nonetheless, available data show that the *contratador de diamantes* (diamond contractor) granted Chica her manumission a few months later. Elaborating on such developments is a rather challenging enterprise; as Hortense Spillers asserts about the dilemma of discussing and theorizing about relationships that unfold within the context of slavery and bondage, "Whether or not the captive female and/or the sexual oppressor derived 'pleasure' from their seductions and couplings is not a question we can politely ask. Whether or not 'pleasure' is possible at all under conditions that I would aver as non-freedom for both or either of the parties has not been settled."[12]

Furtado states that in eighteenth-century Minas Gerais, upper-class women were expected to raise large families.[13] Even though Chica da Silva did not enjoy the social status that would allow João Fernandes to legally marry her,[14] they had thirteen children who later inherited a great portion of João Fernandes's wealth. According to historical records, in 1770, after seventeen years of living in Arraial do Tejuco and maintaining a stable relationship with Chica da Silva, João Fernandes was forced to return to Portugal to administer his father's estate and handle legal matters for his family.

Furtado highlights that Chica's mothering of such a large family is in sharp contrast to the Xica da Silva character whose image has been made popular through carnival parades, poems, plays, soap operas, and Diegues's movie. There, Chica is presented as an over-sexualized, extravagant, careless, and carefree woman—as a lascivious "man-eater," according to Furtado.[15] The movie directed by Carlos Diegues makes no reference to Chica's many sons or daughters. Her image is completely dissociated from motherhood and the responsibilities and caring that are usually associated with parenting, which likely would have brought some redemption to her negative depiction.

Evidence that Chica is typically depicted negatively is seen, for instance, in the movie, where the viewer becomes acquainted with Chica before she meets João Fernandes through her relationship with one of her master's sons. He walks around the backyard, calling Chica for another sexual encounter by producing sounds utilized to gather chickens. She is therefore portrayed as analogous to the farm's animals, or as some "thing" whose basic instincts prevail over rationality. There is no doubt that referencing a woman in this manner is a rather pejorative and offensive attitude—particularly in light of the fact that a chicken in Brazilian slang usually refers to a woman who sleeps around indiscriminately.

## (Mis)Representing Chica: The Historical Figure and the Popular Culture Icon

By the twentieth century, Chica had achieved mythological status. In the 1950s, Diamantia gained greater prominence in the national imagination when Juscelino Kubitscek, who had been born there, became Brazil's president, and the mansion where Chica da Silva and João Fernandes had resided was later chosen as a site of memory by the federal government in an effort to preserve historical and cultural sites in Brazil. In 1953, renowned Brazilian poet Cecília Meireles dedicated a poem to Chica da Silva in her book, *O Romanceiro da Inconfidência* (translated as *Ballads of the Conspiracy*), which discusses historical figures, wealth, and freedom in colonial Minas Gerais.[16]

In 1958, playwright Antonio Callado wrote a play entitled *O Tesouro de Chica da Silva* (*The Treasure of Chica da Silva*).[17] Then in 1963, Chica was chosen by Salgueiro, one of the several samba schools in Rio de Janeiro, as its theme for the carnival parade.[18] In 1976, director Carlos Diegues, inspired by the theme developed in the Salgueiro's carnival parade, transformed Chica's life in eighteenth-century colonial Minas Gerais into a comedy film, *Xica da Silva*, which around eight million spectators watched in the first few months after its release. In 1996, the TV network Manchete brought this historical character back to the limelight in a soap opera entitled *Chica da Silva*, written by Walcyr Carrasco and José de Carvalho, and produced by Walter Avancini and Jacques Lagôa.[19] Since then, it has been shown on the Spanish-language station Telemundo in the United States and exported to several other countries.

In his 1976 movie about Chica, Carlos Diegues recreates the history of an eighteenth-century enslaved woman born in Minas Gerais who gains freedom, power, and prestige by associating herself with a Portuguese Crown official and who became extremely wealthy through the extraction of diamonds in the interior of Minas Gerais.[20] However, as Furtado argues, there are several discrepancies between Chica's life and her representations in Brazilian popular culture. The depiction of João Fernandes's motivations for leaving Arraial do Tejuco in the movie is an example of a significant divergence from the information found in historical records.

According to Furtado, in October 1770, the diamond contractor learned that his father, João Fernandes de Oliveira, had died in Portugal. A few days before his passing, Fernandes's stepmother, Isabel Pires Monteiro, had convinced his father to change the will to leave her half of his wealth. Father and son were also business partners and shared the profits obtained from the extraction of diamonds, and thus the new will could greatly hinder Fernandes's finances.

Hence, he was forced to return to Portugal in November of that same year to protect and maintain his assets.[21]

In Dieguess's movie, however, João Fernandes finds himself under suspicion of mismanagement in his diamond-mining operations, as he had amassed so much wealth and power that he has become a threat to the Portuguese government's authority. Amid harsh criticism for his association with a former slave, rumors about Chica/Xica's[22] purported extravagant and immoral behavior and her unmitigated power had reached Lisbon. At that juncture, a Portuguese revenue agent, the count of Valadares, is sent to the village to examine João Fernandes's professional conduct and his association with Xica. Attempts by Xica and Fernandes to convince Sir Valadares to abandon his investigations and return to Portugal by offering him lavish gifts and other bribes ultimately fail. After Valadares files a motion against João Fernandes, the latter is forced to return to Lisbon by official decree.[23]

According to Dieguess's narrative, Xica is punished and left behind, powerless and unprotected. The director therefore ultimately chastises the character for her attempts to destabilize racial hierarchies and power structures. She is scorned by white elites and stoned by their children, which leaves her no choice but to flee to a secluded monastery, where she eventually rekindles her relationship with the son of her former slaverholder, the one who used to refer to her as a farm chicken.[24] Júnia Furtado, however, has found plentiful evidence that Chica and Fernandes maintained contact throughout their entire lives. After his departure, the couple's main concern was to guarantee social ascendance to their sons and daughters. The sons later joined João Fernandes in Portugal, while Chica searched for the best education for their daughters in Tejuco, her hometown, which was later named Diamantina.[25]

Similar license with the historical data is evident throughout the movie as Chica's body is constantly presented as the only currency utilized in her negotiations with men and society at large. Glaringly underlying her portrayals and representations are racist and stereotypical views of women of African descent. In addition to the plot, the lyrics to the soundtrack, also entitled "Chica da Silva," became a classic in Brazilian popular culture, and it is heavily laden with such stereotypes.[26] In this widely popular song, the soap opera, and in Dieguess's movie, her only power and talent emanate from her sexuality and her instinctive ability to use her body to please men, white men in particular. As stated by cinema studies specialist Robert Stam, "Even the theme song sexualizes her; Jorge Ben Jor's punning and stressed repetition ('Chica dá, Chica dá, Chica dá') suggests in Portuguese that 'Chica gives out.' . . . Furthermore, Chica is 'in bed' with people all over the political and social spectrum, and her desire seems to cloud her judgment; her 'dizziness' which afflicts her whenever she is sexually excited, in this sense, is symptomatic of her political incapacity."[27]

Hence, the musical score, like the movie, portrays Xica as a woman who is always sexually available, almost irrationally trading her body in exchange for favors, someone who is incapable of negotiating through reason, even as she becomes wealthy and enjoys freedom from forced labor. There is one particular passage in the movie that poignantly illustrates this point. After previous failed attempts to convince the Count of Valadares to return to Lisbon and renounce his inquisitive mission, Xica informs João Fernandes that she is going to handle the matter her own way, as Fernandes is on the verge of being forced to return to Portugal and she therefore faces the threat of losing her benefactor. The character starts by resorting to her knowledge of African cuisine and, with the help of her maids, prepares a banquet for the unsuspecting guest.

A dinner table is set up on the floor and no serving utensils are provided, while her maids walk into the dining room one by one, bringing a variety of dishes that are carefully arranged for the visitor's delight. They serve some *cachaça*, or sugar cane liquor, to the illustrious guest, who proceeds to grotesquely swallow the food in a clear allusion to the barbarism and primitivism that is customarily attributed to African traditions and customs. In that sense, the noble European is degraded as he is exposed to the African traditions, which is expressed by his complete loss of etiquette. While he devours the food, Xica's maids, displaying their bare breasts, choreographically walk into the dining room, accompanied by the sound of African drums.

Xica then walks into the dining room, wearing nothing but a miniscule piece of cloth over her pubis. The Count of Valadares at this point is completely astounded by that sight as the sound of some sort of "tribal ritual" of seduction is performed by Xica and her maids. Xica dances and twirls her body as she approaches the table while the rhythm of the drumbeat intensifies. The count suddenly starts to emit guttural sounds, bouncing and swinging his body like a primate, then succumbs to her "supernatural" sexual powers as their bodies fall entwined on the table, rolling over the food and the dishes, as she gets ready to finalize the ritual. The next day, however, she wakes up on the table by herself, and then learns that the count has gone through with his initial plans and that João Fernandes has to return to Portugal. Xica's purported primitive nature had been surpassed and ultimately defeated by the intelligence, the superiority, the rationality, and the moral codes of her enemy. The former slave who dared challenge power hierarchies is therefore punished for her audacity, her immorality, her dishonorable behavior, and ultimately, her blackness.

While Fernandes negotiates with Valadares utilizing words, rational arguments, and his money to persuade the inquisitor to drop the case, Xica utilizes her body, trying to resolve the matter "her way," or the only way she knew, according to Diegues. In that sense, she offers herself to be savored and devoured as part of the African dishes that were served in a ritualistic ceremony aimed at bringing Valadares down to her level, where reasoning is superseded by animalistic instincts. This ceremony is also a clear allusion to rituals deemed pagan by the colonizers, in which flesh is supposedly offered in ritualistic sacrifices to appease the gods, perpetuated in distorting portrayals of African culture that still permeate main-stream media in Brazil and the African Diaspora.[28] This ritualistic reenactment of the encounter between the African and European continents mirrors white Europeans' worst fears: being seduced into the darkness or the unknown, into the mysterious and dangerous world of blackness, where secret rituals involving food offerings to pagan gods, dancing, drumming, nudity, gluttony, and uncon-trolled sexual appetite may result in a loss of the boundaries between wisdom and insensateness.

In Diegues's vision, reason at last prevails over instinct: once the table is plun-dered along with her body, Xica's hedonistic and irrational behaviors are chastised, and her life is destabilized by the subsequent loss of her benefactor, whose reason also prevails in the face of European laws. She is ostracized as João Fernandes re-turns to his world and Xica is abandoned, left to her own devices and punished for her ambitions, her desire to ascend socially and occupy spaces that were reserved for white elites.

Evidently, the filmmaker was not concerned with historical accuracy, as there were archives as well as living descendants of Chica and Fernandes who could have been consulted. Rather, Diegues's vision falls in perfect congruence with portrayals grounded in stereotypes about Africans and their descendants that are quite com-mon in mainstream media in Brazil and the African Diaspora. Misrepresentations of Black women as constantly engaged in dishonorable conduct, sexually available, and therefore undeserving of fair or respectable treatment are indeed pervasive and go far beyond movie and television screens.[29] A critical analysis of movies and television as producers and reproducers of culture points to larger issues regard-ing the sociohistorical "milieu" in which different mass media productions and manifestations of popular culture occur. Historically, mainstream media in Brazil have given much less visibility to those of African descent. Moreover, whenever they are portrayed in soap operas, movies, and commercials, they are usually performing menial jobs or in subservient and secondary roles, or associated with criminality and prostitution. The image of people of African descent is also very often associated with mysticism and with African religious and cultural traditions, but rarely are they seen as entrepreneurs in business ventures, political endeav-ors, or intellectual projects.[30] Within that context, delineations of the historical character of Chica da Silva are informed by and simultaneously reproduce Latin American, and more specifically, Brazilian racial ideologies and (mis)representa-tions of blackness.

## Contextualizing Chica: Historical Narratives and Racial Ideologies

To shed light on the process of transformation of the historical figure of Chica da Silva into an icon in mass media and popular culture in Brazil while conjecturing about explanations for her popularity, it is necessary to contextualize her representations. Portrayals of Chica must be located within the parameters of mainstream discourses and historical narratives that have historically placed great importance on the miscegenation and the whitening of the Brazilian population. As previously stated, the framework provided by the Carlos Diegues film has reduced her to an insensitive former slave who was primarily concerned with her own frivolous and sexual urges. In that sense, it is necessary to locate the icon of Chica da Silva within the context of prevailing traditional ideologies and mainstream narratives about what constitutes a Brazilian. This contextualization may reveal the motivations and the sources of "inspiration" that led filmmakers, songwriters, and other artists to fill the gaps left by the lack of historical documentation about her life in a particularly problematic manner.

A key concept within the framework of sociological conceptualizations about race relations in Brazil is the idea of a Brazilian racial democracy, a concept that is perpetually evoked in traditional narratives about the national identity. Brazilian sociologist Gilberto Freyre is acknowledged as the scholar who most influenced the development of this notion, a paradigm through which Brazil is depicted as a country that historically has not presented legal or institutional obstacles to the upward socioeconomic mobility of people of African descent.[31] In that sense, slavery in Brazil is often portrayed in historical records and sociological texts as an institution that did not preclude the possibility of racial equality, and the historical nature of race relations in the country is often contrasted with the system of de jure segregation that characterized historical developments in the United States.

Sharply contrasting such narratives, historian Robert E. Conrad's *Children of God's Fire: A Documentary History of Brazilian Slavery in Brazil* challenges such inaccurate narratives, evincing the racist projects that have grounded historical records. Conrad seeks to expose these fallacies, such as the benevolence that supposedly characterized the attitude of Brazilian slaveholders toward enslaved Africans and their descendants. As he notes regarding intellectuals who gave credence to scientific racism,

> One of the most influential of these writers was Joao Ribeiro, author of a history of Brazil which was selected in 1900 to serve as an advanced textbook, a function it still served as late as 1996, the year it appeared in its nineteenth edition. For Ribeiro, whose work was read by generations of Brazilian students, the Brazilian master was humane and philanthropic. The African (after surviving the miseries of the slave trade) found a

new and happier life in Brazil. . . . Slavery in Brazil was rehabilitation, he claimed, a new fatherland, peace, and freedom which could have never been enjoyed in barbaric Africa.[32]

As stated by the author, such misleading conceptualizations have permeated the Brazilian educational system for decades. I contend that artists, musicians, film directors, television writers, and *carnavalescos*[33] are therefore informed by and operate within a framework of racial democracy. Notions of national identity in Brazil based on Freyre's romantic view of race relations and racial slavery have infused popular media depictions of blacks in the country, particularly the representation of Black women.[34] Brazil was constructed in his texts as a nation that should serve the rest of the world as a model of how to solve the problems of racial prejudice and racial inequality.[35]

Media portrayals of the historical figure of Chica da Silva similarly induce the audience to forget power relations between the enslaved and the enslaver while romanticizing the cruelty of the institution of slavery, which was fundamentally based on the oppression and exploitation of Africans and their descendants. The character Xica da Silva is hence meant to embody conventional narratives regarding what constitutes and distinguishes the Brazilian nation within traditional discourses about race relations in Brazil. Her depictions produce and reproduce culture precisely because her representations are reinforcing sexual stereotypes of women of African descent and perpetuating an erroneous notion of slavery as a benign institution wherein masters and slaves harmoniously co-existed. Resisting enslavement was therefore almost unnecessary.

Challenging such perspectives, Conrad's research reveals that enslaved Africans in Brazil were brutalized and dispossessed of their humanity and hence resisted bondage in many different ways: "Desperate slaves also turned their violence upon themselves, taking their own lives or those of their children as a way to end their misery, at the same time depriving their masters of valuable property."[36] Yet, such a brutal historical scenario is largely ignored, since the story of a wealthy Portuguese white male who, whether in the name of love or lust for the Black body, faced criticism and antagonism from the eighteenth-century Minas Gerais elite fits perfectly with the romantic vision of the origins of multiracial and multicultural Brazil described by Freyre.[37]

Restricting Chica da Silva's power to a mindless use of her body and her sexuality in mainstream renditions is also in line with Freyre's racist and profoundly sexist notions about women of African descent. Elaborating on the successful blending of races and cultures in the process of formation of the Brazilian nation, Freyre confers rather different roles to the different racial groups. Moreover, he romantically describes the violent process of colonization that was grounded on the violation of African female and male bodies as a harmonious encounter that merged different races and cultures. The idea of a raceless nation is centered on miscegenation, which allegedly took place through consensual sex between the colonizer and the enslaved female. Freyre is particularly enthusiastic in his description of the encounter between virile white male Portuguese colonizers and the ready and willing female slave concubines:

> As for the miscibility, no other modern colonizing peoples exceeded or were even equal to the Portuguese. It was through deliciously mixing with the women of color right at the first contact and multiplying themselves in mestizo (mixed) children that only a few daring machos managed to establish themselves in possessing vast quantities of land and compete with grandiose and numerous peoples in [terms of] the extension of colonial domination and the efficacy of the colonizing action.[38]

The outlandish statement above conveys key aspects of Freyre's understanding of the role of Black women in the process of building the Brazilian nation: they had no objections to sexual encounters and very willingly lent their bodies to the process of conquering and developing the grandiose miscegenated Brazilian nation. In his view, through the possession of the Black female body a new nation emerged, as the author praises white Portuguese males for their ability to conquer new bodies/territories. Gender and racial roles are clearly circumscribed, as he places women of color in passive, subordinate, secondary roles in their contribution, not participation, in the process building the nation.[39] Similarly, in mainstream media renditions of her historical character, Chica's resistance is similarly limited, in perfect alignment with Freyre's views on the lack of agency with respect to women of African descent.

Cultural productions that eternize and mythologize historical events despite incomplete documentation speak largely to prevailing notions about the nature of race relations held and simultaneously contested by Brazilians. It speaks as well to traditional narratives about the institution of slavery, colonization, and nationhood in Brazil. Ultimately, the mythologies surrounding racial slavery created by social scientists provide the framework that Brazilian artists have employed in developing carnival themes and media productions about the history of this eighteenth-century enslaved woman.

## Representations of Chica: The Embodiment of Traditional Discourses

According to cultural studies and literary studies specialist Randal Johnson "Cinema Novo (New Cinema) . . . grew out of a process of cultural renovation that began in the early fifties with the election of Juscelino Kubitschek as president in 1955."[40] Just as Kubitschek was concerned with the economic expansion and the industrialization of Brazil, Cinema Novo was influenced by the same context that guided or inspired the cultural construction of Brasilia. It developed discursive cinematic approaches that were intended to project or probe issues of cultural identity, and race was definitely a central part of such inquiries.[41] Ironically, Cinema Novo, which was meant to transform the technical and stylistic production of Brazilian film, did not lead Diegues to go beyond established paradigms, confront the diminution of Chica's characterization, or critically examine her ability to free herself through the appropriation of her own body. According to Diegues, "Cinema is not the reproduction of reality. It implies the creation of a parallel, alternative, and verisimilar universe. This verisimilitude nourishes itself more on the spirit and ideology of the spectators than on their daily experience."[42] This quote unmistakably expresses how Diegues perceives his role as a cinema director and, more important, how the ideology of racial democracy and the myth of the benign master and his content slave may have informed his rendition of the historical figure of Chica. Traditional narratives about the institution of slavery as a benign institution have not only permeated the Brazilian educational system for decades but Chica's representations as well. The icon she has become can therefore simultaneously be located within these narratives and encompass them. In his analysis of the movie *Xica da Silva*, Robert Stam argues, "An object of desire for the diverse representatives of political, military, and social power, Chica assumes a role that on one level points to the hypocrisy of a society that enslaved Black people and yet desired and exploited Black women. On another level, however, she embodies the fantasy of the sexually available slave."[43]

As previously stated, the historical character of Chica da Silva has become a popular cultural icon whose image has been misappropriated and misrepresented in enduring stereotypes by mainstream scholars and mass media. These depictions tend to overlook the complex roles that the icon of Chica plays in Brazilian society. Her representations illustrate how the Black female body is the site of nationhood in Brazil particularly as conceived in Freyre's view of the role of Black women in the process of colonization located within the ideology of racial democracy. A critical contextualization may thus shed light on her popular appeal and the recurrence of her presence in manifestations of Brazilian popular culture and mass media productions.

## Resurrecting the Myth of Chica da Silva

Chica's image reemerged again in 2004 during a carnival parade in Rio de Janeiro at a time when racial democracy was once again being challenged and exposed as a myth through discussions about the implementation of affirmative-action policies for Afro-Brazilians. These debates and discussions have opened new spaces to counter traditional narratives about the role of race in the access to education and upward mobility in Brazil. Through an intersectional approach that considers race, history, class, sexuality, and nation building, it is possible to further explore the representations of this historical figure in mainstream Brazilian media by movie directors, songwriters, and other artists. Since portrayals of Chica carry numerous overlapping symbolisms, an intersectional approach that reveals both traditional and contested narratives related to the foundations of the Brazilian nation must be employed in order to adequately analyze such complex dynamics.[44]

Hence, scholars must reassess especially the interconnectedness of race, gender, class, and sexuality as an integral aspect of resistance and agency. In that sense, scholar Adrienne Davis elaborates on the sexual economy of Black women's reproduction, production, and fulfillment of white male gratification as an integral element to the system of enslavement.[45] Yet one must also consider that enslaved women like Chica da Silva chose a nonviolent strategy in their alignment with the dominant empowered white male, an act of sexual unity in the face of the oppressive and fundamentally brutal system of enslavement. Along with many other women whose lives were threatened within the brutal confinements of chattel slavery, she utilized her sexuality to equalize the power differential by fully confronting the ambivalent gaze of the white male oppressor turned consort. Whether the enslaved female and the male enslaver derived pleasure from their sexual relationships, Baby Suggs's advice to her granddaughter in *Beloved* (Toni Morrison's novel based on Margaret Garner's life) provides further insight: "Slaves not supposed to have pleasurable feelings on their own; their bodies not supposed to be like that, but they have to have as many children as they can to please whoever owned them. Still, they were not supposed to have pleasure deep down. She said for me not to listen to all that. That I should always listen to my body and love it."[46]

According to Darlene Clark Hine, Southern Black women in the late nineteenth and early twentieth centuries practiced a cult of secrecy that allowed them to hide their inner selves while engaging in their daily routines.[47] The concept of dissemblance recognizes that enslaved women who lacked ownership over their bodies could nevertheless reserve their thoughts for themselves. Perhaps Margaret's words in the opera, "They cannot touch the secret soul," uttered when she is confronted with imminent rape by the slaveholder, best illustrates this idea.[48]

## Moving Beyond Dichotomies

As previously stated, exploring the complexity of sexual encounters within contexts of oppressive systems and highly disparate power relationships is a challenging task, as the dynamics of such interactions may not be unveiled or understood within simplistic dichotomies. Enslaved women's negotiations with their "owners" covered a wide spectrum of strategies. In the case of Margaret Garner, for example, she sought to escape bondage, but she was tracked down by brutal hunters of enslaved Africans and chose to end her children's lives as the ultimate expression of freedom. She thus deprived the slaveholder of what he considered his property through the violent act of infanticide. Though long forgotten, her story is resurrected through bold fictional interpretations whereby her audacious violent act becomes profoundly inspirational. Such complexities are illustrated in the work of historian Joshua Rothman, who also considers the matter of sexual gratification in the eighteen-year relationship between Sally Hemings and Thomas Jefferson, noting that interracial sex in the early antebellum period should be classified as rape: "Perpetrators of these abuses expressed power and contempt rather than sexuality or affection."[49] However, Rothman also acknowledges that relationships between the enslaver and enslaved also might range from blatant sexual abuse to long-term commitment that mirrored legal marriage.[50] Sally Hemings was facing extremely limited options when she decided against a kinless, penniless "freedom" by remaining in Paris on her own. Instead, she returned to Monticello but extracted a promise from Jefferson that her future children would be freed when they reached age twenty-one in exchange for becoming his concubine.[51]

Whether Chica da Silva struck a similar deal with Fernandes is not known, but evidently an understanding existed between the couple that allowed their children to inherit his wealth and with it presumably a degree of comfort in life if not actual higher status. Indeed, although Chica has been crudely objectified in sexual stereotypes, during her lifetime she utilized her erotic appeal to escape bondage and to gain economic advantage. The story of the iconic Chica da Silva reveals that she refused the role of a sexual victim. Black women such as Chica da Silva and Sally Hemings recognized that although they were regarded as inferior, they could utilize their sexual and economic cachet in consensual relationships that were devoid of violence. In that sense, renowned Black feminist Audre Lorde poignantly elaborates on how the erotic is an expression of female power:

> There are many kinds of power, used and unused, acknowledged or otherwise. The erotic is a resource within each of us that lies in a deeply female and spiritual plane, firmly rooted in the power of our unexpressed or unrecognized feeling. In order to perpetuate itself, every oppression must corrupt or distort those various sources of power within the culture of the oppressed that can provide energy for change. For women, this has meant a suppression of the erotic as a considered source of power and information within our lives.[52]

The extent to which Chica da Silva, Sally Hemings, or Margaret Garner were able to retain or reclaim their selfhood by the mental practice of dissemblance is also a matter of speculation. It should be noted that for all three women, their children's futures figured into the options they chose.

The historical integrity of Chica's character has been significantly compromised in fictional reproductions of her life. Popular interpretations of Chica reduce her to a mere sexual object without crediting her with the power that she derived from her sexuality and without acknowledging her strategic reasoning capabilities, obscuring her ability to make tactical and premeditated choices. However, as demonstrated throughout this volume, choosing to unite with an oppressor by honoring one's sexuality is a radical act of resistance to being dehumanized and exploited for someone else's profit. While a different manifestation of resistance than killing one's daughter to save her, both are signal acts of reclaiming oneself.

Clearly, further research on the agency and contribution of women of African descent to histories in the African Diaspora is needed, including their strategic self-determination by any means necessary. To unveil the plights of those whose experiences have been rendered invisible or distorted, literary works, autobiographies, and memorials such as Tony Morrison's *Beloved* offer crucial contributions to efforts of bringing the challenges faced by Black women to the fore. These works also unveil the plethora of strategies historically utilized by Black women to overcome oppression, since they reveal the particularity and intricacy of their experiences within the institution of slavery and its aftermath. Black women's representation in works of the imagination and the media will be transformed when the complex choices made by Black women are properly unveiled and ultimately restored to the public memory.

## Notes

1. I was participating in a symposium about Brazil held at the John L. Warfield Center for African and African American Studies at the University of Texas in Austin as a graduate student. *Cinderellas, Wolves and a Prince Charming* was screened at the Museum of Modern Art (MOMA) in 2009. See *Cinderellas, Wolves and a Prince Charming*, Museum of Modern Art, http://uat.moma.org. There is a review at http://dejiridoo.com/blog1/reviews /full-reviews/cinderelas-araujo (accessed February 26, 2013).

2. See Ella Forbes, "African Resistance to Enslavement: The Nature and the Evidentiary Record," *Journal of Black Studies* 23, no. 1 (1992): 39–59.

3. Even though the movie title spells her name as Xica, according to Junia Furtado's extensive research, her name was registered on her birth certificate as Chica.

4. Stuart Hall, ed., *Representation: Cultural Representations and Signifying Practices* (London: Sage, 1997), 259.

5. bell hooks, *Reel to Real: Race, Sex, and Class at the Movies* (New York: Routledge, 1996), 9.

6. I acknowledge Yamuna Sangarasivam for our conversations and her contributions that helped me formulate these reflections.

7. Nancy Jesser, "Violence, Home, and Community in Toni Morrison's *Beloved*," *African American Review* 33, no. 2 (1999): 325–45.

8. Again, I am deeply grateful to Yamuna Sangarasivam for helping me frame my ideas for this section.

9. See Júnia Ferreira Furtado, *Chica da Silva: A Brazilian Slave of the Eighteenth Century* (New York: Cambridge University Press, 2009).

10. See Furtado, *Chica da Silva*, 265.

11. In the early 1690s, the Portuguese found gold in Brazil, and by the 1720s, diamonds were also encountered. Minas Gerais became the fastest-growing region in eighteenth-century Brazil, and by then the country was the main gold producer in the world. See Thomas E. Skidmore, *Brazil: Five Centuries of Change* (New York: Oxford University Press, 1999), 21, 22.

12. Hortense Spillers, "Mama's Baby, Papa's Maybe: An American Grammar Book," in her *Black, White, and in Color: Essays on American Literature and Culture* (Chicago: University of Chicago Press, 2003), 221.

13. See Furtado, *Chica da Silva*, 123.

14. Furtado argues that their relationship was never legally established because the hierarchical society of colonial Minas Gerais would not allow such a privilege to two people from such extremely different backgrounds.

15. See Furtado, *Chica da Silva*, 123.

16. Ibid., 265.

17. See the online journal *Poiésis - Literatura, Pensamento & Arte*, available at http://www.passeiweb.com/na_ponta_lingua/livros/resumos_comentarios/o/o_tesouro_de_chica_da_silva_peca (accessed February 26, 2013).

18. Each samba school has an individual who develops the carnival theme called a carnavelsco. The most visible carnival parade in which samba groups compete takes place in Rio de Janeiro. These highly elaborate parades are broadcast from Rio to more than a hundred countries every year. See M. R. Faria, "Salgueiro," *Notícia e Opinião* (April 10, 2004).

19. *Xica da Silva*, soap opera (1996). For information regarding the directors, writers, and actors, see http://www.imdb.com/title/tt0138277 (accessed March 25, 2010). See also Robert Stam, *Tropical Multiculturalism: A Comparative History of Race in Brazilian Cinema and Culture* (Durham, N.C.: Duke University Press, 1997), 292–96.

20. The author does not elaborate on the possible implications of the absence of her sons and daughters in the movie, but for a discussion of Diegues's Chica, see Randal Johnson, "Carnivalesque Celebration in Chica da Silva," in *Brazilian Cinema*, ed. Randal Johnson and Robert Stam (Rutherford, N.J.: Fairleigh Dickinson University Press, 1982), 216–24.

21. See Furtado, *Chica da Silva*, 217.

22. The movie character is registered with an X, a discrepancy from her birth certificate.

23. Furtado, *Chica da Silva*, 217.

24. Ironically, in the film, the slaveholder's son was forced to retreat into a monastery due to his involvement with freedom struggles against the Portuguese crown, which were often organized in Minas Gerais. Furthermore, it is also ironic that this character was turned from a racist, sexist figure into a man who fought against Portuguese domination.

25. Furtado, *Chica da Silva*, 246.

26. It has been performed by several prestigious Brazilian artists, such as Jorge Ben Jor, Gilberto Gil, and Milton Nascimento, among others.

27. Stam, *Tropical Multiculturalism*, 294.

28. William Arens, *The Man-Eating Myth: Anthropology & Anthropophagy* (New York: Oxford University Press, 1980).

29. In *In Defense of Honor*, historian Sueann Caulfield contextualizes her insightful investigation of legal disputes over lost virginity in early-twentieth-century Brazil. Her discussion is consistent with my argument about the influence of Gilberto Freyre on national ideas about race and slavery. Sueann Caulfield, *Defense of Honor: Sexual Morality, Modernity, and Nation in Early-Twentieth-Century Brazil* (Durham, N.C.: Duke University Press, 2000).

30. For an excellent discussion of representations of blacks in mainstream media in Brazil, see Joel Zito Araújo, *A negação do Brasil: O Negro Na Telenovela Brasileira* (São Paulo: Editora SENAC São Paulo, 2000).

31. Historian Barbara Weinstein provides an analysis of the process that led to the consolidation of the myth of racial democracy in which she finds that intellectual and political elites during the Vargas regime embraced and promoted his conception of what constituted as well as distinguished the Brazilian nation as it served the purpose of promoting a homogeneous national identity, transcending regional variation, and easing existing tensions between the regions. See Barbara Weinstein, "Racializing Regional Difference, São Paulo Versus Brazil, 1932," in *Race and Nation in Modern Latin America*, ed. Nancy P. Appelbaum, Anne S. Macpherson, and Karin Alejandra Rosemblatt (Chapel Hill: University of North Carolina Press, 2003).

32. Robert Edgar Conrad, ed., *Children of God's Fire: A Documentary History of Black Slavery in Brazil* (Princeton, N.J.: Princeton University Press, 1997), xxii.

33. These are artists who are responsible for elaborating the themes, customs, choreographies, and other elements developed in carnival floats.

34. For an incisive critique of Freyre's work in producing racialized understandings of eroticism and his views on race, racial mixture, and national identity as well as of the material consequences of racial stereotypes in the context of Brazil, see Denise Ferreira da Silva, "Á Brasileira: Raciality and the Writing of a Destructive Desire," *Revista Estudos Feministas* 14, no. 1 (2006): 61–83.

35. See George Reid Andrews, *Blacks and Whites in São Paulo, Brazil, 1888–1988* (Madison: University of Wisconsin Press, 1991), 7.

36. Conrad, ed., *Children of God's Fire*, 360. Conrad's comments and documentation about the violent reactions to being enslaved disproves what is popularly stated about the nature of slavery in Brazil.

37. Gilberto Freyre, *Casa-Grande & Senzala: Formacão da família Brasileira Sobre o Regime da Economia Patriarcal* (São Paulo: Global Ed, 2003).

38. Ibid., 70. I have translated the quote restoring the word "deliciously" which was missing from several English translations I have consulted. It is a key word in terms of expressing the sexual pleasure that Freyre sought to evoke in his vision of the encounter of white Portuguese males and black females.

39. As noted by prominent black activist scholar Abdias do Nascimento, mainstream discourses about the participation of Afro-Brazilians in the construction of the Brazilian nation are usually restricted to "contributions."

40. Johnson, "Carnivalesque Celebration in Chica da Silva," 216–24.

41. Ibid.

42. Ibid.

43. Stam, *Tropical Multiculturalism*, 293.

44. Several Black feminists, such as renowned activist and scholar Angela Davis, have argued that the racial state has applied important instruments of domination (economical, political, educational, and sexual, among others) on black women. These scholars argue that race, class, and gender should be considered as intersectional categories and analyzed as mutually constitutive.

45. Adrienne Davis, "'Don't Let Nobody Bother Yo' Principle': The Sexual Economy of American Slavery," in *Sister Circle: Black Women and Work*, ed. Sharon Harley (New Brunswick, N.J.: Rutgers University Press, 2002), 105.

46. Toni Morrison, *Beloved* (New York: Knopf, 1987), 209. Baby Suggs had also encouraged her fellow enslaved to love their flesh in her defiant prayer ritual in the clearing. Recognizing that they had hearts made for joy and love in defiance of those who denied them all emotional and human capabilities, she told her parishioners that grace was available to them, but only they could imagine and capture it for themselves (87–89).

47. Darlene Clark Hine, "Rape and the Inner Lives of Black Women: Thoughts on the Culture of Dissemblance," in *Hine Sight: Black Women and the Re-construction of American History* (Bloomington: Indiana University Press, 1994), 37.

48. This phrase is taken from Toni Morrison's libretto for *Margaret Garner* (New York: Schirmer, 2004).

49. Joshua D. Rothman, *Notorious in the Neighborhood: Sex and Families across the Color Line in Virginia, 1787–1861* (Chapel Hill: University of North Carolina Press, 2003), 19.

50. Ibid., 15.

51. Ibid., 17–18. Also see Annette Gordon-Reed, who describes the relationship between Hemings and Jefferson as concubinage; Annette Gordon-Reed, *The Hemingses of Monticello: An American Family* (New York: Norton, 2008).

52. Audre Lorde, "Uses of the Erotic: The Erotic as Power," in *Sister Outsider: Essays and Speeches* (Freedom, Calif.: Crossing, 1984), 53–59.

# CHAPTER 9

# THE PSYCHOLOGICAL AFTEREFFECTS OF RACIALIZED SEXUAL VIOLENCE

*Cathy McDaniels-Wilson*

When I was invited to contribute to this anthology on enslaved women—whom I identify as our mothers, sisters, aunts, cousins, and friends—I thought about my years of clinical work with girls and women of color who are survivors of intimate partner violence and sexual abuse and the countless queries from students, colleagues, patients, and others who have asked me why these clients stay in abusive relationships. The answer, unfortunately, is neither simple nor easy to explain. To better understand racialized intimate partner violence, we must acknowledge the bridge between past and present. This process begins by examining abuse in a historical context, drawing on the experiences and actions of enslaved women in the nineteenth-century United States and then moving forward in time to analyze data about victimization and assault gathered from interviews with incarcerated women in U.S. prisons in the late twentieth and early twenty-first centuries.

In contexts past and present, racialized violence warrants particular attention. Instances of intimate partner violence and other sexual violence where the primary perpetrator is a male from the white majority and the victim is a girl or woman of color with less perceived power in the relationship echo powerfully across the generations back to the enslavement of women and girls of African descent. Subjected to what one can only imagine were the most extreme forms of violence perpetrated upon them by their white slave masters, enslaved black women bequeathed to subsequent generations a complex history of trauma and resilience. Woven into the cultural context of enslavement, the emotional sequelae of intimate partner violence and other sexual violence continues to have enduring aftereffects on the psychosexual development of African American women, as well as on their high rates of incarceration.

The parallels between enslaved and imprisoned women can be seen in the life of Margaret Garner, a young enslaved woman of African and Caucasian descent who lived in Richwood, Kentucky, until her early twenties. Sexually entrapped by

Figure 9.1. Edith Jaffy Kaplan, wood-cut, n.d., Alice Walker Collection, Emory University Special Collections. Courtesy of Manuscripts, Archives, and Rare Book Library (MARBL), Emory University. With permission from Jerome Kaplan.

her white master, Garner escaped to Ohio with her family in January 1856. When captured, she murdered her daughter and injured her two sons while attempting to murder them also, not with the pathology of criminal intent but in an attempt to save them from worse violence. When viewed in conjunction with the experiences of incarcerated women in the 1990s and first decade of the present century, Garner's experiences and those of other enslaved women in the nineteenth century offer new insights into the historical theory of "dissemblance," as posited by historian Darlene Clark Hine, and the diagnosis of "dissociation," as understood by psychologists. A broader understanding of the psychological aftereffects of sexual victimization also reveals a key distinction between resilience—the capacity to sustain oneself in the face of extreme adversity or trauma—and healing—the process of self-regeneration that can follow victimization and assault.

## Sexual Victimization, Mental Trauma, and Racist Psychology

S. E. Anderson's work *The Black Holocaust* reminds us that the process of racialized abuse began on the voyage to the Americas. Anderson poignantly describes the brutal and routine victimization that enslaved girls and women were subjected to at the hands of their captors. The process of socialized sexual aggression against enslaved women and girls is highlighted by Marli Weiner in *Mistresses and Slaves*, where she examines the role of gender and race ideologies on the lives of plantation women and how the concept of race and gender defined the limitations and possibilities for all women living on plantations. Many others, including Deborah Gray White, Jacquelyn Jones, Elizabeth Fox-Genovese, Catherine Clinton, and Tera Hunter, have written about the multiple roles and responsibilities of enslaved women, from backbreaking fieldwork to washing, sewing, cooking, and caring for and nurturing not only their own children but the children of slave masters and mistresses as well.[1] These works document a history rife with violence, sexual trauma, exploitation, and evidence of forced breeding. Recent works by Thavolia Glymph, Jennifer Morgan, Stephanie Camp, and Marie Schwartz have provided even more evidence of gendered resistance in the antebellum South and the work of reproduction and the intimate lives of enslaved women.[2]

Nineteenth-century documents confirm that enslaved women and girls suffered extensive racialized intimate-partner violence at the hands of slave masters and of male visitors to farms and plantations. In many cases, the abuse began as soon as a female slave was purchased. Perceived as objects or animals that could be bought and sold, slave women endured brutal sexual conquest. There were slave masters who came to value the intellect and beauty of the black women in their possession and to treat them with respect and dignity, despite an overriding sense of entitlement to her body. But compassionate masters were rare, and in the absence of legal protections against a master's behavior, aggressive sexual attacks could occur at any time, in any venue.[3] Consequently, throughout her life an enslaved woman was subjected to physical and psychological entrapment and identified as a resource for the sexual exploits of the slave-owning class. A woman's body, sexual development, and sexuality were all subject to her enslaver's timetable; what should have been hers was under someone else's control. All an enslaved girl or woman had left in her possession was her spirit, a persistent sense of self-determination that sustained resistance, resilience, and in some cases promoted long-term healing.

Although few formal nineteenth-century records of mental illness, mental instability, or depression exist, written and oral slave narratives recount how "the entire life of the slave was hedged about with rules and regulations."[4] Enforced by individual masters on their own plantations, city ordinances and state laws rigidly circumscribed movement and behavior. A constantly shifting labyrinth of penalties and sentences defined punishment with sadistic precision. Impulsive and inconsistent enforcement of the rules of enslavement left many slaves in a constant state of anxiety or fear. The terror of separation from family haunted many; fear of punishment for trivial mishaps affected all. The punishments meted out to runaways made the decision to escape an almost irrevocable commitment.

Born on a Carolina plantation, Janie Satterwhite had intense memories of being sold "when I was a little tot," telling an interviewer in 1937, "I kin see it all right now." After the woman who owned their plantation died, all the slaves were sold. "I 'member when dey put me on de block," Satterwhite remembered. "When dat man bought me—dat Dr. Henry, he put me in a buggy to take me off."[5] Former slave Edward Glen of the Clinton Brown plantation in Forsythe County, Georgia, told an interviewer in 1937, "Slaves were whipped for small things, such as forgetting orders or spilling food." Punishments included being handcuffed, jailed, and tortured. Sometimes, he recounted, "a slave was treated so bad by his owners he was glad if they put him up to be sold." Glen remembered, "When [a] runaway slave was brought back they was punished. Once in Alabama I saw a woman stripped naked, laid over a stump in a field with her head hangin' down on one side, her feet on the other, and tied to the stump. Then they whipped her hard, and you could hear her hollering far off."[6]

As terrifying as separation and the fear of inhumane punishment could be, historian Jacqueline Jones argues that "the sexual violation of Black women by White men rivaled the separation of families as the foremost provocation injected into Black family life by slaveholders." Jones contends that the 10 percent of the slave population classified as "mulatto" in 1860 provides "a very conservative estimate" of the incidence of "rape or concubinage" on Southern plantations. Sexual assaults on black women by white slave owners were a constant threat, regardless of how fiercely a woman might resist or the ways in which her parents, husbands, or sons might work to protect her. One Louisiana slave reported to interviewers in the 1930s that where he lived, a white man would go into a slave cabin and order the husband "to go outside and wait 'til he do what he want to do" and the husband "couldn't do nothing 'bout it." Jones reported another elder slave who remembered, "What we saw, couldn't do nothing 'bout it. My bood is bilin' now at the thoughts of dem times."[7]

Samuel Cartwright, a well-known physician in the antebellum South, had a psychiatric explanation for runaway slaves, diagnosing them in 1851 as suffering from "drapetomania." Classified as "a disease of the mind," Cartwright defined drapetomania as a treatable and preventable condition that caused "negroes to run away." Literally defined as "the flight-from-home-madness," Cartwright argued that cures for drapetomania included "whipping the negative attitudes out of Africans, treating Africans kindly, feeding Africans well and providing adequate clothes and warmth." Cartwright suggested that slaves live one family per house, consume no liquor, and not be overworked or exposed to inclement weather. Another ailment Cartwright described and named, in 1857, was dysaesthesia "aethiopica," a disease of Africans "characterized by hebetude of mind and insensitivity of body, caused by overworking and bad treatment." Cartwright warned that while dysaesthesia aethiopica was sometimes called "rascality" by overseers, it was actually a state of "mental alienation" that could cause slaves to "fall into a state of impassivity" in which they become "insensible and indifferent to punishment *or even to life*" (emphasis added).[8]

Cartwright's published work established the foundation for what Alvin F. Poussaint and Amy Alexander have referred to as "racism's historic impact" on black mental health. Cartwright's pseudo-science, a potent mix of religion, pro-slavery politics, and medicine, forged a powerful connection between mental illness and race continued by subsequent generations of physicians and psychologists. The consequences of this approach were devastating and long lasting. As Poussaint and Alexander put it, African Americans became "fair game for a host of half-baked studies and experiments in the mental health arena, and to classification by a system of questionable terminology."[9]

## Margaret Garner

Although we have little direct evidence from Margaret Garner herself, we know enough from her court testimony and from local and national newspaper coverage to argue that the psychological aftereffects of the trauma she suffered in slavery and at the time of her capture after attempting to escape influenced her choice to take the life of her baby girl and injure her two young sons. Acting with courage and fortitude, Garner clearly intended to end a multigenerational history of abuse by seeking freedom for herself and her children.

Our understanding of the impact of enslavement, sexual violation, and rape on the psychology of African Americans like Margaret Garner is limited by the ideological and political frameworks within which Garner's actions were understood in the nineteenth century, especially as depicted in the first newspaper report of the family's escape in the *Cincinnati Daily Enquirer*, headlined as a A TALE OF HORROR! on January 29, 1856.

Hastily written for the morning edition of the paper on the day following Garner's capture, this piece opened floodgates of reaction to Margaret Garner. As Mark Reinhardt suggests in *Who Speaks for Margaret Garner?* Garner's killing of her daughter was "presented as born of delirium." The words used to describe her state of mind were "frantic" and "frenzied," which Reinhardt reminds readers are derived from the Latin *phreneticus*, meaning derangement.[10] He points out that the first definition for "frantic" in the *Oxford English Dictionary* is "afflicted with mental disease, lunatic, insane . . . violently or ragingly mad."[11] This framework of frenzy would later resonate with Cartwright's ideas about the "flight-from-home-madness" of drapetomania and the mental alienation of dysaesthesia aethiopica, the racially constructed disease state that caused slaves to become "indifferent to life."[12]

Margaret Garner's mental state during her trial has been recounted in multiple ways. A reporter for the *Cincinnati Daily Gazette* wrote on February 11, 1856, the first day of testimony, that "her eyes during the trial were generally cast down" and that "she would look up occasionally for an instant with a timid, apprehensive glance . . . and her general expression was one of extreme sadness." Two days later, the rendition of the legal arguments made by Archibald Gaines's attorney in the pro-slavery press questioned the validity of Margaret Garner's testimony, writing, "This woman who has barbarously murdered one of her children, whose hands have been imbued in the blood of her offspring. Of what benefit can her testimony be?"[13]

In 2004, the Ohio Chapter of the American College of Trial Lawyers presented a mock trial based on the Margaret Garner case. One of the defense experts involved in this trial represented an "alienist," a nineteenth-century doctor specializing in the treatment of mental illness. He described Margaret as having a "crazed look in her eyes" and stated that "Margaret acted as if she was extricating herself from an ongoing, persistent nightmare of impending rape and violence." He argued that she gave a diagnostic impression of what is currently known as Post-Traumatic Stress Disorder (PTSD), which is marked by having experienced or witnessed events that involve actual or threatened death, serious injury, or threats to the physical integrity of self or others.[14] The trauma experienced by Margaret Garner, both before and after the capture of her family following their escape to Ohio, he argued, would have resulted in myriad symptoms and behaviors, both acute and long term.

## A Contemporary Perspective: Sexual Violation of Incarcerated Offenders

Margaret Garner's sexual victimization and her subsequent entrapment by the legal system is actually remarkably similar to the life histories of many African American women in the criminal justice system 150 years later. Beginning in the 1990s, my work in the area of sexual victimization led me to develop a Sexual Abuse Checklist and a modified version of the Sexual Experiences Survey to obtain a detailed account of 202 incarcerated African American women's self-reported sexual violation and abuse histories. Seventy percent of the women reported at least one violation consistent with what qualified as rape in most U.S. states in 2008. Seventy-eight percent of the women reported having been sexually abused.[15]

Since the late 1970s, feminist criminologists have referred to the link between victimization and trauma with subsequent offences as the "pathways" approach, which identifies girls' and women's (and sometimes boys' and men's) victimization and trauma histories as risk factors for trajectories into offending behaviors. Applications of the pathways perspective have been largely qualitative, often using small samples and identifying trauma and abuse as precursors among women and girls who become offenders within the criminal justice system.[16] The findings in my research support the pathways perspective, and I argue that incarcerated women report significantly higher rates of sexual violation than do non-incarcerated samples of women and girls (70 percent for black women who are incarcerated versus 24 percent for nonprison samples that comprise black women), indicating that sexual abuse is a significant risk factor for women's criminalization.[17]

We do not have parallel documentation to support a pathways analysis in the nineteenth century, but we can draw some connections between past and present in order to understand the psychological sequelae regarding feelings of shame, guilt, and betrayal experienced by enslaved women. Stockholm syndrome, described by twentieth-century psychologists as a phenomenon in which victims display a sense of loyalty or compassion toward their captors in cases of rape, kidnapping, or other forms of terror or trauma, may well have framed the experience of numbers of enslaved women.[18] Women repeatedly raped and traumatized by those they knew intimately, remotely, or not at all may well have bonded with their perpetrators because of the high price slave owners extracted when women rejected their advances or refused to comply with their sexual demands: separation from family, beatings, lynching, or even death. Female victims, left with feelings of helplessness and powerlessness, were forced to adapt to the demands of the situation.

Contemporary incestuous or child abuse relationships mimic this situation, and it has been well documented that trauma exposure lends itself to both immediate and chronic aftereffects. From a developmental perspective, the results of sexual trauma can range from immediate physical deformations and/or lacerations to emotional responses such as anger, guilt, anxiety, depression, suicide, and, in the more extreme cases, dissociative reactions that include the disruption of memory and consciousness. These processes of detachment, disengagement, and disconnection undoubtedly increased survival levels and enabled women and girls, past and present, to withstand repeated sexual victimization.

Twenty-first-century contexts for the abuse of women and girls of color are remarkably similar to those experienced by enslaved women. Such women and girls are often exposed to random acts of violence, sexual victimization, and rape. Early-twenty-first-century social safety nets remain chronically inadequate and often place women of color at a greater risk of being victimized. Programs developed specifically to support and protect women and children, such as foster care, child advocacy programs, domestic violence shelters, and rape crisis centers, often fall short of meeting needs, providing support, and establishing a protective base, particularly for women and girls of color. Given the structure of the legal system, a woman's cry for help often results in additional criminalization. For example, when a young girl suffering incestuous sexual violation at home responds by running away, she is frequently arrested for prostitution or drug use. Once imprisoned, women and girls are subject to decreased contact with others. One woman described it as "not [being] able to ever talk about this even in prison, they only want to punish me. No one ever asked why I became an addict, or why I did the things I did." Routine strip searches and the constant supervision by male officers demonstrate a basic insensitivity toward the large number of women with a history of intimate partner violence. The effects of this treatment perpetuate the cycle of violation. A female inmate described the effect this way: "Officers yanking open the door to my cell at any time. . . . their screaming, shouting, and firm-fisted approach to maintaining security often causes me to have post-traumatic episodes or flashbacks."[19]

Women like this often fall through the cracks of psychological studies that focus instead on the high rates of suicide and ongoing mental-health crisis among African American men. Such studies, including the work of Poussaint and Alexander in *Lay My Burden Down*, report that African American women have an unusual capacity to survive ongoing and horrendous abuse, from verbal insults to physical sexual attacks, and continue their capacity to function, to work, attend school, and care for children. On the other hand, studies of sexual victimization that analyze the high levels of abuse among women in the United States usually focus on predominantly white populations and argue that there are few major racial differences in sexual abuse prevalent among black and white women in a given community.[20]

In *The Invisible Woman*, Joanne Belknap identifies four categories of intimate partner violence: physical battering, sexual battering, psychological battering, and destruction of pets and property. Physical battering may consist of slapping, hitting, burning, shooting, stabbing, or any other form of nonsexual physical violence. This is probably the most common form of abuse. Sexual battering occurs when there is a sexual nature to the violence, such as beating on the breasts or genital, or oral, anal, or vaginal rape. Psychological battering is often minimized but is potentially extremely harmful. Indeed, many women report psychological battering as the most damaging type of abuse. The victim is demeaned, criticized, and devalued on a consistent basis, which often leads to feelings of decreased self-esteem, self-worth, and feelings of helplessness. It is also not unusual for a batterer to destroy a woman's property (anything from clothing to automobiles or even her home) or to abuse or kill her pets. Belknap suggests that the underlying message is "if I can do this to your pets, imagine what I can do to you."[21]

While Belknap's work includes some cross-racial data, according to a national survey, 29 percent of African American women and 12 percent of African American men report at least one instance of violence from an intimate partner. African Americans account for one-third of the intimate partner homicides in the United States and have an intimate partner homicide rate four times that of whites. Black women represent 8 percent of the U.S. population but account for 20 percent of the intimate partner homicide victims.[22] We know that many external variables or external contexts can increase an African American woman's vulnerability and risk of exposure to violent episodes, including unemployment, deficient educational opportunities, drug and/or alcohol dependency and abuse, or a prior history of intimate partner violence.

In *Compelled to Crime*, Beth Ritchie discusses the socially constructed concept of "gender entrapment" to explain women's involvement in criminal behavior in American society in the late twentieth century. She argues that from a historical perspective, this concept fits the circumstances of enslaved women as well.[23] Culturally sanctioned violence against women and girls dominated the social landscape during that period. African American women's and girls' forced vulnerability to men's violence in intimate and other sexual relationships was inexorably linked not only to their gender, but also, as Ritchie points out, to their racialized identities. These women's culturally expected gender roles involved disempowerment, lack of control over their lives, and the violent nature of their intimate and other sexual relationships.

My survey of 391 women incarcerated in Ohio in 1996, combined with an understanding of the racial construction of sexuality in the nineteenth century, tells a different story. The sample included 202 African American women (54.7 percent) and 167 white women (45.3 percent). The data indicate that the white women reported more of almost all forms of sexual abuse than did the black women. For example, while 50 percent of black women reported having been raped, 60 percent of white women reported incidents of rape. Moreover, while 78 percent of the black women in this sample reported having experienced some form of illegal sexual abuse, 83 percent of the white women reported the same. These differences persist across all forms of abuse.[24]

The question is, why? The answer lies in the complex legacy of trauma and resilience passed down to African American women from generation to generation. I offer two hypotheses, both of which draw on the legacy of slavery and on what I have learned from my clients. The first is that the high levels of sexual violation experienced by enslaved black women rendered rape and sexual abuse normative. Consequently, black women would be less likely than white women to identify a particular behavior as sexual abuse. The second is that black women make conscious choices not to report black men as abusive, a consequence of a criminal legal system that has made men of color targets for high rates of arrest, criminal conviction, and harsh sentences.

One of the most frequently cited sociocultural explanations of violence against women and girls is based on feminist theory, which suggests that violence against women emanates from potent socializing messages from families, peer groups, the media, the legal system, and other institutions of a sexist society which have led to a widespread acceptance and normalization of gender-based violence. When these theories are uniformly applied across cultures, however, they ignore the various ethnocultural differences and similarities that may adversely affect women's resistance to abuse from male partners.[25] Given the limited documentation of information pertaining to the emotional or psychological aftermath of these assaults, one is left to surmise or make assumptions about the impact of such assaults on the psyche of specific groups of women and girls. Furthermore, what we do know about the aftereffects of trauma applies only to those who have survived ongoing attacks. We understand much less about the intrapersonal process of empowerment that sustains and energizes African American women.

## Dissemblance versus Dissociation

Darlene Clark Hine has written powerfully about the racial construction of sexuality and the history of Southern black women's vulnerability as victims of rape and sexual violence.[26] Hine's work underscores the importance of understanding the effect of rape or the threat of rape as it relates to the underlying motivations that led African Americans to escape from enslavement and to seek freedom from abuse and violence. She argues that many enslaved mothers, perhaps in an attempt to protect their daughters from being traumatized, refrained from sharing with them the "truth" that lay before them. Ironically, this placed young girls at an even greater risk for the sexual assault and violence they would likely experience because they had no warning or preparation.

Margaret Garner exercised an even more extreme form of protection by terminating her daughter's life rather than allowing her to be victimized repeatedly over the course of her life, as Garner herself had been. Unlike the fictionalized version of her life story in *Beloved*, Garner was in fact criminalized and tried in a court of law as an escaped slave. The focus of the trial, interestingly, was not on the fact that she had taken the life of her daughter, but that she was an escaped slave who had destroyed the property of the man who enslaved her. That is, the focus was not on the psychological sequelae of the trauma she lived through and its possible relationship to her motivation to commit what some may refer to as an "act of mercy." We can only surmise that the repeated trauma that Garner experienced left deep emotional scars. We know from examining the enslavement process that female children in particular were accessible and vulnerable; the slave masters held all the power and utilized their authority to gain access and control over the women and girls they "owned."

One way in which African American women were able to survive the recurring bouts of victimization, decreased sexuality, and forced breeding to which they were exposed is described by Hine as "dissemblance," which she defines as the "behavior and attitudes of Black women that created the appearance of openness and disclosure but actually shielded the truth of their inner lives and selves from their oppressors."[27] This act of resilience used a "façade of calm" as a way of coping with repeated victimization and of resisting stigmatization and feelings of guilt and shame. A self-imposed form of secrecy, dissemblance is a conscious act that involves choosing to present oneself in a certain light and is not the same psychological process as dissociation, a complex psychological mechanism characterized by an alteration of normal integrated awareness and self-identity. Rather, disassociation is an unconscious process that involves the disruption of memory, consciousness, identity, and general perception of one's own self and surroundings.[28] Margaret Garner's responses after the death of her child, her capture by Archibald Gaines and a posse of federal marshals determined to return her to slavery, and her appearance in court in Cincinnati exhibited serious symptoms of dissociative behavior.

Although Hine has established the historical origins and efficacy of dissemblance, this form of interaction continues to be used by many African American women and as such is not only a process of the past. As a practicing clinician working with women of color who are experiencing traumatic events in their lives, I frequently see dissemblance serve as an important way of coping with twenty-first-century economic, relational, and social challenges. A woman may come into my office well dressed and composed, speaking in a gentle voice as she talks about the events of her life. But underneath that seeming composure, she may be losing her job or her home or being beaten at home. Black women often seem to have an amazing way of pulling it together, physically, psychologically, and spiritually. Until they decide to let you in, you may never know what is actually going on in their lives, which constitutes dissemblance.

But neither the conscious process of dissemblance nor the unconscious mechanism of dissociation goes far enough in explaining the silent or subtle internal processes that sustain women emotionally and intellectually. In both processes, women engage in a form of mental protection that allows them to deny reality and even perhaps fantasize that things will change for the better, that the abuse will stop. The women I see in my practice tend to fall into two primary groups: those who report a solid sense of identity and may have some level of financial and economic independence, and those who have fewer internal and economic resources to facilitate their distancing themselves from the abuse. Although women in the first group may appear only mildly affected intrapersonally by intimate partner violence, those in the second group, often those with a greater dependence on men, are in most cases unable to remind themselves and to affirm that "I am a good person; this is not my fault."

## Healing and Resilience

Women who are able eventually to transcend experiences of intimate partner violence remain aware of the dynamics of victimization. They seem to engage in little minimization of the facts, distortion of reality, or denial of problems as they undertake a process of reconstruction that allows them to manage the realities of their lives. Most therapists examining this process describe a model in which some level of reconstruction takes place internally that serves to create balance, centeredness, and a genuine sense of calm.

In *Wounds of the Spirit*, Traci West emphasizes the difference between resilience and healing, describing resilience as "having the power to resist, using coping mechanisms and/or strategies to withstand recurring bouts of violence despite the sociopolitical climate and lack of social support for one's problems." Healing, she argues, is a "regenerative process that repairs the damage of violence."[29] That is, resilience is a way of coping, utilizing strategies to survive, while healing is a process of intrapersonal reintegration of a spiritual and psychological sense of self. When healing takes place, the emotional and spiritual costs of violence have been transformed. This distinction can be seen in both contemporary and historical contexts.

To heal properly, a survivor of abuse must reclaim the "spirit" that was once vibrant and alive inside her; her healing should not be equated with self-numbing.

She must learn to create space for reflection, perspective, and regeneration of herself. Rather than simply coping, managing, or deflecting her perpetrator's angry words to feel less pain, she must turn inward to find that "light" she has been protecting from both immediate and systemic abuse and restore its energy. This is what Margaret Garner must have done during her enslavement, as she not only survived sexual servitude to a white slave master, but she also went on to form a loving partnered relationship and a keen sense of caring for her children. The final tragic outcome of Margaret Garner's life was the result of external rather than internal forces. Within a brutal system of enslavement, her resilience nurtured a sense of what was possible; her strong spirit powered her escape.

## NOTES

1. S. E. Anderson and Vanessa Holley, *The Black Holocaust: For Beginners* (New York: Writers and Readers, 1995); Marli Frances Weiner, *Mistresses and Slaves: Plantation Women in South Carolina, 1830–80* (Urbana: University of Illinois Press, 1997); Deborah G. White, *Ar'n't I a Woman? Female Slaves in the Plantation South* (New York: Norton, 1999); Jacqueline Jones, *Labor of Love, Labor of Sorrow: Black Women, Work, and the Family from Slavery to the Present* (New York: Vintage, 1986); Elizabeth Fox-Genovese, *Within the Plantation Household: Black and White Women of the Old South* (Chapel Hill: University of North Carolina Press, 1988); Catherine Clinton and Michele Gillespie, eds., *The Devil's Lane: Sex and Race in the Early South* (New York: Oxford University Press, 1997); Tera W. Hunter, *To 'joy My Freedom: Southern Black Women's Lives and Labors after the Civil War* (Cambridge, Mass.: Harvard University Press, 1997).

2. Thavolia Glymph, *Out of the House of Bondage: The Transformation of the Plantation Household* (Cambridge, New York: Cambridge University Press, 2008); Jennifer L. Morgan, *Laboring Women: Reproduction and Gender in New World Slavery* (Philadelphia: University of Pennsylvania Press, 2004); Stephanie M. H. Camp, *Closer to Freedom: Enslaved Women and Everyday Resistance in the Plantation South*, Gender and American Culture (Chapel Hill: University of North Carolina Press, 2004); Marie Jenkins Schwartz, *Born in Bondage: Growing Up Enslaved in the Antebellum South* (Cambridge, Mass.: Harvard University Press, 2000); Marie Jenkins Schwartz, *Birthing a Slave: Motherhood and Medicine in the Antebellum South* (Cambridge, Mass.: Harvard University Press, 2006).

3. Morgan, *Laboring Women*, 105; Susan Dwyer Amussen, *Caribbean Exchanges: Slavery and the Transformation of English Society, 1640–1700* (Chapel Hill: University of North Carolina Press, 2007), 64; Renee K. Harrison, *Enslaved Women and the Art of Resistance in Antebellum America* (New York: Palgrave Macmillan, 2009), 63. Regarding the absence of legal protections against the abuse of black women, see Thomas D. Morris, *Southern Slavery and the Law, 1619–1860* (Chapel Hill: University of North Carolina Press, 1996), 303–21.

4. Federal Writers' Project and Library of Congress, *Born in Slavery: Slave Narratives from the Federal Writers' Project, 1936–1938*, Georgia Narratives, vol. 4, pt. 4 (Washington, D.C.: Library of Congress, 2001), 322.

5. Ibid., 340.

6. Ibid., 328.

7. Jones, *Labor of Love*, 37–38.

8. Samuel Cartwright, "Diseases and Peculiarities of the Negro Race," originally published in *De Bow's Review*, vol. 11, New Orleans, La., 1851, reprinted in the *Africans in America* Resource Bank, pt. 4: 1831–1865, Antebellum Slavery Historical Documents, PBS Online, WGBH Educational Foundation, 1999. Available at http://www.pbs.org/wgbh/aia /part4/4h3106t.html (accessed February 26, 2013).

9. Alvin F. Poussaint and Amy Alexander, *Lay My Burden Down: Unraveling Suicide and the Mental Health Crisis among African-Americans* (Boston: Beacon, 2000), 70.

10. Mark Reinhardt, *Who Speaks for Margaret Garner?* (Minneapolis: University of Minnesota Press, 2010), 36.

11. Ibid.

12. Cartwright, "Diseases," 1851.

13. Quotations from Reinhardt, *Who Speaks for Margaret Garner?*, 97, 109.

14. "*Margret Garner*, Project Description," Michigan Opera Theatre, in Animating Democracy, A Program of Americans for the Arts, available athttp://www.artsusa.org /animatingdemocracy/labs/lab_078.asp (accessed May 26, 2011). For the diagnostic symptoms of PTSD, see Michael B. First, Allen Frances, and Harold Alan Pincus, *DSM-IV-TR Guidebook*, 309.81 Posttraumatic Stress Disorder (Washington, D.C.: American Psychiatric Association, 2004), 234; see also 249–67.

15. Cathy McDaniels-Wilson and Joanne Belknap, "The Extensive Sexual Violation and Sexual Abuse Histories of Incarcerated Women," *Violence Against Women* 14, no. 10 (2008): 1090–127.

16. William V. Arnold, *Pastoral Responses to Sexual Issues*, (Louisville, Ky.: Knox, 1990); Meda Chesney-Lind and Noelie Rodriguez, "Women under Lock and Key: A View from the Inside," *Prison Journal* 63, no. 2 (1983): 47–65; Fran Sugar and Lana Fox, "Nistum Peyako Séht'wawin Iskwewak: Breaking Chains," *Canadian Journal of Women & the Law* 3, no. 2 (989): 465–82; Emily Gaarder and Joanne Belknap, "Tenuous Borders: Girls Transferred to Adult Court," *Criminology* 40, no. 3 (2002): 481; Mary E. Gilfus, "From Victims to Survivors to Offenders: Women's Routes of Entry and Immersion into Street Crimes," *Women and Criminal Justice* 4, no. 1 (1992): 63–89.

17. McDaniels-Wilson and Belknap, "Extensive Sexual Violation," 1109–10.

18. American Psychiatric Association, *Diagnostic and Statistical Manual of Mental Disorders DSM-IV-TR*, 4th ed., text rev. (Washington, D.C.: American Psychiatric Association), 2000; Dee L. R. Graham, Edna I. Rawlings, and Roberta K. Rigsby, "Love Thine Enemy: Hostages and Classic Stockholm Syndrome," in *Loving to Survive: Sexual Terror, Men's Violence, and Women's Lives* (New York: New York University Press, 1994). Also see Judith Lewis Herman, "Captivity," in *Trauma and Recovery*, revised ed. (New York: Basic Books, 1997), which contains a useful analysis of Stockholm syndrome.

19. Excerpts from interviews with incarcerated women conducted by Cathy McDaniels-Wilson. See Cathy McDaniels-Wilson, "The Relation of Sexual Abuse History to the

MMPI-2 Profiles and Criminal Involvement of Incarcerated Women" (PhD diss., University of Cincinnati, 1998).

20. Gail E. Wyatt, Tamra Burns Loeb, Beatriz Solis, Jennifer Vargas Carmona, and Gloria Romero, "The Prevalence and Circumstances of Child Sexual Abuse: Changes across a Decade," *Child Abuse & Neglect* 23, no. 1 (1999): 45–60.

21. Joanne Belknap, *The Invisible Woman: Gender, Crime, and Justice* (Belmont, Calif.: Wadsworth, 2010).

22. From "Uniform Crime Reports," Uniform Crime Reporting Program, Federal Bureau of Investigations, U.S. Department of Justice, available at http://www.fbi.gov/about-us /cjis/ucr/ucr (accessed February 26, 2013), and "The Institute on Domestic Violence in the African American Community," University of Minnesota, School of Social Work.

23. Beth Richie, *Compelled to Crime: The Gender Entrapment of Battered Black Women* (New York: Routledge, 1996), 132–58.

24. McDaniels-Wilson and Belknap, 1118–21.

25. Rebecca Campbell, Sharon M. Wasco, Courtney E. Ahrens, Tracy Self, and Holly E. Barnes, "Preventing the 'Second Rape': Rape Survivors' Experiences with Community Service Providers," *Journal of Interpersonal Violence* 16, no. 12 (December 2001) 1239–59; G. E. Wyatt, "Sexual Harassment and Prior Sexual Trauma among African-American and White American Women," *Violence and Victims* 9, no. 3 (Fall 1994), 233–47.

26. Darlene Clark Hine, "Rape and the Inner Lives of Black Women: Thoughts on the Culture of Dissemblance," in *Hine Sight: Black Women and the Re-construction of American History* (Brooklyn, N.Y.: Carlson, 1994), 37–48.

27. Ibid., xxviii; 37.

28. Christine Courtois, *Healing the Wounds of Incest* (Norton Professional, 1988); American Psychiatric Association, *DSM-IV-TR*.

29. Traci C. West, *Wounds of the Spirit: Black Women, Violence, and Resistance Ethics* (New York: New York University Press, 1999), 151.

# CHAPTER 10

# ART AND MEMORY

## Healing Body, Mind, Spirit

*A Conversation with Carolyn Mazloomi,*
*Nailah Randall Bellinger, Olivia Cousins,*
*S. Pearl Sharp, and Catherine Roma*

The Gendered Resistance Symposium, sponsored by Miami University and the National Underground Railroad Freedom Center, featured the artwork of seven contemporary women. Fabric artist Carolyn Mazloomi opened the conference with *A Piece of My Mind*, a powerful quilt exhibit on the history of sexual abuse and violence, which she prepared for the conference. Performance artist Vanessa Johnson brought a series of historical documents to life in *Griot Stories*, an original interpretation of the boundaries between slavery and freedom. Anthropologist and poet Irma McClaurin's keynote, "ReVisioning a World without Violence against Women," wove a tapestry of words revealing a transcendent future of autonomy and peace. Choreographer Nailah Randall Bellinger and her dance troupe transformed Toni Morrison's words into movement in an energetic evening performance of Bellinger's original work, *Dancing Beloved*. Spiritualist and medical sociologist Olivia Cousins introduced conference participants to filmmaker S. Pearl Sharp's documentary, *The Healing Passage/Voices from the Water*, a retrospective film designed to create paths to healing from the present-day residuals of the Middle Passage suffered by enslaved Africans as they came to the New World. Vocal works performed by MUSE, Cincinnati's Women's Choir, directed by Catherine Roma, closed the Gendered Resistance Symposium with resistance songs from the United States, Argentina, and Zimbabwe.

In this chapter, several of the artists who participated in the symposium reflect on artistic expression and the process of memory, healing, and transformation, discussing the role of art, dance, poetry, performance, and music as bridges between the past and present. In written responses, or in the case of Carolyn Mazloomi, through excerpts from a previously recorded oral history interview, they answer four specific questions posed to them by the editors of this volume as they consider the role of the arts in shaping historical memory and examine the self-knowledge

Figure 10.1. "Flight for Peace" quilt by Carolyn Mazloomi. Image courtesy of Carolyn L. Mazloomi.

and activism that evolves out of artistic work. Each of these artists shares her vision of the arts as part of a transformative educational platform and speaks about the role of the artist in conveying stories of gendered resistance.

## Question 1: What do you seek to accomplish as you create and then share your work?

*Carolyn Mazloomi, fabric artist, author, historian, and curator[1]*

Women have to be celebrated and lifted up because they have the most important job on the planet—the most influential job on the planet. And you see these recurring themes in my work because I like for young people, young women, to see that work, to know that they have power. Because a lot of times they don't know it. And they have to be reminded of it. I have this power. Older women have to be reminded that they have this power of influence over all humanity because we, as first teachers, influence all human beings, and every human being on the planet comes through us regardless. It can be the teacher, it can be the president, it can be the doctor, it can be the maid. It's everybody. So that's awesome when you think about influencing all of humanity with your teaching your children. That's power. So we have that—an innate, intuitive wisdom. Only women have it, and young women sometimes don't even know that. They don't think about that, the intuitive wisdom of women. Men don't have it. Most men don't. But to me they, young girls, have to be reminded through the quilts.

*Nailah Randall Bellinger, dance educator, performer, choreographer*

The primary objective of creating the dance performance of *Dancing Beloved* was to offer an alternative way of discussing the content of Toni Morrison's masterwork and to show how dance, as well as other art forms, has been used historically to culturally identify the African and African American experience. This project considers dance as text and fuses dance performance and cultural memories of the past. At times considered an anomaly, dance is often reduced to entertainment. However, as Toni Morrison shows us in her novel, dance provides another way of knowing, in an attempt to understand one's present existence.

*Olivia Cousins, medical sociologist, educator,*
*spiritualist, community history advocate*

I came to the Gendered Resistance Symposium to screen S. Pearl Sharp's documentary film *The Healing Passage/Voices from the Water* and to lead a guided reflection at the Freedom Center. As S. Pearl was making this documentary, I was attending an event for healing from the Middle Passage, known as Maafa, at the St. Paul Community Baptist Church in Brooklyn, New York. Familiar with the connections between illness and disease in groups of free Blacks in the colonial period, I was examining the connection between post-traumatic slave syndrome and the legacy of slavery. I was following a line of research that looked specifically at Black women, the enslavement legacy, and reproductive disease and illness. When S. Pearl interviewed a group of women attending the Maafa, my daughter and I became a part of this extraordinary documentary. For the past fifteen years, a lot of my work has been centered on enabling women to become more aware, alert, and attentive to opportunities for healing—self and others. What has emerged in this work, front and center for both me and my students, is a consciousness of the ways in which artistic expressions—sight, sound, taste, smell, and touch—can be used as vehicles for healing. For re-membering. For re-storing. For re-imagining, re-visioning, and re-creating individual and collective lives. For putting back together bodies, minds, and spirits that have been torn, ripped apart through unspeakable, unbearable, devalued, violent acts that have muted and/or stolen our collective memories and voices. For me, it begins with the collective stories of women in general and of Black women in particular; with my mother, grandmothers, great-grandmothers, and great-great-grandmothers who were African, Irish, and Native American. Creation. Oppression. Resistance. Struggle.

*Catherine Roma, Founder and Artistic Director of MUSE,*
*Cincinnati's Women's Choir*

Our program for the Gendered Resistance Symposium was diverse, having an eclectic sampling to address many relevant issues by way of our music. A number of MUSE members consider ourselves cultural activists, and through music and artistic expression, we establish our stancing, to use Bernice Johnson Reagon's term from her essay "Battle Stancing: To Do Cultural Work in America."[2] This stancing, chosen collectively by our membership and manifested individually by the choices we make in our separate communities, provides a locus of empowerment from which we can work for and facilitate change in ourselves and in the space we inhabit. Adopting this strong stance has been the foundation upon which we build and mount our resistance to the oppressions offered to us by a patriarchal society that privileges whiteness, wealth, maleness, and heterosexuality over other forms of experience. By creating a strong, collective stance in our choral community, we simultaneously liberate and intertwine one another. Women's rights and the celebration of womanhood is core to who we are as an organization. We include all women, everywhere, in our musical exploration.

## Question 2: What is the relationship of your art to memory, especially the memory of enslavement and resistance, in both the past and the present?

*Carolyn Mazloomi*

When they (young girls) can look at my quilt *Wise Woman* [Wise Women series, 2002–2003] and see this owl in this woman's belly and know that it symbolizes wisdom—she's surrounded by moons, the lunar cycle, that allude to birth-giving—that's powerful. They have to be reminded, and what better way than to remind them through these quilts with this woman surrounded by fire and water, the life sign and the sign of so many trials and tribulations. Women walk through fire every day. Every day they walk through fire, every day by virtue of being women and not having so many things. Not being privy to education in so many countries; being a part of a workforce that makes or creates seventy percent of all working hours but yet owning only a fifth of the world's wealth.

And being the most undereducated. The world's refugees are mostly women. But yet they have the most important job. Sometimes in the weight of living on this planet as a woman, we have to be reminded of who we are. Quilts help to serve that purpose of reminding women about their power.

### Nailah Randall Bellinger

Toni Morrison in *Beloved* emphasizes the importance of memory throughout the plot. Her use of the dance metaphor is one of the vehicles she employs to invoke remembrance. Through numerous references to the dance trope, Morrison explores the concept of *lieu de mémoire* used by the late literary scholar VeVe Clark, following the French historian Pierre Nora. The symbology and function of dance forms a lieu de mémoire—a site of memory—that serves as a nonverbal communicator of historical events and thus lends itself to the creation of collective memory.[3] Dance in *Beloved* helps the characters in the novel remember their past by recreating the traditional rituals of their ancestors. When Baby Suggs gathers the community together to deliver her powerful sermon, she demands that her listeners become active participants in their own lives through dance, as a means of taking ownership of their destiny. Suggs's sermon is filled with inference of the kinesthetic attributes of self-discovery. Morrison describes the gathering as a staged performance:

> It started that way: laughing children, dancing men, crying women and then it got mixed up. Women stopped crying and danced; men sat down and cried; children danced, women laughed, children cried until, exhausted and riven, all and each lay about the Clearing damp and gasping for breath.[4]

Toni Morrison, understanding the power of dance, treats the Clearing as the stage site where Suggs is able to choreograph the improvisational dance that calls for a community to recognize their importance through this ritual of self-affirmation. She continues:

> in this here place, we flesh; flesh that weeps, laughs; flesh that dances on bare feet in grass. Love it. Love it hard. Yonder they do not love your flesh. They despise it. . . . This is flesh I'm talking about here. Flesh that needs to be loved. Feet that need to rest and to dance; backs that need support; shoulders that need arms, strong arms I'm telling you. . . . And all your inside parts that they'd just as soon slop for hogs, you got to love them. . . . More than lungs that have yet to draw free air. More than your life-holding womb and your life-giving private parts hear me now, love your heart. For this is the prize.[5]

While this is the most highlighted description of dance in the novel, it is not the single one. The dance trope appears more than a dozen times throughout the novel, beyond the point of mere coincidence. Deliberate use needed to be examined and this was the objective of my project.

*S. Pearl Sharp, filmmaker*

"Channel Poem" (excerpt), by S. Pearl Sharp, from *The Healing Passage/ Voices from the Water:*

> *From the first ship to*
> *the last whip*
> *was for this moment.*
> *Our bodies were taken*
> *to render us unconscious*
> *and our cells filled with fear*
> *and yes, we slept through our beliefs*
> *but now you hold the seed.*
> *You remember.*
> *You know our full nature*
> *not just the pain*
> *walk that memory*
> *You submitted to the collective way*
> *walk that memory*
> *Your law was the sacredness of life*
> *recall that sustenance*
> *walk that memory*
> *water this seed.*

When the African American artist Riua Akinshegun was asked if she would like to visit the slave port in Lagos, Nigeria, she responded, "What do I want to see that for?" and refused to go. Fifteen years later, on her third trip to Africa, she could finally "hold up the mirror" and descend into the emotional memory steeped in the rooms where captured Africans were held. She returned from Gorée Island and created the art installation "The Most Mutinous Leapt Overboard," which she describes as "a burial ground for ignored spirits."

Akinshegun's installation became the foundation for my documentary film, *The Healing Passage/Voices from the Water*, a journey of more than ten years. At a point when the direction for the film had me completely stumped, I received, from artist Tom Feelings, this quote by Toni Morrison: "There's so much more to remember, and to describe, for purposes of exorcism, and purposes of celebratory rites of passage. Things must be made. Some fixing ceremony, some altar, some memorial, something, somewhere, where those things can be released, thought, felt. But the consequences of slavery only artists can deal with . . . and it's our job!"

Gradually, the film wrapped itself around these words, and other artists and healers entered the film—Sweet Honey in the Rock's Ysaye M. Barnwell, film-maker and descendant of slave owners Katrina Browne, photographer Chester Higgins Jr., and the founder of the healing Maafa Conference, Rev. Dr. Johnny

Ray Youngblood. Toni's words, the artists, the healers, all began to weave themselves into a fabric that affirmed the role of the artist to be directly involved in a community's healing. The crucial component here is the artist's acceptance of this role, this task.

What had strongly impacted Riua's spirit was the sense of resistance by our ancestors. Some Africans made the choice to leap to certain death into the Atlantic Ocean rather than be enslaved. However, in the re-telling of the African Holocaust, or Maafa, this aspect of our resistance is often discarded or questioned.

*Olivia Cousins*

Freedom journeys have burst through conscious memories in the viewing of films such as *Follow Me Home, Sankofa*, and *The Healing Passage*. With an unflinching focus on women's stories, one film deals with the Native American concept of "soul wounding" (acculturation and genocide); another with spirit breaking (dehumanization and marginalization); and the last with cultural erasure (degradation and amnesia). All three films deal with themes that explore how culturally based violence tears the body apart, colonizes the mind, and deadens the spirit. It is in the storytelling, filming, scripting, singing, weaving, writing, imaging, framing, creating, painting, and collaging that we as women share individual stories with the collective for expressed purposes of reflection, meditation, and healing. For some, the notes, the dance, the words, the pictures, the frames, serve to lift veils crossing not only our faces but our eyes, allowing or enabling us to see the connections between violence visited on our beings and the illness and dis-eases that attack our bodies, our minds, and our spirits.

My first large-audience screening of *The Healing Passage* took place in the Langston Hughes Auditorium of the Schomburg Center for Research in Black Culture in New York City. The place was packed. There was an air of expectation. Images, memories, songs, reflections, and meditative words. Artists speaking, sharing, singing their work led the audience through the gut-wrenching, spirit-splitting images of enslavement. The artists' voices held, comforted, and led the audience (racially, gender, and age mixed) through stories of dehumanization, torture, resistance, struggle, freedom, and healing. From where I sat (purposely in the middle), one could hear the sobs, groans; see the tightening of the bodies and the clenched fists; see the tears streaming down faces without Kleenexes to stop the flow. Feel the anger. And as the stories and songs and reimaging moved across the screen, so many of these reactions, responses, and emotions gave way to smiles and cheers—pride in resistance and survival. Women and men, Black and White, and so many more, were visibly moved. At the end of the screening—first silence—and then the thundering applause. Time and again, people spoke about how this documentary made them feel, remember, claim, and release. It spoke to their spirit.

The screening of *The Healing Passage* in Cincinnati at the Freedom Center was different. Smaller and less racially mixed, but with a larger percentage of women, many of those present had just "passed through" a reconstructed slave pen acquired from property in Kentucky (some of the original markings were still observable on the walls). What was striking was the silence in this particular space. It was challenging to get people to share what they had experienced after watching the documentary. It was even harder to gauge their reactions and responses, given that the auditorium was shaped more like a small amphitheatre. The conversations were more at arms-length, with the most poignant and emotional responses coming from a family and set of biological sisters who had not yet been through the slave pen replica. Interestingly enough, it was after the screening that women came down the stairs to share emotions and feelings that were akin to the ones observed in the Schomburg screening. The one-on-one conversations were freer, peppered with thoughts about how the film had made them feel or remember. I recall in particular the reactions and responses of the two young people who were the technician (male) and assistant (female) for this screening. The same range of emotions observable in the Schomburg crowd was observable with them when I glanced their way. Both African American, they softly whispered "thank you" as they returned the film, vowing to send away for a copy.

*Catherine Roma*

Our program for the conference included the following repertoire: "Wanting Memories," by Dr. Ysaye Maria Barnwell; "Set Her Free," by Ruth Huber; "Imagine My Surprise," by Holly Near; "Sayitshaya," a traditional Shona piece from Zimbabwe, taught to us in workshop; "A Small but Fateful Victory," by Roger Bourland; "Duerme Negrito," by Atahualpa Yupanqui, an example of *nueva cancion*; "I Ain't Afraid" and "Foolish Notion," by Holly Near. Each of these songs is, in its own right, a song of resistance. While "Duerme Negrito," a lullaby, makes a literal reference to slavery, other works such as "Set Her Free" and "A Small but Fateful Victory" refer to domestic conditions of women in patriarchal society. The linking of these three works reminds us that the enslavement of women takes many forms, and that no matter what form it occupies, it must be resisted and overthrown.

In the lullaby, Argentinean folk composer Yupanqui utilizes double entendre, where one meaning is implied but another meaning is understood. References are made to the brutal practice of cutting a person's foot off to prevent escape and to the sick mother working hard to care for her children. The text also implicates the necessity of instilling fear, necessary for children of color to know how to protect themselves:

And if the black one doesn't go to sleep, the white devil will come and
zap! he'll eat your little foot, chica bu; hurry, chica bu!
Sleep little black one, your mama's in the field, little one. She's working
hard, working, yes, working and they don't pay her, working, yes,
working and she is coughing, working, yes, for her sweet little black
one, for her little one yes.

On the surface, the song seems to recount a variant of the "bogeyman" story
used in many cultures to frighten children into good behavior. Viewed through
the lens of cultural resistance to slavery, however, the seemingly playful threat to
cut off the child's foot to prevent escape becomes a cold reference to a real-life
punishment for Argentinean slaves. Similarly, the bogeyman motif itself takes on
a deeper meaning as it underscores the need to instill fear as a survival instinct
for children of color.

Women held in bondage and the drudgery of domestic chores resist in "A Small
but Fateful Victory" when the woman "smashes her kitchen stove into bits." She
gives voice to her anger but uses humor to convey her message. "Foolish Notion"
is staunchly anti-war and links the notion that both capital punishment and war
purport to be righting wrongs, but in reality, such measures demonstrate exerting
power over marginalized people. The words in the song, written several decades
ago, ring true today:

Why do we kill people who are killing people
To show that killing people is wrong?
What a foolish notion, that war is called devotion
When the greatest warriors
Are the ones who stand for peace

In an American climate so poised in 2005 to equate the pursuit of war with the
support of patriotism, such words were revolutionary and resistance indeed. To
bridge the past and the present, MUSE sang "Sayitshaya," which enacts a competi-
tion between old and new and the conflict between young and old religion and
culture in contemporary Zimbabwe. The fundamental message is shared in the
music that we all, regardless of the changes in our culture, are able to join together
and respect our differences.

"Wanting Memories" figures the grandmother as the past, in her departure
from the life of the young girl, and the girl as the future, reflecting on how much
the grandmother meant to her. This work operates on many levels, intertwining
women defining themselves, supporting one another, tying one generation to
another, the connection to ancestors and support from elders. The young teenage
girl sings, "I am sitting here wanting memories to teach me, to see the beauty in

the world through my own eyes." As the song progresses, she realizes that although her grandmother has left her, there are lessons that remain with her forever. "*I know that I am you and you are me, and we are one.*"

Question 3: What message do you want to convey, especially to young people, who see or hear your work? What is special about the way your particular artistic expression delivers that message?

*Carolyn Mazloomi*

When I talk about a force for healing, I'm thinking about those remembrances of our ancestors. It's a spiritual thing. Even though we're Americans, we know that our roots are in Africa, and these ancestors have had such tragedy—lived such tragic lives. Why not celebrate those lives? I do, a lot, in my quilts. One of the first quilts that I made was a narrative quilt about the slave trade, and it was a huge piece, now in the collection of a national African American museum. But in the center of this quilt it shows a woman of color dressed in African garb holding this much darker child and surrounded by a line of African warrior shields, and she's symbolic of that African ancestor whose child she and her child brought to this country. It's indicative of all the hues that we come in as so-called black folk. She and her child are different colors, and behind her is a huge outline of a slave-ship with the slaves lying in the bottom of the hull of this ship. And in the water surrounding this woman and child are skeletons, symbolic of all those enslaved persons that lost their lives in the slave trade.

*Nailah Randall Bellinger*

Dance can be used as an empowering voice to tell our stories as a people. And dance should be considered as a meaningful subject in any academic curriculum. Dance offers an alternative means of acquiring knowledge. Through using more of the left side of the brain, dance allows visual learners to take in information in another way.

*S. Pearl Sharp*

I first experienced Akinshegun's unique art installation on healing from the trans-Atlantic slave trade in 1994, and knew that it should be documented. Its interactive framework is compelling. The installation only exists if the public helps to create it, and they are invited both to help with and learn from the story of enslavement and recovery from enslavement. The public's interaction with the installation begins with a challenge to claim this African Holocaust and their connection to it, regardless of their racial DNA. This is hard for some people to do. Even some Africans born on the continent are in denial about their inherited connection to slavery.

Observing this, the landscape then became, for me, the need to focus on our condition in the present. People are usually stumped when asked to identify some of the present-day residuals resulting from the trans-Atlantic slave trade. The artist and the healer allow us to acknowledge the past while dealing with the present, and to make a clear, active connection between the two. One power of working in film is the ability to juxtapose images to project a specific message and to direct an interpretation of that message. In *The Healing Passage*, we project a correlation between the sale of Black women on the auction block during slavery and the sale of women today via a media auction block. Our daughters are coerced onto it, believing it is their right to be sold, believing it is the norm. Because they act out of an ignorance of the significance of their ancestors' herstories, they are therefore unable to recognize an auction block when it is presented to them. An auction block, be it wood or digital, can reappear in the twenty-first century only where memory is absent. When screening the film, I challenge teens and young adults in the audience to acknowledge and respond to their manipulation by and submission to the media. Cognizance precedes resistance.

On the other end of the age spectrum, Riua and I are helping Black women reclaim the color red, taken away from us during slavery and years of post-slavery. A Black woman wearing red signaled whore or slut, and dark-skinned sistuhs were trained to be embarrassed in such a vivid hue. Many of us inherited this stigma. So I was overjoyed to witness dozens of women, at the film's screening at the Schomburg Center, standing and waving red scarves, red hats, jackets, shoes, celebrating their freedom to be vibrant.

## Catherine Roma

Music is a timeless form of communication. It transcends the boundaries of geography and culture, the limitations of language, and the confines of either recorded history or contemporary events. The art is in the thought and the words, and if it strikes a chord with the listener, it is also able to transcend cultural and generational differences. While some of our pieces may be seen as "political," for women everywhere the songs are personal and relevant. They speak to the common elements of our humanity—a desire for peace, a love of beauty, a hope for a better, brighter future for self and family. In the stories we sing, our commonality unites us. Some of our music brings forth views about the denial of liberty for women in other countries. Some pieces share thoughts about the struggles of everyday life for women. Others are more about confronting issues that threaten our freedom, our society, our equality, and our lives.

Each time we sing, we inform our collective consciousness and that of our audience. We are awakened to new awareness of the work that has been done on our behalf and the work that is left to do. We share this awakening with our audience, and we are empowered, both collectively and individually, by a music-making experience that is constantly teaching us about the past and present, and ultimately inspiring us to continue sharing our message, as we have for more than twenty-five years.

## Question 4: How are you and the world changed through your art, music, storytelling, dancing, or filmmaking? Explain how you see creative work as a form of resistance?

*Carolyn Mazloomi*

A lot of my quilts deal with, especially early on, social and political issues that affect me as an African American living in this country. I can't help but be touched by events and actions that affect me as a human being here, and I have to get them out sometimes in my work. I may not have a voice that can be heard nationally on a certain issue, but I have this medium of quilt-making where I can create a quilt that can be seen by hundreds or thousands of people that are in attendance at a museum or gallery show that will voice my concerns about racism. Voice my concerns about AIDS. Voice my concerns about violence in the African American community. Voice my concerns about the daily theft of a legacy of art created by African Americans. I have a wider audience in the creation of quilts that are shown at museums to address certain issues that bother me.

I've had viewers who have been strongly affected by quilts that I've done on the topic of racism. Particularly, I made a quilt two years ago for an exhibition about the Underground Railroad. That exhibition took place at Oberlin College [in Oberlin, Ohio], and I chose to not make a quilt to celebrate the Underground Railroad movement but my own childhood experiences growing up in Louisiana and having one of my young friends lynched by members who we assumed were in the Klan. And this quilt was a very visual representation of that memory. That memory of finding my friend. That memory of seeing Klansmen with torches and lighted crosses, burning crosses, crossing the highway.

A lot of work deals with women. I have the image of women on every other quilt that I make, and it's to celebrate the status of women and their specialness in the sphere of things here on this planet. As special people. It is to remind young women, especially, too, that they're powerful. They're very powerful. Sometimes they don't know how powerful they are, because they have the most important job on the planet and that's raising children. So through the raising of our children, we influence all of humanity. It's a powerful position to be in: mother. It's great. So I like to celebrate that in my work.

And I also have a lot of Africanisms in my work. When I say Africanisms, I mean I love to use African cloths—and the color is exciting—and African beads and shells in my work. I love that. I love the color, the movement from the color and design of the fabric. So always that will be an integral part of my work as well. In the near future, I want to start painting. Whenever I am afforded that time, I would love to paint, so it's coming.

## Nailah Randall Bellinger

What I discovered was that this dance project introduced Toni Morrison's *Beloved* to a wider audience who may not otherwise have taken the time to read the book. Many viewers of my staged performance commented that the dance performance inspired them to pick up the book and read it.

More than a form of resistance, I found that choreographing the story was self-empowering. This performance study transformed the lives of all of my dancers and me by reliving the experience through our artistic journey. The whole idea of lieu de memoire offered each performer the opportunity to personalize the mnemonic experience through the body. The process of creating *Beloved* served as a springboard to my creation of a nonprofit organization, JANBE, offering an annual summer intensive workshop to young aspiring dancers in Port-au-Prince, Haiti.

## Olivia Cousins

Over the years that followed the screening in Cincinnati, I have shown *The Healing Passage* in other parts of New York, Ohio, and even in South Africa. The conversations usually begin with a release of feelings and emotions followed by a movement to provide sociocultural and oftentimes political analyses—for example, colonialism versus slavery paradigms. First and foremost is the power of memory to awaken awareness. In my Women's Health Concerns classes, the showing of this film has visibly ignited conversations around the collective pain, wounding, and healing of women. Bosnian women, Korean, Chinese, and Japanese women; African women, West Indian, and African American women; women from the United States, Central and South America, and Mexico who refer to themselves as Hispanic, Latinas, or Chicanas; and Euro-American and European women all have referenced the oppression, atrocities, struggles, and violence that has continued in the lives of women, from the enslavement of African Americans to the forced prostitution of women and girls in Asia and the United States.

Discussions of the collective bring light for individuals engaged in ongoing or past experiences with violence and exploitation by virtue of being a female in any given society. Stories are shared about individual and collective violations and acts of violence inflicted on bodies, minds, and spirits. Conversations are moved towards "closure"—endings awaiting new beginnings—with stories about how women have reclaimed their voices/spirits through their creative sides. Singing

their songs, dancing their dances; writing their journals/stories/poetry; painting; visual imaging, costuming, weaving and fashioning, and filming; claiming/
reclaiming; losing/finding; visioning/revisioning women-centered ways of being
to heal bodies, minds, and spirits.

*Catherine Roma*

Who MUSE is, where we perform, and what repertoire we sing is informed by
our philosophy:

> MUSE is a women's choir dedicated to musical excellence and social change. In keeping
> with our belief that diversity is strength, we are feminist women of varied ages, races,
> and ethnicities with a range of musical abilities, political interests, and life experiences.
> We are women loving women; we are heterosexual, lesbian, and bisexual women united
> in song. We commission and seek out music composed by women, pieces written to
> enhance the sound of women's voices, and songs that honor the enduring spirit of all
> peoples. In performing, we strive for a concert experience that entertains, inspires,
> motivates, heals, and creates a feeling of community with our audience.

We raise our voices for peace and justice as a women's choral community. Much
of the music we program is chosen by a small, self-selected collective from within
that we call Dreamers, Eaters, and Philosophers. Every performance begins with a
reflection upon the message we will be sharing with our music, and the choir as a
whole contributes thoughts about the history of the music, the various interpretations of the lyrics, and the personal experiences members may have had regarding
the impact of the piece. We value our connection as women, and our being able
to use music as an instrument of change.[6]

## Conclusion

Those working in the visual arts, dance, and music have long produced representations that probe the history of slavery by powerfully revealing the contradictions
that underpin the ideals of liberty and freedom. Art provides a map that shows us
the way back home, a representation that can heal the body, mind, and spirit. The
voices of the artists included here describe various practices of representation that,
as S. Pearl Sharp suggests, lead us to memory made tangible in the present: to the
rooms where captured Africans were held before the Middle Passage; to the dance
in *Beloved*; to a young friend lynched and burning crosses on the highway; to the
collective histories that bind together the shared and often tattered fabric of our
lives. As Catherine Roma reminds us, the common elements of our humanity—"a
desire for peace, a love of beauty, a hope for a better, brighter future for self and
family"—strike a chord that transcends the cultural and generational differences

that divide us. Art is a form of resistance without which we remain strangers to ourselves, the proverbial outsiders in that foreign country that is the past—the *obruni* from across the sea, as young Ghanaian children called writer Saidiya Hartman when she traveled the Atlantic slave route in search of her ancestral home.[7]

Margaret Garner, whose story inspired *Gendered Resistance*, lived in a world both alien and familiar to us as twenty-first-century Americans in a global society in which the struggle over slavery and freedom continues to pervade our collective consciousness. The history of this remarkable woman has been larger than life since the moment she decided to resist the slave system into which she was born. Over the past 150 years, her life has quite literally been transformed into art: in poems, paintings, novels, film, and opera. The power of these representations has transformed what we know about the history of enslavement and resistance into compelling symbols that we can hold in our memory—tapestries of words and images that have the power to shape our vision of the past, inform our understanding of the present, and give us hope for the future.

## NOTES

1. Excerpts from "Oral History Interview with Carolyn Mazloomi," interview by Joanne Cubbs, Archives of American Art, Smithsonian Institution, September 17–30, 2002, available at http://www.aaa.si.edu/collections/interviews/oral-history-interview-carolyn-mazloomi-11504 (accessed February 27, 2013).

2. Bernice Johnson Reagon, "Battle Stancing: To Do Cultural Work in America," in *Voices from the Battlefront, Achieving Cultural Equity*, ed. Marta Moreno and Cheryll Y. Greene (Trenton, N.J.: Africa World Press, 1993).

3. According to Pierre Nora, "A lieu de mémoire is any significant entity, whether material or non-material in nature, that has become a symbolic element of the memorial bridge of that community." Pierre Nora, "From lieux de mémoire to Realms of Memory," in *Realms of Memory: Rethinking the French Past*, vol. 1, ed. Lawrence D. Kritzman (New York: Columbia University Press, 1996), xv–xxiv, quoted in "Sites of Memory" by Cornealius Holtorf, available at https://tspace.library.utoronto.ca/citd/holtorf/2.6.html (accessed May 18, 2011). Although Nora was referring to France in his depiction, other scholars, such as VeVe Clark, have applied the concept to the Black American experience and the world of dance. See VeVe Clark, "Performing the Memory of Difference in Afro-Caribbean Dance: Katherine Dunham's Choreography, 1938–1987," in *History and Memory in African American Culture*, ed. Genevieve Fabre and Robert O'Meally (New York: Oxford University Press, 1994). See also Lillian Ashcraft-Eason, Darnise C. Martin, and Oyeronke Olademo, eds., *Women and New and Africana Religions* (Santa Barbara, Calif.: ABC-CLIO, 2009), 124.

4. Toni Morrison, *Beloved* (New York: Plume, 1987), 88.

5. Ibid.

6. Contributions from MUSE members Amanda Schear, Debbie Piper, Diana Porter, and Deb Meem are greatly appreciated.

7. Saidiya Hartman, *Lose Your Mother: A Journey along the Atlantic Slave Route* (New York: MacMillan, 2008), 103–4. Hartman notes that these Ghanaians were also separate from their own history, a consequence of colonialism. "Slavery had made us strangers," Hartman writes, quoting Frederick Douglass, meaning that African Americans who return to visit their "homeland" are not recognized as having once been kin.

# CONTRIBUTORS

**Olivia Cousins** is a sociologist who received her doctoral training in both medical and community sociology from Boston University. She holds a master's degree in Afro-American studies from Boston University and a master of arts in education and social policy from Harvard Graduate School of Education. She completed her undergraduate work in psychology at the University of Dayton. With a specialty in women's health, she has conducted research projects in the United Sates, Africa, and China. A former board chair of the National Women's Health Network, Cousins is also a former chair of the Health Education Department of Borough of Manhattan Community College, CUNY. She has developed and taught courses in urban health, stress management, human sexuality, and black women in the Diaspora. A founder of the BMCC Women's Resource Center, Cousins is the owner and steward of the John Mercer Langston Historical House and the founder of the John Mercer Langston Institute.

**Mary E. Frederickson** is professor of history at Miami University, Oxford, Ohio and visiting professor in The Graduate Institute for Liberal Arts at Emory University in Atlanta, Georgia. Her doctorate is from the University of North Carolina at Chapel Hill. In 2010 she was a Public Policy Scholar at the Woodrow Wilson International Center for Scholars in Washington, D.C., and was awarded the Distinguished Teaching Award by the Ohio Academy of History. Her book, *Looking South: Race, Gender, and the Transformation of Labor from Reconstruction to Globalization*, was published in 2011. During 2012–13 she was a Visiting Fellow at the James Weldon Johnson Institute for the Study of Race and Difference at Emory University.

**Cheryl Janifer LaRoche** is a historical and archaeological consultant who focuses primarily on eighteenth- and nineteenth-century free black communities, the black church, and the Underground Railroad. She served as a cultural heritage specialist for the President's House archaeological site for the National Park Service in Philadelphia. She was one of the authors of the National Significance of the Harriet Tubman Historic Area for the National Park Service. She has worked as an archaeological conservator for the African Burial Ground Project in New York City. LaRoche teaches a broad-ranging course on African American History, Visual Culture and Identity for the University of Maryland, College Park. Currently she serves as the vice chair of the Maryland Commission on African American History and Culture. Her first book, *Free Black Communities and the Underground Railroad: The Geography of Resistance*, will be published later this year by the University of Illinois Press. In 2011, the Society for Historical Archaeology awarded LaRoche the John L. Cotter Award for her exemplary work in bringing a multidisciplinary approach to the study of African American archaeology.

**Carolyn Mazloomi** is an artist, author, historian, and curator acknowledged as being among the most influential African American quilt historians and quilting artists of the twenty-first century. In 2003 Mazloomi was awarded the first Ohio Heritage Fellowship Award. She is author of the book *Spirits of the Cloth*, given the Best Non-Fiction Book of the Year award by the American Library Association. *Threads of Faith*, written by Mazloomi in 2004, was published by the Museum of the American Biblical Art. An exhibition based on the book toured the United States for two years. In addition, she wrote *Textural Rhythms: Quilting the Jazz Tradition* (Paper Moon, 2007) and *Quilting African American Women's History: Our Creativity, Champions and Challenges* (Paper Moon, 2008). A former aerospace engineer, she has been involved in the economic development of women through the arts for more than twenty years. Her organization, WCQN, has been recognized by the International Labour Department in Geneva and the United Nations for its developmental programs to help advance women.

**Cathy McDaniels-Wilson** is the director of University Counseling and Health Services and the coordinator of Disability Services at Capital University in Columbus, Ohio. Throughout her career as an educator and clinician, she has developed programs and training opportunities to increase students,' colleagues,' and organizations' awareness of their levels of comfort and discomfort with respect to their interactions within diverse cultural contexts. As a consultant at the National Underground Railroad Freedom Center in Cincinnati, McDaniels-Wilson developed and implemented the Dialogue Zone, aimed at engaging participants in listening, reflecting, and inquiring within a "safe" environment. She also developed the Freedom Center's protocol to enhance basic knowledge and awareness about the ever-expanding role of diversity and race relations for doctoral students in Xavier University's PsyD program in clinical psychology. In addition to the examination of race relations, McDaniels-Wilson's research interests include intimate partner abuse, sexual victimization, and incarceration of women and girls. She served as president of the Ohio Psychological Association in 2009 and is currently on the American Psychological Association Council of Representatives. McDaniels-Wilson also maintains a private psychology practice in Columbus, Ohio, where she works extensively with survivors of sexual trauma.

**Nailah Randall-Bellinger** holds a master's degree in interdisciplinary studies from Lesley University in Massachusetts and a bachelor's degree in Franco-African literature from Scripps College in California. For many years in the Dance Department at Dean College in Franklin, Massachusetts, she now teaches modern dance technique, dance composition, dance history, and dance in film survey at Harvard University. A dance educator and performer for more than twenty-five years, Randall-Bellinger has served on the dance panel for the National Endowment of the Arts and has taught master classes for the American Dance Awards and at national conventions for Dance Masters of America. The artistic director of RootsUprising, a Boston-based contemporary dance ensemble that she founded in 1998, Randall-Bellinger also co-founded the JANBE institute, a small cultural performing arts organization, based in Port-au-Prince Haiti that focused on the preservation of culture through the language of dance.

**Catherine Roma**, DMA, is professor of music, Wilmington College, Wilmington, Ohio, and founder and artistic director of MUSE, Cincinnati's Women's Choir. For twenty-five years she has been creating vibrant choral communities in southwestern Ohio that reach across barriers of race, religion, class, sexual orientation, and age. She works to translate the values of social justice and inclusion into fundamental experiences of community for both audience and singers. Roma's work in the Greater Cincinnati area serves as a model for bringing the choral arts to a wide community, a community where differences are celebrated and men and women of many colors, ages, cultures, and lifestyles come together in harmony.

**Huda Seif** holds a master of arts, a master of philosophy, and a doctorate in social/cultural anthropology from Columbia University, New York City, and a bachelor of arts in anthropology and economics from the City University of New York. Her focus is on political and legal anthropology, human rights, and humanitarian crisis. She was a Human Rights Fellow at the Center for the Study of Law and Religion, Emory University Law School, where she worked to develop a legal platform to address the constitutional rights of minority ethnic groups in Yemen. She has worked extensively with the United Nations agencies (UNDP, UNICEF, UNESCO, and OCHA) in Afghanistan, Kenya, Somalia, Sudan, South Sudan, Yemen, and Zimbabwe. Seif was a co-founder and co-director of Alternative World: Partnership for Equitable Development and Social Justice, under which she authored an Alternative Report to the United Nations High Commission for Human Rights on human rights in Yemen and parallel to the Yemen State Report on 2006. She also served two terms as a Political Advisor for the European Union Special Representative (EUSR) for Sudan during the Darfur crisis. Currently based in Brussels, she is a freelance consultant and part-time lecturer at the Institut d'Etudes Politiques (Science Po), Lille, France. She is the author of numerous UN documents and scholarly articles.

**S. Pearl Sharp** is an award-winning filmmaker. Her work merges art, history and healing, including *The Healing Passage/Voices From The Water* and *Picking Tribes*. She is the author of *Black Women For Beginners*, the poetry w/jazz CD, *Higher Ground*, and her commentaries and essays are broadcast on NPR. Both a student and advocate of holistic health and healing, Sharp conducts workshops on "Reclaiming Your Ancestral Power" and "Writing Wellness."

**Jolene Smith** is co-founder of Free the Slaves, a nonpartisan and politically independent organization that has worked since 2000 to end slavery worldwide. Free the Slaves researches real-world solutions to eradicating slavery and helps those released from slavery to rebuild their lives. This work has taken Smith across the globe as Free the Slaves collaborates with governments, businesses, international organizations, and local communities to end human trafficking and slavery. She has recently returned to United States after living and working in Ecuador for more than three years.

**Raquel Luciana de Souza** was born in Minas Gerais, Brazil, where she received a bachelor's degree in languages, literature, and translation studies at the Federal University of Ouro Preto (UFOP). In 1999 she was awarded a Fulbright Scholarship in interdisciplinary studies, and in 2001 she earned a master's degree in American studies in the Political Science Department at the University of Maryland, College Park. She received a second master of arts in history with a focus on Latin America in 2004, also at Maryland. She is currently a doctoral candidate in social anthropology in the John L. Warfield Center for African and African American Studies at the University of Texas in Austin. Her areas of interest include issues of race, gender, sexuality, Black social movements, intersectional identities, popular culture, and media representations of the African Diaspora.

**Veta Smith Tucker** holds a doctor of arts in English from the University of Michigan. She directs the Kutsche Office of Local History in the College of Interdisciplinary Studies at Grand Valley State University in Allendale, Michigan, where she has taught American Literature, African American Literature, and

Women and Gender Studies since 1995. She served as coordinator of the African/ African American Studies Program from 1997–2003. She has developed courses on the History of the Underground Railroad, Black Women's History, and the Modern Civil Rights Movement. Her current research focuses on the Underground Railroad and abolitionist movements in Michigan and the experiences and representation of nineteenth-century African American and Afro-Canadian women who participated in those movements.

**Delores M. Walters** began researching the story of Margaret Garner while directing a family/local history training program at the National Underground Railroad Freedom Center and teaching at Northern Kentucky University. As a member of the Margaret Garner Steering Committee, her articles and presentations helped introduce the historical Margaret Garner in Greater Cincinnati and later in several Northeastern cities. She is the director of faculty recruitment and retention in the Office of Community, Equity and Diversity and associate dean for diversity in the College of Human Science and Services at the University of Rhode Island. She directed the Southern Rhode Island Area Health Education Center, aimed at reducing health care disparities in the College of Nursing at URI. From 2007–09, she directed a Ford Foundation grant to diversify the member centers of the National Council for Research on Women. In 2010, she received funding from the Rhode Island Council for the Humanities and Providence Inner City Arts for an arts/education pilot project highlighting the cultural/historical legacies of African Americans and other people of color in the Ocean State. Walters earned a doctorate in cultural anthropology from New York University after conducting field research among an African-identified group in Yemen. Subsequently, she produced articles and a film on Yemeni women's roles in promoting healthcare and social inclusion.

**Diana Williams** is assistant professor of history and law at the University of Southern California. She received her doctorate in American civilization from Harvard University in 2007 and taught at Wellesley College until 2009. Her research focuses on nineteenth-century African American and women's history as well as mixed-race history. Her dissertation, *"They Call It Marriage": The Louisiana Interracial Family and the Making of American Legitimacy*, won the 2008 William Nelson Cromwell Dissertation Prize in Legal History.

**Kristine Yohe** is an associate professor of English at Northern Kentucky University, Highland Heights, where she has taught since 1997 after receiving her doctorate from the University of North Carolina at Chapel Hill. Her teaching and scholarship focus on African American literature (especially Toni Morrison), on Underground Railroad literature, and on Afro-Caribbean writers, including Edwidge Danticat and Jean-Robert Cadet. In 2005, Yohe served as conference director for the Toni Morrison Society Fourth Biennial Conference, "Toni Morrison and Sites of Memory," which took place in conjunction with the *Margaret Garner* opera, in Cincinnati, Ohio, and at Northern Kentucky University. She is editor for *Word-Work: The Newsletter of the Toni Morrison Society*. Yohe recently published a chapter on teaching Morrison's novel *Love* in *The Fiction of Toni Morrison: Reading and Writing on Race, Culture, and Identity* (NCTE, 2007), edited by Jami L. Carlacio.

# INDEX

THE NEW BLACK STUDIES SERIES

The University of Illinois Press
is a founding member of the
Association of American University Presses.

_____

Composed in 10/13 Minion Pro
by Lisa Connery
at the University of Illinois Press
Designed by Dennis Roberts
Manufactured by Thomson-Shore, Inc.

University of Illinois Press
1325 South Oak Street
Champaign, IL 61820-6903
www.press.uillinois.edu